The Intelligent Woman's Guide to Dating and Mating

Books and Monographs by Albert Ellis, Ph.D.

Published by Lyle Stuart:
Sex Without Guilt

The Art and Science of Love

The American Sexual Tragedy

Creative Marriage *(with Robert A. Harper)*

Reason and Emotion in Psychotherapy

If This Be Sexual Heresy . . .

Sex and the Single Man

The Origins and Development of the Incest Taboo

The Intelligent Woman's Guide to Man-hunting

Homosexuality

The Art of Erotic Seduction *(with Roger O. Conway)*

Is Objectivism a Religion?

Murder and Assassination *(with John M. Gullo)*

Executive Leadership: A Rational Approach (Citadel Press)

The Sensuous Person: Critique and Corrections

Sex and the Liberated Man

Published by Others:
An Introduction to the Principles of Scientific Psychoanalysis

The Folklore of Sex

Sex, Society and the Individual *(with A. P. Pillay)*

Sex Life of the American Woman and the Kinsey Report

How to Live with a "Neurotic"

New Approaches to Psychotherapy Techniques

What is Psychotherapy?

Sex and Sex Education: A Bibliography *(with Flora C. Seruya and Susan Losher)*

The Psychology of Sex Offenders *(with Ralph Brancale)*

The Place of Value in the Practice of Psychotherapy

The Encyclopedia of Sexual Behavior *(with Albert Abarbanel)*

A Guide to Rational Living *(with Robert A. Harper)*

Nymphomania: A Study of the Over-sexed Woman *(with Edward Sagarin)*

The Case for Sexual Liberty

Suppressed: Seven Key Essays Publishers Dared Not Print

The Search for Sexual Enjoyment

How to Prevent Your Child from Becoming a Neurotic Adult *(with Janet L. Wolfe and Sandra Moseley)*

Growth Through Reason: Verbatim Cases in Rational-Emotive Therapy *(with Ben N. Ard, Jr., H. Jon Geis, Paul A. Hauck, John M. Gullo, and Maxie C. Maultsby, Jr.)*

The Civilized Couple's Guide to Extramarital Adventure

How to Master Your Fear of Flying

A New Guide to Rational Living *(with Robert A. Harper)*

How to Live With—and Without—Anger.

Overcoming Procrastination *(with William J. Knaus)*

Handbook of Rational-Emotive Therapy *(with Russell Grieger)*

Brief Psychotherapy in Medical and Health Practice *(with Eliot Abrahms)*

The Intelligent Woman's Guide to Dating and Mating

by ALBERT ELLIS, Ph.D.

Foreword by JANET L. WOLFE, Ph.D.

LYLE STUART INC. • Secaucus, N.J.

Published by Lyle Stuart Inc.
120 Enterprise Ave., Secaucus, N.J. 07094

Published simultaneously in Canada by George J. McLeod Limited
Don Mills, Ontario

Address queries regarding rights and permissions to Lyle Stuart

Manufactured in the United States of America

Library of Congress Cataloging in Publication Data

Ellis, Albert, 1913-
   The intelligent woman's guide to dating and mating.

   Bibliography: p.

   1. Dating (Social customs)   2. Courtship.   3. Mate selection.   4. Sex instruction for women.   I. Title.
HQ801.E4   1979   301.41'4   78-26858
ISBN O-8184-0277-6

Contents

Acknowledgments

Grateful acknowledgment is made to Bernard Geis, for collaboration on the original idea for this book; to Fiddle Viracola and Rhoda Winter Russell, who read the first edition of this work when it was still in manuscript and made valuable suggestions; to Eileen Brand and Edward Sagarin for helpful editing; and to myself, myself, and myself, for invaluable assistance in typing the manuscript and editing the goddam galley and page proofs.

Foreword

Janet L. Wolfe, Ph.D.

Sleeping Beauty slumbers until her desires are awakened and fulfilled by the kiss of her prince; Rapunzel waits in her tower for the prince who will free her body from its imprisonment. Reared on a diet of "Be nice, be sweet," "Don't make waves, or appear too brainy," "Put other people first," and programmed to feel that if they are not mated, they are incomplete, half people, women have tended to go about the pursuit of a primary sex/love relationship with a fair amount of desperation and a lot of suffering.

He looks deeply into your eyes, tells you he loves you and can't live without you. You are swept off your feet and forget while the relationship lasts that you are an independent person who runs a large and successful department. The person with whom you have spent several bittersweet years goes through a life-cycle crisis and decides to take off. Depressed and resentful, you sit home night after night. Or you halfheartedly show up at a social event or two, but remain utterly convinced you'll never find another partner you could be happy with.

Women have an inordinate talent for blocking out negative features in the person they want; and a knack of going for the same kind of person their past experience indicates is bad news.

Not to mention passing over nice, gentle people who treat them well and care for them. We've been taught that, sooner or later, "Mr. Right" will come along. The problem is, there aren't too many Knights around, and lots of "Ladies." And if we remain sitting demurely waiting, we are likely to wind up with a lot of mismatching or no match at all. We pay the price of commonly feeling incomplete when lacking a partner. Feeling incomplete, we continually seek fulfillment in another; then expend a lot of energy either looking for someone to match up with; or cling fearfully to a poor relationship; or stay alone and feel unwanted and depressed, not enjoying the many things we *do* have.

Although heir to a truly botched-up set of values about mating and dating, we are fortunately living at an exciting time when millions of women are carving out new definitions for themselves of what a fulfilled human life consists of. We are beginning to replace romantic fantasies that never came true with more realistic expectations about relationships, to examine and extend the choices that are open to us, and to pursue our own goals more actively.

But, lo! Having begun to give up the White Knight myth, do our eyes deceive us—or is that a knight in shining armor on the horizon? There is probably no male writer around who has argued so forthrightly and courageously for women's assertively going after what they want in their sex/love relationships than pioneering writer, psychologist, and stamper out of sexual ignorance, Dr. Albert Ellis. When he published the first edition of this *Guide* in 1963, the present-day women's movement barely existed. Betty Friedan's *Feminine Mystique* had gone to press just as Ellis was putting the finishing touches on his volume, in which he inveighed against women's buying into relationships where they did all the giving and got little in return; and he implored women to fight against mores which put them into the back seat as far as initiating dates and having input into shaping their relationships was concerned. *The Intelligent Woman's Guide* is the first book that clearly came out for women's being as sexually assertive as men. It aroused great opposition on the part of many critics, including many of Ellis' professional colleagues, because it frankly advocated women's literally picking up male companions in public places, just as men had been customarily allowed to pick up women for countless previous decades.

Chapter Four of the original edition of the *Guide* was titled, as it still is in this new edition, "How to Become Assertive Without Being Aggressive," and it again turned out to be a pioneer piece of writing that sparked some of the later outstanding writings on assertion training. Other espousers of assertiveness training, such as Andrew Salter and Joseph Wolpe, had previously done some pioneering work in this area; and this was further developed by Robert Alberti, Michael Emmons, Arnold Lazarus, Arthur Lange, Patrica Jakubowski, and others during the 60's and 70's. But *The Intelligent Woman's Guide to Man-Hunting* may well have been the first major work that clearly differentiated between assertion and aggression and that unequivocally encouraged women to be just as assertive as men not only in general but specifically in sex-love relations. Others of Ellis's previous writings on sex, especially his famous essay "Is the Vaginal Orgasm a Myth?" and his books, *Sex Without Guilt* and *The Art and Science of Love,* all of which were written in the 1950's, also championed the notion that women have as much right to sex satisfaction as men and that it is often better for them to focus on achieving orgasm through noncoital means rather than through penile-vaginal copulation. Though Ellis has developed some of his early ideas further, partly through the influence of subsequent writings of the women's liberation movement, a perusal of the original edition will show that his major views were stated there. The 1963 version is something someone unaware of the identity of the author and publication date would speculate had been written by an ardent female supporter of women's rights in the 70's. Updated, it is a more remarkable book than ever—a gift to millions of women struggling to clarify their goals, feelings, and behavior in relationships that are being radically redefined.

Over the years that this extraordinary book has been out of print, awaiting revision by the astonishingly busy Ellis, I have personally received several dozen requests from women whose lives had been remarkably affected by the first edition, who had lent out their only copy, and who were frantically trying to track down a copy of the book for themselves or for a needy friend, perhaps as an "emergency ration" to keep them from sinking into the quicksand of a problematical relationship. I have seen at least 200 clients in my clinic over the last several years to each of whom I would have greatly liked to have given a copy of this book had I had one. My last two copies have long since disappeared—stolen, I think. Women by the score keep asking about this book—or comment on the great results they got from reading it. Many met their husbands or lovers through heeding some of its advice. Others, even though still unmated, benefited considerably in regard to some of their emotional problems. It has helped more women I know—friends as well as therapy clients—than any other book I've ever recommended to them.

What is so special about this book? Although in recent years women writers have begun to write articles and books encouraging women to question some of their assumptions and values in regard to sex/love relationships, rare has been the male who has assertively argued for women's equality; for their inalienable right to be treated with dignity and respect; and for the importance of their getting out of relationships which have a lot of negative aspects before too many years of self-sacrifice and too much emotional energy has been expended. And for the millions of women still hooked on the possibility of a good male / female relationship, it is indeed important to know that there are at least some *men* out there who support egalitarian relationships and assertiveness in women—men who stalwartly fight the anti-feminist attitude that males are the only ones with the right to go after what they want. And someone who provides a system for mobilizing anger at male oppression of females into constructive remedial action.

Ellis does not merely show women how they allow themselves to be doll-puppets, pulled by others; he gives them the technology for stopping their dependency and their excessive need to please others. He warns against falling into the traps of appearing helpless, of always nurturing others rather than themselves, and of being an eyelash-batting, sweet-talking lackey in order to attract a mate. He is acutely aware, through his over 30 years as a therapist, of the price that is eventually paid in terms of loss of personhood and, frequently, contempt by the mate the woman has allowed to use her as a doormat.

Ellis encourages women who want to be themselves to stay away from prospective male chauvinists who believe men were born to master women and who feel women are imposing on them when they ask for things that please them. He argues for relationships in which the people concerned can help nurture each other, and be nurtured; but where they can also both be strong, independent units who can drive nails, sew buttons, and do other tasks that most adult humans of either gender are perfectly capable of doing.

He is explicit in his guidelines about the wheres and how-tos of actively looking for a good sex/love partner, while at the same time sensitive to the limitations imposed by kids left over from the last marriage, exhaustion from working and keeping house, or being poor, aged, or handicapped. Unlike many other experts, he offers specific, highly practical suggestions on how to proceed to find suitable partners and how to initiate acquaintanceships without pressuring oneself to have a stock of brilliant opening lines.

Ellis's greatest contribution, however, lies in his use of his unique self-help system for helping people rid themselves of their blocks to successful mating, dating, and relating: anxiety, guilt, depression, low self-esteem, fear of rejection, and hostility. He shows women how, by using the principles of rational-emotive therapy (RET), they can replace the enjoyment-crippling scripts ("I couldn't approach a strange man!" "It's *awful* to be rejected!") poured into them by their parents and society, with new, more rational self-messages. He indicates how women can learn to be rejected without feeling their life must end, and how they can refuse to desperately *need* a relationship and thereby often doom themselves to failure. He demonstrates how women can be *themselves,* rather than some pale reflection of what others would like them to be. He teaches them how to express annoyance without blasting and blaming; how to accept their partners' mistakes without being a doormat for their whims; how to encourage positive change in a mate without cramming it down his throat; and how to calmly deal with a neurotic, treat him/her kindly, and if kindness doesn't work, how to leave and look for someone who more naturally behaves in a way more to their liking.

These guidelines for refusing to make oneself miserable about the trials of dating and mating are wise and profound; and—best of all—applicable to not making oneself miserable about practically every other area of life as well. Hopefully, this work will (along with its strongly feminist companion book, *Sex and the Liberated Male*), provide major ammunition in a revolution that will ultimately liberate men and women from constricting sex-role expectations and allow them to experience new highs of self-actualization and egalitarian relating. There are, alas, still far too many males around who, unlike Ellis, do not always flock to the woman who is vibrant, alive, self-assertive, and sexually direct. Warning: this book is not for women who want to knuckle under to male chauvinism and continue to play the eyelash-batting pussycat game. It is for women who want to bring themselves and the people with whom they have chosen to relate closely to a new level of caring and sharing and comfort.

Society has taught us a lot of rules we would better learn to start ignoring. Ellis teaches us a whole new set of guidelines about how to relate to others and ourselves that we'd better *not* ignore. If we keep following early teachers and models, we will probably lead uninteresting and unfulfilled lives. If we heed Ellis' wise teachings, and on a daily basis practice working against our self-downing, terror of rejection, desperate need for a partner, and hostility and blame when we don't get what we want, the world is ours—with or without a mate.

Introduction to
the First Edition

Let's face it: practically all books and articles on How to Get Your Man and Live Happily with Him Forever After are full of hogwash. Why? Because to a large extent they are written by women.

What would a woman in our society know about the sex-love responsiveness of men? Even a clever woman? Not too much. Obviously, being a woman, she is not a man. Nor, in this respect, can we legitimately pull the old chestnut about *vive la difference*. A man, just because he is a man, knows what it takes to encourage him to relate to a woman. A woman, just because she is a woman, knows relatively little about what he wants. She may, of course, find out. But not, you may safely bet, from another woman.

Why? For several reasons.

First of all, most women in our culture really don't *want* to know how to go about improving their dating and mating relations. They want to know, rather, where to find a male who is "naturally" pleased with the ways in which they prefer to date and mate. Which is quite a different thing!

Take, for example, a woman's making frank overtures toward

a man. Practically all males love women to make frank, open, undisguised friendly overtures toward them: to pick them up on street corners, give them their telephone numbers, ask them for a date, call them when they are lonely, and start taking off their own and the male's clothes when they are alone together. This is what the Walter Mittys of the world daydream about constantly, and what the less inhibited men imagine as the greatest—and rarest—of delights.

But will women deign to make such unvarnished overtures to the males they prefer? No, a thousand and one times no. Because they like to believe—as a result of their *own* fear of failure and rejection—that the men don't want them to take the initiative, but would rather show what red-blooded, assertive, rootin-tootin males they are.

The hell they would! The very last thing the poor male things want to risk is failure or rejection. And the very best way for a woman to make sure that they are gratefully, undyingly hers is for her to ensure that her male friends can't possibly fail—because she herself sticks her neck out and takes all the risks that they, theoretically, should take. But will women ever, to themselves or their sisters, admit this? Naturally not. For if they did, they'd have to get off their derrières and do what *they're* most afraid of doing: taking risks, making firm commitments, and being honest about showing their feelings.

Secondly, most women are much too conventional to admit to themselves or to learn from each other the gory details of the real art of searching. For, in most modern societies, the female is not *supposed* to unzip her clothes and fully and freely *give* of herself to every prospective husband that she meets. But, as almost any village idiot will quickly tell you, this is usually the easiest, and often positively the only, way that she is likely to impress her (no pun intended) womanly virtues on almost any sane and intelligent man she encounters.

Consequently, in the vast majority of cases, the modern American woman bows to convention—and bows out of another possible prenuptial affair. Worse, she pigheadedly and wrongheadedly then rationalizes her stupidity by maintaining that no respectable man would marry her if she did surrender her chastity to him. And she has no trouble in convincing herself—and her equally other-directed (i.e., other-*women*-directed) sisters that her false views are true.

In the third place, American women almost invariably set up the ground rules of their manhunting activities so that these rules are beautifully designed *not* to net them an intelligent, sane, and cultured husband but to bag a boorish dunce, a male supremacist, or what H. L. Mencken aptly termed, a typical member of the booboisie.

Millions of contemporary males even in this last quarter of the twentieth century do insist that women are *never* to take the initiative in a sex encounter and that the one who wins her mate by giving away free premarital samples of her bedworthiness is, mister, no real lady. And just about every one of these millions of "real men" is, clearly, ignorant or stupid or seriously emotionally disturbed. Practically none of them, moreover, is likely to make anything but a narrow-minded, woman-downing, double-standard-bearing mate who will have about as much real respect for his wife as a human being and a person in her own right as he will have for Marcel Proust or Leonardo da Vinci or Albert Einstein.

Well? Well, *this* is the type of average man whom our females allow to set the rules of their man-snaring game. And, with all due poetic justice, this is the kind of man, at best, on whom the trap door before the altar generally swings shut. With consequent misery to both husband and wife, naturally, until divorce (if it can be mercifully arranged) does them part.

In other words; if, inspired by our woman-promulgated mating codes, a modern miss is highly "successful" in getting her man— and, as the vital statistics show every year, she much more often than not eventually is—she is almost guaranteed to mate with an undemocratic, woman-downing satrap while leaving the few truly woman-accepting males of her acquaintance to fall to her unsqueamish, "cheap" sisters—or to the everlasting joys of bachelorhood. The more she follows the rules of the usual female-endorsed man-baiting manual, the more likely is she to end up with the same kind of authoritarian-minded cad who married Mom and Grandmom. And the less likely she is to be, before, during, and after mating, herself.

Women, then, know as much about finding, fascinating and stimulating, and mating men as they do about the gentle art of mustache-tweezing. They usually insist on playing the tunes of twentieth-century dating on a medieval psaltery. And when, as is generally the case, they compromise by taking a man they really don't want, they frequently ascribe this sad result to their not having followed the conventional rules of the mating game, when in truth it is the consequence of swallowing them whole; and they run for yet another batch of hard-cover or paperbacked treatises on HOW TO BE CHASTE BUT CHASED.

Enough! *One* book one day had to be written telling the female of the species, plainly and in unsaccharined language, how to meet, greet, and treat the man—and I really mean *man*—of the tribe. This, ladies, is it. Much of what you are about to read, you probably won't like. Some of what follows, you will positively abhor. Tough. Strong medicines rarely tickle the palate. But they often, if taken regularly, settle the stomach. Or strengthen the guts.

Let us, too, get this straight at the start: the present book, *The Intelligent Woman's Guide to Dating and Mating,* is not carelessly titled. This volume is *not* designed for the average feminine dunderhead. It assumes that its readers are intelligent: women who can, want to, and do read. And think. And read some more. And think some more. And think still more.

It also assumes that these intelligent, reading women primarily want to relate to a similarly intelligent man. Not that they might not enjoy Don Juan's looks. Or Hercules' strength. Or Casanova's love-making ability. Doubtless, they would. But these intelligent, reading women, it is assumed, mainly want a long-lasting, well-wearing mate and companion; not a dependent slob; or a woman-dominating autocrat; or a nose-to-the-grindstone business tycoon; or an ears-glued-to-the-TV fanatic. But a bright, cultured, firm but kindly *person:* a *mensch.*

These, then, are the main questions that this book will attempt to answer: Where can the intelligent woman find a suitably intelligent, truly strong, not too emotionally disturbed man? How, when she finds him, can she unanxiously relate to him? What, specifically, can she do to help herself win and keep him?

Now that hundreds of women magazine writers and scores of authoresses of books have had their say in giving what are mostly the wrong answers to these questions, what are, from a *man's* point of view, some of the right ones? We shall, in the following pages, see!

Introduction to
the New Edition

It is indeed a pleasure to revise this edition of my earlier book *The Intelligent Woman's Guide to Man-Hunting* and to bring it out for a new age in a substantially new form. For of the more than forty books and monographs that I have written, none has been more enthusiastically received by its readers than this one. The original edition of this book has been out of print for several years; but the demand for its return has been most insistent, largely because, as Dr. Janet L. Wolfe notes in her Foreword, the original volume has helped so many women in their dating and mating encounters.

Naturally, I am pleased by this response. Most of the books I have written have, in one way or another, been used as self-help manuals by professional and lay readers. And a few, like *A New Guide to Rational Living,* which I co-authored with Dr. Robert A. Harper, are among the most popular of such books, and continue to bring me unsolicited testimonials, in the form of letters, poems, therapy referrals, and verbal appreciation. But not like the *Intelligent Woman's Guide!* If I were still capable of being embarrassed—which, after using rational-emotive therapy (RET) on myself for a number of years, I no longer seem to be—I would positively blush at hearing some of these encomiums. Instead, I thank those who like it and feel highly pleased that the original edition of this book has seemed to do so much good.

Why, then, has the *Guide* been out of print for several years? For a number of reasons, first and foremost of which is my usual busyness. As the contemporary sexual revolution that I helped to initiate over a quarter of a century ago has resulted in some significant changes in our social-sexual customs and mores, I have known for some time that some of the material in the book had better be updated. One of the main changes in this respect is the fact that, when I published the original edition some fifteen years ago, almost all the single women in Western civilization were enormously interested not only in a sex-love relationship with a man but in legal marriage. Many or most, of course, still are. But innumerable women today, especially before they finally end up legally wed, want to experience a mateship rather than a marriage: that is, they want to have a one-to-one relationship on a somewhat prolonged basis, often including domestic sharing; but they do not, at least as yet, actually want to marry, nor to have children. Some of them even want to have children—but still not to marry.

A remarkably bright and attractive reporter, for example, told me a couple of years ago that she, at the age of thirty, had a fine career, many good friends in New York, and a love relationship with a man, and that she wanted to go on with these same arrangements but quite probably would never legalize them or any other relationship. She also said that several of her close female friends felt exactly the same way she did, and never intended to marry, even though they all wanted some kind of a heterosexual affair, either on a long-term basis or from time to time.

I do not suggest that this woman or her female friends are in the majority today; nor that they ever will be. But certainly legal marriage is far from their minds much of the time; while extralegal mating is one of the things they most want. I have therefore deliberately retitled this book, *The Intelligent Woman's Guide to Dating and Mating,* to emphasize the fact that if a woman wants a steady male companion, she does not have to marry him; but if she definitely wants legal marriage, that is fine, too—and she can still use all the techniques of self-actualization and of enhancing relationships that are outlined in this work.

Another reason for making a fairly thorough revision of this book has been my increased use of rational-emotive therapy (RET) during the past two decades and the greater incorporation of its methods into my writings on sex and love, as well as in those on psychotherapy and general self-help. For as I have said repeatedly during the last two decades, Freud and his followers are mistaken when they state or imply that emotional problems of living stem from specific sex problems—such as the Oedipus or Electra complex, castration fears, penis envy, or fixation on oral eroticism. On the contrary, as Alfred Adler, Karen Horney, Erich Fromm, George Kelly, Eric Berne, Rollo May, myself, and other leading therapists have shown, both male and female sex difficulties often arise from general, nonsexual disturbances; and love problems, in particular, again usually stem from general emotional blocks rather than from sexual hassles.

Although RET was a comparatively new and unproven form of treatment for emotional disturbances when I wrote the first edition of *The Intelligent Woman's Guide,* it has now come of age, and is at the center of the cognitive-behavior therapy revolution. As the bibliography at the end of this revised edition will show, scores of experimental studies have now been published which attest to its effectiveness, and thousands of therapists throughout the world use it as their main technique. In this revised *Guide* I have included a great deal more material on RET than I included in the original version, just as I did in the case of *Sex and the Liberated Man*—a completely rewritten version of my old popular book, *Sex and the Single Man.* Any woman (or, for that matter, man!) who reads this new *Guide* will be able to understand, I hope, most of the basic principles of RET and to apply them to problems of dating and relating. I believe that the more she does so, the better she will relate to people and achieve a satisfactory sex life. This seems to have happened in the case of tens of thousands of women who read the first edition of the book; and it is to be hoped that it will happen, in even greater numbers, to those who read this revised edition.

Another significant change in American life that has taken place since the early 1960's is our acceptance of lesbian relationships. It is not that the proportion of women who are lesbians has increased; but more lesbians now acknowledge long-term homosexual relationships, and many more women than before now have at least occasional lesbian experiences. Although the present revision still assumes that the vast majority of Western women strongly desire to have sex-love relationships with a man rather than with another woman, virtually all the methods of encountering, choosing, and getting along with suitable partners can be easily applied to lesbian affairs. There is no attempt in this revision to promulgate the doctrine that women *should* or *must* have male partners or that they are emotionally disturbed if they choose females. Compulsive homosexuality, like compulsive heterosexuality, may well stem from disturbance; but preferential sex-love affairs, with same-sex or other-sex partners, are not in themselves neurotic.

A final word about the women's movement. When I published the first edition of this *Guide* in 1963, the present-day women's movement hardly existed. Now it is a vital and important force in our lives. Good! But for all my liberalism regarding women, I am still of course a male, reared in a male chauvinist culture. I am therefore inclined to have a biased outlook on what females had better do and not do. To counteract possible prejudice, I have therefore arranged with an outstanding feminist, Dr. Janet L. Wolfe, a psychotherapist, sex therapist, and associate director of the Institute for Rational Living and the Institute for Rational-Emotive Therapy, to go over the contents of this revision and to write a Foreword to it. I have found her comments and suggestions most valuable, and I am sure that the readers will also profit from them.

Anyway, I have finally found the time to finish this revision of *The Intelligent Woman's Guide.* Once again: happy dating and mating!

Albert Ellis, Ph.D.

Institute for Rational-Emotive Therapy
45 East 65th Street
New York, N.Y. 10021

The
Intelligent
Woman's
Guide
to
Dating and
Mating

1

What Women Think a Man Wants in Women

What women *think* a man wants in women, and what most intelligent, sane men actually do want are as different—well, as masculinity and femininity. Women are generally, in this respect, the victims of projection. They essentially, if unconsciously, ask themselves: "What would *I* and my sainted mother (not to mention my cousins and my sisters and my aunts) want in a person, especially in a close woman friend?" Then they project this peculiarly feminine set of preferences onto the males they know, and rashly assume that *they* must want the same things in a woman, too.

Nothing could be more misleading. Certainly, there are *some* men who look for, in a female, exactly what females look for in another woman. Mama's boys, for example, and the seriously neurotic, and males obsessed with proving their manhood and other assorted kinds of kooks. But who the devil wants them?

Take Jonathan, for example. Jonathan was a very well brought up boy, whose mother made a kind of substitute lover of him from the age of eight, when she kicked his father out of her bedroom and encouraged him to go fly his kite elsewhere (which, with his secretary and a series of maids, he promptly did). Mama took Jonathan with her everywhere: including even women's rest rooms, when she could possibly sneak him in.

Naturally, he grew up to be a real, fine boy: courteous, pleasant, and quite devoted to women. And naturally, he always wanted a girl just like the girl who married dear old Dad—that is, a girl just as super-refined, pluperfect, and sexless as Mama.

When he finally married Marilyn—who had been chased around so many living rooms by one-track-minded males that she was delighted to find one of the brute breed who was perfectly content with a good-night peck—he asked nothing more of her than he would have thought of asking of his own mother. Namely: that she look like a well-groomed doll twenty-four hours a day; that she never use an expletive stronger than "Oh fudge!"; that she keep her sneaky little hands off him while he laboriously waded through the *New York Times* and the *Wall Street Journal* every evening from seven till eleven; and that she stop that terribly disgusting heavy breathing and panting whenever, every other Saturday evening, they had the kind of relations which, alas, were necessary for the procreation of a Jonathan, Jr.

So much (as Marilyn finally said to herself and her lawyer) for Jonathan. Certainly such "men" exist. And certainly their ideals of womanhood are remarkably close to those of Queen Victoria. But that's *their* problem; and the intelligent woman of today who would make it hers had better hie herself, fast, to a competent psychotherapist.

Fortunately, such males as Jonathan are among the small minority. Even so the majority of educated and cultured young men are batty enough, and usually have amply more than their fair share of unassertiveness, withdrawal, and impotence. Or (as a mask for these very traits) they have varying nauseating degrees of false confidence, and are demanding and domineering. Too bad; and I really sympathize with the women of our society who have to keep putting up with this kind of rot.

The fact remains, however, that most American males definitely do *not* want the kind of females that most American women seem to think that they want. And the brighter and saner the men are, the less does their notion of the ideal woman approximate that of their tradition-bound mothers and sisters. Let us, by way of illustration, run down the list of some of the main traits which men are supposed to crave in their Dream Woman, and let us see to what extent they actually do.

Respectability

Perhaps the main thing that the average woman *thinks* a man
wants is respectability. His prospective mate should be—she
feels—the kind of person who, like Caesar's wife, is above suspi-
cion; whom no one would even think of saying a nasty word
about; who is as pure as the unpollinated flowers that bloom in
the spring, tra-la. What is more, she should come from a fine
family; live in a most respectable neighborhood; have an expensively furnished and tastefully decorated apartment; be living
with her family rather than by herself; etc.

Well?

Nonsense! The truly intelligent and mature contemporary
male has about as much use for this kind of respectability as he
has for a shaving mug. This is not to say that he wants his partner
to be so totally unrespectable that his friends and his boss will
literally be shocked when she wears blue jeans to a cocktail party
at the Waldorf Astoria or invites his buddies to share their bed as
well as their board when they come to visit. After all, there are
some limits to how disheveled, disorganized, and "disreputable"
a man wants his mate to be.

Nonetheless: today's bright young man generally wants a
woman to have had some sort of sex life before she met him, and
he has no objection to her friends, and his, knowing perfectly
well that she is not the Virgin Mary's maiden aunt. He frequently
prefers that she not come from a fine, hoity-toity family that will
forever after prove to be a royal pain in the backside to him, as
they insist on garish, expensive parties, attendance at stuffy
weekly dinners, and all kinds of other showy family rituals. He
usually *prefers* his woman to live by herself, in a not too prim
neighborhood where he and she and their friends can come and
go as they please, without being subject to Gestapo-like prying
neighbors or service people. He often does not give a hoot about
the furnishings and the decor, as long as the chairs and beds are
comfortable.

Sue came around to her group psychotherapy sessions bitterly
complaining for weeks that she couldn't make out well with any
of the men she kept meeting because she didn't dare take them
up to her sleazy apartment-hotel room, and therefore was only
able to kiss them good night in the taxi. At first, most of the

women in the group agreed with her, since she did live in a pretty crummy hotel, and the furniture in her room was, to use her term, quite ghastly. But the males in the group couldn't see this at all, and insisted that the appearance of a woman's place was the very last thing they concentrated on if and when they finally got inside.

Finally, Sue's complaints became so repetitious that one of the other members of the group, Maryann, got suspicious. "Look," she said to Sue with some degree of annoyance, "you keep blaming your poor social life on your stupid apartment or room or whatever you call it—"

"Room!" exclaimed Sue, almost in tears. "Let's face it: it's a really awful place. And I can't—"

"All right, all right!" Maryann interrupted. "So it's ghastly. Let's say it is. But how about your best friend, Joan, that you keep telling us about so enviously. *She* makes out quite well with men, doesn't she?"

"She sure does! But she's not afraid to take men up to her place and let them stay, even all night if she wants them to. And now she's found a lover who seems ideal. The luck I have!"

"Luck?" Maryann persisted. "It seems to me that your friend, Joan, *makes* her luck. Just like you make yours—only in reverse. And where, may I ask, has Joan been living these last few months, when she's been doing so well with men, and now about to marry one?"

"Oh. Right down the hall from me."

"Oh! The same sleazy hotel? And what kind of a room does she have there, may I ask?"

"Well—I, I guess it's about the same—no, I even have to say a little smaller and worse—than mine."

"So! Even a little smaller and worse than yours."

"Oh, Oh, I see what you mean. Oh."

And Sue did see what Maryann meant. From that time on, she began to invite a few, selected male companions to her room, either before or after she went out with them. Her complaints to the group about her troubles with males considerably diminished.

The fact remains, then: while respectability and putting on the Ritz may be most appropriate for the woman who lives in a town like Stillwater, Iowa (perhaps 3,000 pop., most of them residing — but not exactly living— there since the days of the

Indian wars), or for the one who wants to find a stuffed shirt with solid gold cuff links and a chinchilla bow tie, the woman who lives in any sizable modern city and wants to relate to a real person rather than a bank account needs this kind of respectability like she needs a hole in her diaphragm.

Shyness and unassertiveness

Nineteenth-century novelists eulogized the unassuming modesty, the demure shyness (not to mention the shy demureness) of their ineffably beauteous, inexpressibly charming (and inestimably vacuous) young heroines. That, among other good reasons, is undoubtedly why the three-decker novel died a horrible, long-overdue death.

Many female (and, incredibly, a few male) journalists are still bent on exhuming this pre-twentieth-century ideal of abashed young womanhood; and it is to be feared that only when many women's magazines find their way to the Happy Hunting ground for anachronistic publications will this inane image finally be annihilated.

There are several significant reasons why the shy and unassertive woman, especially when she has reached her midtwenties, has as much chance of ensnaring a fine, alert, mature man as I have of becoming Pope Albert the First. To wit:

1. Her less shy and eminently saner sisters have been gratuitously given, by her tight-lipped and tight-buttoned retreat, hearts, spades, diamonds, and clubs in the game of love; while she has left herself with the facsimile on the outside of the card box.

2. Her tied tongue and locked legs are no longer attractive in a world where women commonly open up their heads and hearts to new acquaintances as well as would-be lovers.

3. The shackles with which she binds herself may still be appropriate for the *hoi polloi* of the hinterlands; but they are sadly misapplied to the members of the urban smart set.

4. If, when she has reached the age of thirty her pathological shyness has not helped her—as we may well predict, statistically, that it will not—to snare a mate, she will have by that time missed out on most men who are keen on

pairing off with women. She then will be forced to try her ineffective ways on the remaining really difficult customers. *That* will give her something to be shy about!

5. Timidity and unassertiveness are just as healthy for the average young female as is a thrice-daily dose of cyanide. Being alive and kicking means, in the first and final analysis, *being* and *expressing* oneself. Self-imposed inhibitions on self-expression are equivalent to suicide; only, in terms of extended suffering, much worse. The woman who sells her soul for a mess of pusillanimous pottage is, whether she mates or not, a zero. And what man in his sound mind wants to marry and live with a cipher?

When Jane S. came for psychotherapy, because she felt depressed a great deal of the time and could find nothing worthwhile to live for, it became immediately apparent that a large part of her depression was closely linked with her pathological shyness. But when I quickly brought to her attention the fact that she was terribly shy, and that there was no reason why she *had* to be, she strongly resisted my suggestions and stoutly contended that she was *naturally shy,* and she sort of *felt* good to be that way.

"Perhaps so," said I, "but what does it *get* you to be this shy — or, to use a harsher-sounding (and truer) term, to be scared stiff of people?"

"*Get* me? Does it have to *get* me something?"

"No, it doesn't have to, in the sense of your deriving some special benefit from being shy. But it does have to get you something, in the sense of disadvantages."

"And they are?"

"They are what you've already indicated: lack of man friends — or, for that matter, woman friends; a dull existence; and, in the final analysis, depression, or the feeling that what's the use of going on if life is this empty."

"All those things stem from shyness?"

"Wouldn't they almost have to? Can you imagine anyone as shy as you who would *not* lack friends, have a dull life, and finally feel depressed?"

"Hmm."

"Hmm, indeed! And let me go one step further. Not only can we ask, 'What does shyness *get* you?' but also, and perhaps more importantly, 'What does it get *you?*' "

"*Me?*"

"Yes: *you.* Your*self,* that is. Or maybe we'd better stress it differently: *your*self. For while you are shy, you are of course not being *you.*"

"Who am I being, then, if not myself?"

"Obviously: the puppet of *others.* These others, you think — or, rather, you *un*thinkingly imagine — are going to be terribly critical of you if you *are* yourself, if you express your you-ness. Probably they won't be. Or they may even like you much better if you are you. Anyway, you're afraid they won't. So, to please *them,* you shyly, fearfully withdraw, and refuse to be you. You become what *they,* presumably, want you to be. Or, at least, you become so neutral, so hard to see, that they'll never notice that you are *not* what they want you to be. So you dance, in effect, to their pulling of *your* strings. Except, ironically, they aren't even pulling the strings. *You* are! You therefore make yourself into a do-it-yourself puppet, and absolutely refuse to be *you.*"

"By trying to please them, then, I'm giving up on pleasing and being *me?*"

"Exactly. While if you tried, really tried, to keep being *you,* to do what *you* basically wanted to do, you in all probability would still win more of them over to your side than you're now doing; and, whether you did or not, at least you'd have your*self.*"

Jane S. was a difficult client, and it took me a good many more sessions before I finally convinced her that she had everything to lose and nothing to gain by making herself behave shyly. When she started to see how *un*natural her "natural" timidity really was, and when I got her to persist at her therapy homework assignments of meeting, by hook or crook, at least one new man or woman every week, she not only lost most of her shyness but actually began to enjoy being self-assertive. Within six months she was living with a man after accepting the third offer she had received during this period. Her male acquaintances found her shyness to be as attractive as skunkweed. Once self-deodorized, and blooming like an unblushing rose, she became much more mateable.

Brainlessness

Numerous mating manuals warn the young woman never, oh

never, to let her natural braininess show through to her suitors. Males, these manuals say, simply can't *stand* a girl who is as right as are they; their poor, dear masculine egos are sorely offended by female wit and sagacity; and they must be continually led to believe that only they, of the heterosexual couple, have a well-nourished brain beneath their pointed heads.

Bosh!

Certainly there are many men, including highly intelligent men, who break out in hives when women display any degree of knowledge or wisdom, and who prefer to associate (euphemism for climb in the hay) with flibbertigibbety sexpots who haven't— or at least make sure that they don't express—a serious thought in their heads. But how many of these truly bright males want to live with thoughtless, harebrained women? Dammed few.

One of the most frequent complaints I hear, in fact, in the course of the marriage counseling sessions I do every week, is that Mrs. Jones or Mrs. Smith or Mrs. Doe seemed to be such a bright, interesting young thing before the chiming of the wedding bells; but now that she's comfortably married, she doesn't read, discuss, or think at all; and she's consequently such a horrible bore that the sooner she runs off with the supermarket manager, the better!

Naturally, the woman friend or mate who snottily uses her brain power to show her male up (particularly before others!), or who keeps ceaselessly proving to him (with facts, figures, and witnesses) that his stupid ideas are much inferior to her unexcelled gems of sagacity, is not going to endear herself greatly to him. But neither will the woman who deliberately acts like a dumb Dora whenever her male is around, just to show him what a gweat big bwight man he is. Sure he will think, under such circumstances, that he is God's intellectual gift to humanity— and that why the devil should he waste this gift on such a hopelessly stupid female?

If, moreover, a woman selects an otherwise keen male who actually does insist that she behave like an orangutan when she is in his presence, what does she need him for? If he is *that* emotionally insecure, she'd be better off to *use* her brain and eliminate him as a good prospect rather than scuttle her good sense just to trap him into mating. Having an *affair* with such an egg may have a kind of fascination all its own. But living under the same roof with this kind of character is quite another thing.

Stylishness

It has often been said that women in our society normally do not dress for men but for other women. Let me, with unabashed repetition, say this again. Certainly, some men insist that their women friends adopt the very latest Telstar-relayed Parisian mode. Which men? Well, playboys for example. And weaklings who want their so-called egos raised by having an up-to-the-minute fashion-draped Ms. America on their arms.

But the above-average, independent-thinking man? Rarely! As soon as he notes that his weekend date has closets of expensive clothes, shelves full of makeup, and racks of many-splendored shoes, he begins to ask himself some interesting questions. Such as: How much is all this stuff going to cost *me,* if we get mated? How long am I going to have to wait, every time we go out, for her to put on her armor and war paint? What has she got to *hide* behind all that fancy camouflage? Has she any *other* thought in her pretty little head than clothes, clothes, clothes?

More important still: long before he even thinks of intimately relating the biologically normal male is far more interested in how a woman *undresses* than in how she dresses. Her foundation garments may be just the thing, thinks she, to pull in her tummy and bulge out her breasts. But, thinks he: how the devil am I going to get beyond that coat of mail to see what delights are underneath? Her fresh-from-Bonwit Teller dancing dress may be wonderfully eye-catching, she tells herself, and bound to set his heart swiftly beating. But, he asks himself with his heart gently purring and his genitals roaring: how can I even *touch* her, with that horribly fragile, easily crushable gown between us?

The healthy, eager male, in other words, is primarily interested in one kind of feminine style: bed style. If the woman he dates is to wear anything at all, he prefers it to be a negligée. Or a bikini. Or any reasonable facsimile thereof. And noisy night clubs, crowded cocktail lounges, Sunday church services, and even a good Broadway or off-Broadway show are at most of second-rate interest to him, especially at the beginning of a relationship. He will take his date to a fashionable club or resort because *she* wants to go there; and, being interested in getting certain obvious ultimate rewards, he aims to please. But what *he* really wants is a private room—almost *any* old room—and clothes which are as casual and removable as possible.

Does this sound as if the male is terribly crass and insulting, with little interest in style, flair, and finesse, and his one-track-minded absorption in getting to bed firstest with the mostest? On the contrary!—it is the ultra-modishly-minded female, if anything, who is the actual, if unintending, insulter. For the man is literally going for what *every* woman presumably eagerly wants him to go for: *her.* Her outer vestments, her dyed hair, her artificial eyelashes, and her various other store-bought charms she can, to his way of thinking, throw down the drain.

He craves *her* body, *her* kisses and caresses, *her* conversation, *her* responses to his overtures. And how, prithee, is he to find *her* if she is hopelessly lost in all the expensive, armoring, look-but-don't-touch trappings of haute couture? Does he insult her by his honest, lustful interest? Heavens, no! If denigration exists in their relationship, it is much more likely to be her *self*-deprecating insistence that she cannot possibly offer herself to him as she *is,* because he obviously would not accept her if he knew what a twerp she *really* was.

Away, then, with the super-stylishness hokum! If you want to dress tastefully, individually, and even (if you can really afford it) expensively, go right ahead: be yourself. If you want to live in the finest neighborhood, be seen at the best places, go only to the hoity-toitiest resorts: fine. If that's your cup of tea, swig it to the dregs. But don't delude yourself that this kind of modish behavior has anything—except, probably, negatively—to do with your finding and keeping a real, yourself-loving man. Such a man will be interested in you, naked—and I mean naked—you, and not your fashionable, up-to-the-minute trimmings. Or, as Confucius could have said: To trap with trappings is to trap yourself.

Mothering

Every man, so some books written by women say, wants to be mothered. Make him feel that you are always there, with his slippers at night and his rubbers (the kind you wear on rainy days, that is) in the morning, and he will become so unalterably attached to you that no other vixen can possibly erase your mark with her bushy tail.

What claptrap! Even little boys—yes, four-, six-, and eight-year-old little boys—frequently do not like to be mothered. The male, if he is biologically anything, is a pretty independence-

seeking, why-the-deuce-don't- you-leave-me-alone kind of ani-
mal. That's why small boys play hooky, stay out late, at times
even run away from home. That's why big boys often remain
bachelors.

Do *some* presumably grown-up males dote on being mothered? Yes, ma'am; and if truly wise you were, you'd leave them
to just that: their mothers. You'll probably never be able to drag
such a man away from her anyway; and even after she (Allah be
praised!) kicks the bucket, he'll still be with her, in spirit, in the
coffin. Who needs it — *you?*

Come, now: let's face reality. A real mothering type of mother
is almost always a pain in the neck, as is any other form of
strangulator. She worries too much — and thereby restricts her
child's freedom. She plots, schemes, and plans — and prevents
the kid from thinking for himself. She bans pleasant, exciting
experiences; enforces the dullest and deadliest of routines; and
generally kills with "kindness." Is *this* what you want to do to
your dearly beloved man?

Besides, what male above the age of eighteen really wants
(except in the Freudian fairy tales, euphemistically termed case
histories) to copulate with his mother? Cleopatra's step-son?
Well, perhaps. But who else?

If you feel terribly motherly, beget and breed your own children. Or open a nursery school. Or mate if you dare with a
schizophrenic. But if, perchance, you happen to encounter a
reasonably grown-up, moderately mature man, for God's sake,
lady, keep your cotton-pickin', mothering hands to yourself.

Be nice to this man, yes. Give him understanding and succoring *if and when* he asks for it. But don't spend your idiotic life
looking ceaselessly for things to do for him, for ways to abdicate
your selfhood by making life effortless for him. You may, in that
way, win his attention and attachment as a lackey or an underling
wins him. But not very much more than that. And, very likely,
you won't even win that: since after a while he may well find your
services onerous and insidiously demanding. For a real man to
want to stay with you and to love you deeply, you'd better have
his respect as well as his domestic involvement. And what spoiled
brat actually respects his mother?

Do services rendered before mating help yank a man out of
his determination to lead a completely single life? Very definitely,
in many instances. Take your boyfriend's suits to the dry-clean-

ers. Meet him at the airport when he is coming in from out of town. Help him on the research project he is doing. Show him, in many such ways as these, that you really care for him, are interested in his work, and will do anything you can to be of service — when he *asks* for it. Even volunteer certain services that you know perfectly well he would like you to do but that he is too timid or too considerate to ask you for.

All this, however, is not mothering. Mothering is done by a woman who is convinced that she knows what her (little or big) boy wants much better than he does, and that if he does things the way *she* thinks they should be done, he will be efficient and happy. Mothering is a *condescending*, holier-than-thou kind of behavior. It is also, perversely enough, mixed in with the credo that the mothering individual is no damned good *unless* she is of service to someone else: that her intrinsic worth as a human being *depends* on her telling another what to do, and sometimes doing it for him.

Although the mothering person's intentions are mostly good, she actually deprecates both herself and her victim by her determined self-sacrifice. By managing to get both above *and* below her often all-too-willing victim, she makes it impossible for them both to achieve male-female complementarity and true equality.

So read, if you must, those blubbery, let's-make-John-happy-by-mothering-him articles in some women's magazines. Then do the opposite of what they say.

Romance-seeking

Everyone who sees Hollywood films knows, of course, that mating directly springs from romance, that the way to live with a man is to get him to fall violently in love with you, and that the only true method of keeping him from straying is to keep romance fiercely burning for *every* moment of your life sentence in glorious Technicolor. How? Well, as everyone who reads Madison Avenue's best efforts knows, by annually applying some six thousand, two hundred and eighty-three dollars and fifty-two cents worth of Alluring face cream, Come-hither cosmetics, Yougetmerightbelowthebelt perfume, and WhyshouldMmepompadourhaveanythingonme hair dye.

Everyone knows all this, obviously — except highly intelligent, reasonably sane, cultured males. Such curious beings, normally enough, have more than average propensities for romance; and, given half a chance, they will violently commit themselves to heterosexual passions that, while not exactly putting poor old Abelard, Petrarch, and Dante in the shade, have a resplendent glory that is uniquely their own. High-level males, in other words, distinctly can love in a high-level romantic manner; and frequently they do.

But romantic love, to a man of this type, does not necessarily equal mating: otherwise, as I have noted in *Sex and the Liberated Man,* most of them would have ended up living with one of their first schoolteachers. Love is just not enough. And, as I keep repeating to my clients, although it is usually foolish, these days, to live with anyone whom you *don't* love, it is even more foolish to live with everyone you do.

Nor, apparently, am I alone in noting this. Years ago, when I did a study of the love relationships of college women, I discovered that even suggestible, highly romantic teenagers were hardly overly determined to mate with the first man whose physical attributes quickly set their virginal hearts pumping. Rather, they somehow managed to ask themselves, in most instances, such questions as "How bright, really, is he?" . . . "What are his chances of getting on well in life?" . . . "What kind of a father do I think he'd make?" . . . and "How much does he really think of *me?*" — all this before they let themselves "spontaneously" and "romantically" slide.

So, too, I later found, with most sensible males. "Hooray!" they consciously or unconsciously shout to themselves, "for Sylvia's matchless cold-creamed skin, flawless lotioned hands, peerless carmined lips!" But, a little more cautiously they add: "*Who* is Sylvia? *What* is she?" And only after that *who* and *what* are, with more than a slight degree of practical evidence, reasonably answered do they allow themselves to "fall" in love with Sylvia and consider her as a housemate.

What is more, love is not all — not at least to the man who has most of his marbles. Sure, he can love Gloria because of her baby-blue eyes, Edith because she is so sweet, and Harriet because she puts a lady rabbit to shame. But he is also quite capable of remembering that Gloria doesn't shut up for a single minute, Edith falls apart when company is present, and Harriet hasn't cleaned her little apartment for the last seven and a half weeks. And who needs, thinks he to him, *that* kind of stuff?

If even erstwhile romance is not likely to charm the above-average bachelor into parting with a sizable chunk of his life savings to set up a *menage-à-deux,* his enthusiasm for romance in perpetuity is usually even more fragile. Sure he would like to feel ultra-impassioned about his mate and to devote oodles of time to keeping her romantically agog — *if* there were not endless bills to pay, housewares to be fixed, office work to be done, children to make arrangements for, etc., etc.

What's so damned romantic, anyway, he wants to know after dating a woman for several months, about looking into her eyes and softly holding her hand until three in the morning — when it's so late that she's too tired to do anything else, and he probably wouldn't be very good at doing it even if she wanted to? Or about telling her sweet nothings for a couple of hours every time they meet, when he really wants to know what she thinks about religion and child-rearing? Or about listening to schmaltzy music in a crowded, uncomfortable cafe, when they could be having a fine intellectual discussion with some interesting friends?

The road to amative hell, in other words, is paved with unrealistic romantic expectations. Living steadily under the same roof with a man, or even seeing him two or three times weekly for months on end, ultimately becomes just about as romantic as living, after the first fortnight, in a new hotel or a boarding school. High romance is based largely on novelty, excitement, adventure; and *steady* dating or mating just cannot be *that* perpetually novel, exciting, or adventurous. The woman, therefore, who overemphasizes the romantic — as against, say, the intellectual, the companionable, the sexual, or the every-day aspects of dating is almost invariably going to be demanding the impossible from both her partner and herself. And probably the quickest and most effective way of irritating a man is to demand what he or anyone else cannot possibly give.

Suggest if you will, then, an *occasional* walk in the wilds, or a look at the sunset, or hand holding at the top of a mountain. But, for cupid's sake don't expect a *steady diet* of this kind of romantic frippery. Life largely consists of practical matters, small talk, amusement-seeking, intelligent discussion, physical pleasures, and half a hundred other quite down-to-earth, unethereal things. Use the brains beneath your hairdo to make *these* kinds of everyday contact with your boyfriend as vitally alive and non-boring as possible. And for the most part, leave the high-flown romanticizing exactly where it belongs — in Hollywood.

2

What Men Really Want
in Women

Assuming that highly intelligent, not too kooky males do not want in women what some lady journalists want them to want, the obvious next question is: Well, what do they *really* crave in their female partners? A whale of a lot, actually. Including:

Assertiveness

The stupid man, be he honestly mousy or false-facedly gruff, frequently cannot bear an assertive woman who knows her own mind and tells it to anyone who asks. Needing to be in the spotlight himself (even though he may do nothing to get into it), he shies away from anyone who is closely identified with him and who gets her own due share of public approval. Not always, of course: since some unassertive men mated with assertive females seem to thrive on their mates' forwardness. But the weaker a man feels himself, the more he tends to be a male supremacist and the more he attempts to keep his woman from, to his own distorted way of thinking, "showing him up."

The moral of this? Patently: if you, as a woman, want to be yourself and speak your piece when the spirit moves you, stay away from male chauvinists who act "assertively" to cover their inherent weakness.

O.K. Now let us suppose you follow this sage advice and you set your cap at a male who is neither numbskull nor nut. Should you unassertively walk on eggs with him? Over his (and your own) dead body!

The bright man usually *wants* a woman who, without being obnoxious or querulous, has a real mind of her own, and does not hesitate to use it. He wants her to be able to join him, when they are by themselves or with their friends, in a protracted, well thought-through discussion of the show they have just seen, the latest events in China, or the care and feeding of mothers-in-law. If she fortuitously happens to agree with him on these kinds of questions, and is articulate as to why she agrees, fine: he is well pleased with her position. But he definitely does not want a yes-woman, who merely agrees because she knows she'd damned well better if she wants him to love her. *That* kind of woman he can easily find in a brothel; and even then she bores him after a suprisingly short time.

Assertiveness, as we shall show in more detail in a later chapter, is not equivalent to aggressiveness. To be assertive is to know what you want to say and to say it, or to know what you want to do and to do it. To be aggressive is (especially as usually applied to a woman in our society) to be determined, at all costs, to get what you want, and to fight like a vixen, in a hostile manner, to get it. Men rarely like aggressive or so-called "castrating" females (though at times they may masochistically be subservient to them). They do, however, want a woman who is vibrant, alive, and self-assertive.

Even when an intelligent man is rolling in the hay with his inamorata there is likely to be, especially over some period of time, as much talking and discussing as rocking and rolling. If, during the periods of palaver, she is all saccharine agreement and no firm dissent, he might just as well answer his own questions and indulge in soliloquy. Moreover, as the months and years go by, what have a man and woman to give to each other, more than their own inimitable *selves*? This means, of course, their *own* views on life, literature, love, and what have you. To *grow* with another person essentially means to *learn* with that person; and how is a man to learn from his mate if she isn't able to open her mouth and say boo?

Assert, then, your own real being. Think what you think and say what you think. When your man violently differs with your views, politely but firmly differ with his. Don't be browbeaten into becoming a nonentity. If you can't respect yourself sufficiently to stand up for your own opinions, how long will it be, do you think, before you lose your man's admiration and respect? The male you keep by forcing yourself to be a mouse will be a mouse-lover —not a you-lover. Is that the best you can *really* do?

Guts

Being assertive and having guts are in some respects the same, but in other respects quite different. Many people who assert themselves freely, in that they tell you what their views are and try to get what they want out of life, nonetheless balk whenever their views or desires seriously buck up against social convention.

Females, in particular, in our society, will often be quite forward about speaking in public, meeting strangers at a cocktail party, or something of that order; but when it comes to clearly unconventional acts, such as asking a man to go to bed with them, they will be just as shy and gutless in this respect as they are gutsy and forward in the more traditional social issues.

The vast majority of American women, in fact, are sexually ungutsy, and even the bravest among them hold, as a rationale for their sexual inhibition, the idea that men abhor sexual directness in women, and immediately conclude that any female who is anything but indirectly suggestive is a whore.

Is this idea correct? The hell it is!

Uneducated, stupid, inept, and fascistic-minded men usually feel that a woman who has sexual (or almost any other kind of) guts is a low-down tramp. But who, we must keep ceaselessly asking throughout this book, wants *them?* Let them stew in their own goldarn fascistic juices—with, for poetic justice, the pusillanimous, sex-shy types of females who normally become their mates.

The brighter and better males, however, are in quite a different class when it comes to labeling the woman with guts as one of the sluts. Nothing pleases them more, in most instances, than the lass (be it her first or fifty-first date with them) who frankly and clearly indicates that the lovely dinner and that fine show are only the preliminary parts of the evening, and that the real show goes on at home, after midnight.

Take, by way of illustration, the case of Rhonda G. Rhonda

came to me for premarital counseling because, although she was twenty-nine, unusually attractive, well-educated, and socially adept, the men she was most interested in never seemed to stay around long enough for any attachment to grow. The creeps she met, to be sure, adored her, and would keep calling and dating her, if she let them, forever. But the really good guys, whom she would meet once every few months or so, would show her a grand time for one date, possibly two, occasionally three—and that was it.

"What kind of people are these 'good guys' that you keep talking about?" I asked her.

"Oh, rather unusual, I'd say," was her reply. "Frankly, I think I know a good thing when I see one. And the good guys I'm talking about are sort of the cream of the crop."

"Meaning—what?"

"Well, they're not too young, since I don't particularly like young men. In their early forties, say. Usually doing exceptionally well in business or some profession. Single, of course, since I don't fool around with married men. Definitely on the highly intelligent side. And—I might as well admit it, since I have a weakness for good-looking men—almost always tall, well-built, and almost any woman's idea of an attractive guy."

"You really do pick them!" I smilingly said.

"Yes. But, naturally, they don't sell them at the supermarket, so I have to wait a reasonable length of time before the next one comes around to take my mind off the last one—who unfortunately scooted out on me several months before."

"O.K. So let's say that the men you choose are, by normal standards, pretty desirable. Now, what exactly do you do with them, when you see them on first and second dates?"

"Do? What, I guess, everyone else does. Dinner, usually. Then maybe a show. Then back to my place for coffee and a long conversation. Sometimes, like the one I saw a few weeks ago, and who still hasn't called back, and who I might as well admit is a lost cause by now, all-night conversation."

"*Only* conversation?"

"Sure. At first, that is. Not that I wouldn't do anything *later,* you know. I'm really not exactly a virgin. I have had affairs with men, and thoroughly enjoyed the sex. But these are *first* dates, mostly, that I'm talking about. And *that's* different!"

"Perhaps so," I said. "But couldn't we also say that these may be *first* men, too, with whom you're having these dates; and that maybe, well, *that's* different, too?"

"What do you mean by *first* men?"

"Simply that the type of men you seem to be having these dates with—the ones, that is to say, you're concerned about not later losing—are, from your own description, la crème de la crème—right?"

"Yes, I guess you could call them that. They're certainly outstanding compared to most of the other creeps who keep calling."

"And they're not only outstanding to you, but most probably would be, also, to other young, eligible, good-looking women in New York City. True?"

"Oh, definitely. I hardly delude myself that I'm the only one who would find them attractive—or the only one whom they might want to take out."

"Yes—or to take *in*. The type of man you describe is obviously a good catch for other women besides you; and by the time he's reached the age you're selecting and has got a few financial or professional successes in life, he knows perfectly well that he *is* a good catch and that lots of women will want to catch him in bed long before they insist on catching him in church."

"In other words: my competition is keen."

"Right: damned keen. And while you're making your subtle distinctions between first, second, and umpteenth dates, and just how far, sexually, you can go on which date in the series, these other partners, or at least some of them, are quickly surrendering their 'all' without any internal or external debate. And to whom, if you were in *his* position, would you choose to return?"

"Oh, but that's not fair! How does he know that, if he just is a little patient with me, I won't be far better in bed than any of those other chippies who flop into the sack with him immediately? And I probably am, you know, I really am!"

"Yes, you probably are. But that's just the point: how *does* he know. From what he can see, you may put him off for weeks, or may never go to bed with him at all, or may, when you finally do break down and welcome him sexually, be entirely frigid. All the evidence that he has at his disposal—namely, that you play a great game of *talking* all night—hardly encourages him to conclude that you are the greatest thing worth waiting for since Helen of Troy."

"Do you really think that he might get the idea, from my first or second date behavior, that I am actually *frigid?*"

"Why not? Or puritanical. Or determined to sell your sexual responsiveness at a price so high that it would hardly be worth paying for. Or—don't forget—he might think none of these things, might even believe that you are a pretty hot number once the bedspreads are down—but also believe that you are not especially interested in *him* that way. Why not? Why shouldn't he think such things."

"Yes, I see now. Why shouldn't he? And me, fool that I've been, I've been thinking all the time that if I did let him have me the first or second date he'd surely think that I was promiscuous, was interested in anything in pants, was not really worth having. Evidently the male and female mind work quite differently!"

"Evidently they do. The thoughts that you have been putting into your dates' heads could certainly be held by *some* men. But honestly, now, do you think that the specific kinds that you have been seeing—or, worse luck! *not* seeing after your initial encounters—are likely to have such thoughts?"

"No, I guess not. *I* had the thoughts. But I guess very few of them do. As you say, they probably mostly think that am a prude, frigid, or not interested in them. Christ! have I been stupid!"

"No. you mean you acted stupidly. That doesn't make you a stupid person. Let's not have you beating yourself over the head, now, for your stupidity. So you made mistakes. So we all do. The point is: blaming ourselves for these mistakes will help us not a whit to eradicate them. On the contrary, it will probably help us—no-goodniks that all of us feel that we are for making the mistakes!—to make still more of them. So none of that crappy self-blaming! The sane question is: What are you going to do *next* time? That's the thing you should almost exclusively be concentrating on."

"Yes. What am I going to do *next* time? No worse, I think I can promise you. And maybe a lot better!"

Next time, somewhat to my surprise, came with amazingly rapidity. "You won't believe it," Rhonda exclaimed when she came to see me the following week, "but Judson is so turned on to me now that he actually wants to live with me."

"Judson?" I asked. "Isn't he the man you thought you lost out on a few weeks ago? Did he actually get in touch with you again, in spite of the fiasco of a first date you thought you had with him?"

"Get in touch with me, hell! And he never was going to again, from what he told me."

"Then—?" I asked with a puzzled look.

"Oh, yes. You mean, how could he tell me he never was going to see me again without actually seeing me to tell me. Well, he just wasn't—until I, right after I saw you last week, called him. What the devil, I figured: 'You have nothing to lose, kiddo. You've already loused up the deal, but good. So find some damned excuse to call him, and see if it's not possible to stir up a few embers again.' So I did. I called him that very night.

" 'Look,' I said, 'you'll never guess why I'm calling.' 'You're right,' he said, 'I guess I never will.' 'Well,' I grimly plodded on— oh, I was determined, really determined about that *next* time we had spoken about that afternoon—'I don't think you ever will either. I—' and I hesitated just a split-second, but then I muttered to myself 'Screw it! Nothing at all to lose!' and plunged: 'I was so goddam hot, when you left at seven in the morning that last time we met, and I was so damned mad at myself for letting you go— when that was the last thing I really wanted, myself, that, well, I've been kicking myself around the block every day ever since. And I'm still hot—mad at myself, that is, and in the other way, too.'

"There was a dead silence on the phone for several seconds. 'O.K.,' I said, 'you can put your teeth back in now. And how soon can you come over?' 'In about twelve and a half minutes,' he said. And he did. And *we* did. Ever since. And along about the sixth, or was it the seventh, time we did it that following morning—coincidentally, I think, about seven a.m. again—we decided that this sort of thing was too good to be wasted on single people, and that maybe we should apply for some kind of monopoly on it. Which, on second thought, third thought, and fourteenth thought, we're still very much thinking of doing. So there! Next time, perhaps, there won't have to be any next times. Not, at least, while I'm still single!"

So gutsiness came to Rhonda G. As it has also come to many of the other women I have worked with in counseling and psychotherapy sessions.

For what self-respecting male, given the choice of a scintillat-ing conversation or a fully enacted bedtime story with an attractive young woman, would be likely to choose the former? And who would want him if he did?

Competence

The woman who gets the strong, hard man is often supposed to be an inept, fragile little thing who can't even put her panties on straight, and who has to run for masculine aid every time she has a light bulb to be changed. Such exemplary feminine weakness, we are variously told, will cement male-female relationships so solidly that Samson himself (were he interested) could never rend those dependency-succoring bonds asunder.

True? Certainly: in a few cases. The average above-average man, however, is about as thrilled with catering to the flaunted incompetence of a potential inamorata as he would be to running a two-person relay race with his partner on his back.

Remember this: The outstanding man in our society is almost always *busy*. No goofer or playboy, he; but usually an incredibly alive-and-kicking student, scientist, entrepreneur, sportsman, or other variety of activity-bent person. And consequently, when he thinks seriously about mating with some keen Young Thing, he is rarely notably encouraged by her lying abed until noon each day; taking four and three quarter hours to be ready, at nine o'clock, for a seven o'clock appointment; or insisting that he rearrange the living room furniture that he moved for her yesterday because, oh dear, she forgot, yes, you know how it is, just plain forgot that the pattern of the living room rug, that really, yes, she was really so sure that it ran this way, actually does run, yes, now that you look closely at it in the broad daylight, my god yes!—actually runs *that* way.

On the contrary! The truly active, going-places man ordinarily wants a woman who, even if she is not the greatest helpmate in the world, at least does her share. Preferably, the better hostess, housewife, efficient mother, wall painter, rug cleaner, etc. she is, the better he likes it. He may really want to be there with her, pitching in on all the partying and housecleaning chores. But he would damned well like to see her in there pitching, too.

The woman similarly, who simply can't handle her own emotional problems, and is continually calling up her friend to ask his advice, cry on his shoulder, and get him to come right over and comfort her—*maybe* she'll find a more than willing do-gooder who likes nothing more than to rush around in her hour of need to prove what a big strong man he is. But, among the truly up-and-coming males of our generation, she probably won't.

Moreover, even when she finds that, early in the mating game, her broad-shouldered lover is more than willing to listen to her every gripe and moan, she is likely to be sadly disillusioned when she discovers how short a way that same griping and moaning is going to get her. Nothing can be more boring than repeated complaints about oh, the horror of it all, and ah, the injustices of the world. And women who are so palpably incompetent that they not only cannot find suitable solutions to most of life's little inequities, but who also actually *create* considerable hassles where few actually exist, are as likely, eventually at least, to be about as popular with vitally absorbed, empire-building men as are fleas at a dog show.

The solution to the problem of your being competent enough to attract and keep a man who himself is in the highly competent class is not very neat or obvious.

What you can do, though, is at least give up your noble efforts to be *in*competent. Rid yourself, and fast, of the idea that ineptitude and feminine weakness are the royal roads to romance and stop convincing yourself that even smart males like their women beautiful but dumb. Whatever brains you happen to have been born with, use; and don't hesitate to show your best male prospects that you can, rather than that you can't, do various things well.

More specifically: plan (with paper and pencil, if necessary) some of your Saturday night activities yourself; then (tactfully, tactfully!) get lover-man to accept your plans. See that the tight-rimmed pickle jars are pried open *before* he comes to dinner. Get the superintendent of your building to fix the wretched window that is most likely to stick when you try to open it while your not-overly-handy manfriend is there. See that you have ample maid or butler service for the evening if you happen to give a big party. Talk to him only briefly when you call him at the office, unless he absolutely insists that the conversation go on and on.

More hints along this line: Be, in general, well-organized, and let him see that you are. Organize your appearance and your home; don't be too sloppy; but don't go to the other extreme of being compulsively tidy and clean. If he comes to your apartment, try to see that the place is reasonably in order—no curlers, stockings, and tampons all over the place! Show your prospective mate that you know how to shop, to cook, to serve, to clean up after meals.

A preparer of gourmet menus by the dozens you do not necessarily have to be (though that may help in some cases!). But at the very least know *something* about domestic affairs, and indicate that if your boyfriend is thinking seriously of living with you, he need not worry about your needing two maids and a business manager to keep your household in order.

Competence about *you* doesn't hurt either, and may be distinctly helpful. Are you overweight? Do you take vitamins daily? Do you drink like a fish and get in everybody's hair when you are looped? Is your posture reasonably good? Do you know what to do, and sensibly do it, when you are sick, or tired, or out of sorts? The more you show your chosen male that you can ably, fairly-onsistently handle yourself, and that you are not too likely to need *his* continual succoring, the more he is apt to conclude that you will not be too much of a burden on him and that he can spend most of his time enjoying rather than bolstering you.

This does not mean, now, that you must show your friend that you can and must do *everything* for yourself, and that any help on his part is as welcome as a kick in the shins. It is far better to let him do *some* things to help you, from time to time—while you still, in the main, competently go about helping yourself in his presence and behind his back. As usual, attaining the mean between the two extremes of utter helplessness, on the one hand, and complete lack of need for *anyone* else, on the other, is generally the best course you can take. Perhaps almost every man would, in some part of his psyche, want to have a child-mistress; but it is highly questionable how many males truly enjoy a child-mate.

Get the idea, now? The things that you have to do in his presence, manage to plan in advance and do reasonably well. The things, especially the onerous and failure-inviting things, that he has to do in your presence, manage to eliminate, to reduce to a minimum, to assume some of the responsibility for, to ease, or to help him with. Give him, at least some way back in his mind, the impression that when he is with you, as well as when you are with yourself, life somehow goes pretty smoothly, and hassles are relatively few and far between.

Let me repeat, don't try to be a thoroughly competent jill-of-all-trades who is so well oiled and in such good working condition that she seems to be entirely *un*feminine. But squelch the I'm-such-a-poor-helpless-creature-that-I-desperately-need-a-big-strong-man-like-you-to-take-endless-care-of-me line, too. There surely is *some* kind of reasonable mean between these two undesirable extremes.

Permissiveness without ingratiation

The habit of blaming, as I spend so much of my life saying, is the root of much evil. To say to children or adults that what they have said or done is wrong or self-defeating can be very helpful; to call them lice or idiots is mere abuse. It is important to make a clear distinction between the condemnation of an act or an opinion and the condemnation of the person as a whole.

If John gratuitously kicks Jim in the teeth, it is sensible for me to say to him, "Look, John, you've done the wrong thing by kicking Jim in the teeth." If, however, I say, "Look, you dirty so-and-so, you shouldn't have kicked Jim in the teeth, and you are a horrible man for doing so," I am not only assessing John's act as wrong, but assessing John himself as a bad person.

Showing people that they are responsible for their mistakes and that it would be better for them to change the nature of their acts in the future is to be rational and helpful. To accuse people of being altogether worthless slobs because of some wrong action is to be irrational and unhelpful.

Blaming humans *even* when they are clearly in the wrong practically never helps to change them for the better and almost always helps to change you for the worse—for they remain pretty much the way they are, while you wind up with a needless angry pain in your guts.

This particularly goes with your best-beloved male. Wrong he may decidedly be about his words and deeds relating to you, others, and the world at large. All right: so he is wrong! The real, and only relevant, question is: How are you going, for his sake and your own, to induce him to be less wrong. Yes, *less* wrong, not perfectly right, nor even plain darned right.

For as long as he is a human, rather than (as you might possibly like him to be) an angel or a god, he is going to be enormously, ineradicably *fallible;* and fallible people—even as you and I—are never, for any serious length of time, right: they are always, at best, less wrong.

The sane and wise thing to do when your lover makes the

latest of his normal large batch of mistakes is to accept them without damning him as a wrongdoer. Not *like* him for his bloopers. Not cheer him on to make more. But calmly accept the fact that he has made another error, and that it is too damned bad that he has, but there it is: he has. *How* can you accept this when he has made that very same mistake, that you told him about eighty times previously, once again? Very simply: the same way that you accept the rainy day that you prayed would be sunny, or that you accept your mother's appendicitis attack just when she was going to help you move to another apartment. To accept something undesirable does not mean that you like it, or want it, but (when there is just no other choice) that you see that the only sensible thing is gracefully to lump it.

Permissiveness will usually go a long way toward winning the undying devotion of a man (or child, or patient, or employee, or almost anyone else with whom you are in a close relationship). But servility or obsequiousness will only go a long way toward winning (from another as well as yourself) contempt.

"But how," you may ask, "am I to remain permissive without simultaneously becoming spineless and ingratiating?" A good question. And the answer: define, in the most concrete sentences possible, the behavior of which (a) permissiveness and (b) obsequiousness consists.

Take, first, permissiveness. To be permissive toward someone who is acting unangelically toward you is to be thoroughly convinced of the following self-statements: "I don't like the way he's behaving, and I wish to hell he wouldn't behave that way. But he has a perfect right, as a human being, to behave any way *he* likes, even though *I* don't like it. Now, if I don't want him to behave the way he is acting, then I'd better calmly accept, temporarily, this way; point out to him that I don't like it, even though I am temporarily accepting it; and try my best to induce him, by various means, to modify his way of behaving. If I can get him to change, fine. If I can't, tough. I *want* him to act better, but I don't *need* him to. And if, finally, he doesn't change enough to suit me, and I still don't like the way he is behaving, I can always leave him and look for some other person who normally behaves more to my liking."

Take, now, ingratiation. To be ingratiating to someone who is acting badly toward you is to tell yourself and to be quite convinced of the following kinds of self-sentences: "I don't like the way he's behaving, and I wish to hell he wouldn't behave that way. But I can't *stand* the thought of his not loving me or of his leaving me. I *must* have his acceptance and approval. Therefore, no matter *what* he does, I simply can't afford to tell him I dislike his behavior, and I certainly can't try to get him to change it. Therefore, I'd better bow low, lick his bottom, sacrifice myself in every possible way, and thereby see that there is no possibility whatever that he will ever leave crummy little me, even if in the process I thoroughly lose his and my own respect."

Permissiveness, then, springs from self-acceptance, while ingratiation derives from self-hatred and utter dependency on others. And if you can manage to train yourself to be permissive toward an erring male, you not only will probably win him, but you will invariably also win yourself. Permissiveness follows the pattern of firm kindness to others. Ingratiation follows the pattern of *un*firm kindness—which leads to poor results. Unpermissiveness, or angry retaliation, follows the pattern of firm *un*kindness—which also produces, especially in a love relationship, dismal consequences. (Compare, A. Ellis: *How to Live with a Neurotic.*) You puts up your money and you takes your choice. Which choice will you make?

Concern without worry

About half the males who come to see me to talk about problems with their sweethearts or wives complain that these women are not sufficiently concerned with their welfare, do not care if they work themselves to death, show no interest whatever in their business or professional affairs, and generally don't give a plugged pfennig for what they think or say or do. The other half complain that their female partners are much too concerned with their welfare, are always worrying about their working themselves to death, show too much interest in their business or professional affairs, and generally plague them with overabsorption in every little thing they think or say or do.

Does this prove that you just can't please those lousy hairy-chinned creatures, and that you might as well not try? Not necessarily. It often proves, instead, that women are supremely indifferent to some of the most vital concerns of the men they insist they madly love—or else that they are obsessively worried about every little thing their man does or does not, and keep plaguing him incessantly about this, that, and the kitchen sink.

There is, of course, a middle ground. It is possible for you to be duly concerned about your man friend's affairs without being unduly worried over every little step he takes. And men—especially, busy, bright men—do want their mates to be sincerely interested in their doings. They want to be able to talk about their work, from time to time, and not just relegate it to the "Oh, yes, that's the beastly sort of stuff that you unfortunately have to do for a living" class of thing. They want to have their partners ready and able to help throw a fine dinner or cocktail party for their business associates, or put in a good word for them with the head of the laboratory, or help them talk out at home a problem that could well use ventilation before they work it out at the office.

So standoffishness from your lover's affairs won't exactly help. And it may well encourage him to seek, elsewhere, someone who is just as good in bed as you are—and more interested in his nonsexual doings as well. On the other hand, reminding your man, every few moments, that he really is in a terrible fix with his business partner; or that he'd better sell that mining stock he has fast, before it goes down to next to nothing; or that if he gets drunk once more, yes, just once more, at Dean Smith's semiannual cocktail party for the faculty, he might just as well kiss his job, yes, kiss his job goodbye and apply for a fine spot, and I mean a fine spot, on the Bowery right now, yes dammit right now; reminding your man of *this* kind of stuff is not likely to endear him to you, either.

As noted before in the case of permissiveness and ingratiation, the dividng line between sincere concern and anxiety can fairly easily be seen if you look at the kinds of internalized sentences that you are telling yourself to create both of these feelings. To be concerned about the man you love, you are probably saying to yourself something along these lines:

"I wonder what kind of a day he's been having at the office today. I really would like to know, so that I can better appreciate his life and make myself a greater part of it. And maybe I might be able to help him with some of his problems, too—as I'd certainly like to do. Of course, he may not care to tell me, right now, how things actually have been going today. Maybe he's too tired; or just doesn't feel like talking about it; or has had enough of this kind of thing for one day and would just like to relax and talk about something else. O.K.: If so, I'll soon find out and switch to another topic. I don't *have* to talk to him about his work, even though I'd really like to. But why not try? What have I got to lose? If he's eager to talk, we'll both enjoy it; and if he's not, we can easily switch to another topic. Anyway, let's try it and see"

To be overconcerned, or worried sick, or naggingly anxious (and anxiously nagging!) in regard to the man you most care for, you keep telling yourself sentences such as these: "God! He looks tired. I'll bet that he had a simply *terrible* day at the office. And he probably feels just *horrible* about it. Now, let's see what I can do to help him. I've *got* to help him. I can't *stand* his being as upset and messed up as he seems to be.

"And if I can't help him with his worst problems, then what good am I to him at all? And what's the purpose of my being mated to him, or even going on in this dreadful life? Oh, I *must,* I just *must* help take that load off his back. I'm sure he must want me to. He *couldn't* not want me to. And if he doesn't talk to me about it, as he sometimes doesn't when he's all upset like this, I just won't be able to take it again. I just *won't.* That'll really be the end between us. One more rebuff, like the cruel one he gave me when I tried to be so helpful to him last week, and I'll just about *crack.* That'll be it. The end. I just won't be able to bear it!"

Obviously if we examine these two sets of sentences, we can see the clear-cut differences between them. The concerned woman *wants* to help her man, but can find other fish to fry if he, for any reason, doesn't at the moment go along with her wanting. The worried woman *needs* to help her man, and can find no other fish, flesh, nor foul for her cooking pot in case he wants to solve his problems by himself.

The concerned woman really accepts herself and therefore, at any given time, does not *have* to be fully accepted and approved by her mate. The worried woman does not really like or respect herself and therefore *has* to devote herself to her mate's cause if she is to view herself as being in the least "worthwhile." Where the concerned woman is preferentially *motivated,* the worried one is compulsively *driven.* Not only, then, is the latter sick, but the chances are enormously high that she will, by her driven behavior, create a neurotic relationship with the man she wants most to mate with.

The moral is as obvious here as it is in the various other points we have raised in this chapter. Want what you want, and even at

times want what you want when you want it. But in your relations with yourself and the man of your dreams, don't make the
sad mistake of unconsciously or consciously transmuting your
wants into needs. Babies (who would of course die without
external care and succoring) need; healthy adults *need* very little
(except for food, clothing, and shelter, without which they might
actually die) but have many wants or preferences.

Go after, then, what you want. Be assertive—express the
things you want to say, do the things you want to do. Have
guts—find out what your sex-love preferences really are (and not
what your mother and your maiden aunts *think* they ought to be)
and let your man know what they are. Be competent—discover
what *you* think is the efficient way of doing things and don't try to
act as if you haven't got anything in your head but Hollywood
scripts. Be permissive—try to get the results you *want* to get from
your chosen male, but accept (at least temporarily) without tears
the results that you could well live without. Be concerned—
endeavor, if you can, to help your mate with his life problems,
but do not think that you have to worry yourself sick if he refuses
your help or if he fails in spite of it.

Will you, if you closely follow all the do's and don'ts which we
have so far outlined in the first two chapters of this book, be
absolutely sure of winning and keeping the kind of strong, sane,
highly cerebral kind of man that you want? You know perfectly
well you won't be. But you will be surer of getting your heart's
desire than if you follow the usual "ladylike" ways. And whatever the ultimate outcome, even if it be the relatively sorry state of
eternal singleness, *you* will be a much saner and happier person
to live with. By, of, for, and with—if necessary—yourself.

3

How to Prevent Yourself
from Being in Desperate
Need of a Man

Probably the worst possible way to win the man of your choice is to be in desperate need of having him—or of having any man whatever. For as soon as you are convinced that you *must* have someone, that your life and well-being literally depend on your winning the esteem of this person, you are most likely to do all the wrong things to get him.

The need to be loved is usually a need to prove one's own worth; and is a function of basic insecurity and anxiety. In order for you to prevent yourself from being desperately in need of a man, you'd better tackle this underlying insecurity. Let us see, in this chapter, some of the main methods by which this can be done.

What makes you anxious

The main difference between practically all so-called normal and neurotic behavior is (as we have been noting from the start of this book) the difference between *wanting* or *preferring* something and *needing* or *demanding* it. The more you *demand* from life, and thereby imagine that you cannot possibly live happily without, the more likely you are, of course, not to achieve your demands. And not only will their nonachievement lead to enormous disappointment and disillusionment—frequently accompanied by horrible feelings of depression and inadequacy—but the mere thought that you *may* not get what you are utterly certain that you need will probably lead to hypertension and anxiety.

Most of my rational-emotive therapy (RET) clients are over-anxious, quite insecure individuals who feel that they simply must be loved and approved by others, particularly their mates, or else they might as well end it all. Miriam S. is a good case in point. Miriam kept coming around to her group therapy sessions every week and often complained about how unloved she was, and how she never had the energy to do practically anything she wanted to do in life, largely because she kept depressedly ruminating about how none of the men she was interested in ever really liked her, and how even her women friends were not completely on her side.

One day Miriam came in more upset than usual. The night before, she had gone to a movie just to pass the time, and had seen a rather boring science-fiction film, in the course of which some dreadful technicolored monsters kept attacking the inhabitants of the earth. She was rather upset while watching the film, but became even more frightened when she started to notice after returning home that the same kind of monsters she had seen in the film—pink and green and purple and whatnot— seemed to be lurking in the dark corners of her room, under the bed, in the recesses of her closets, etc.

Hardly knowing what to do about this dreadful situation, Miriam did what she normally did when confronted with any serious difficulty: she immediately called the latest of her long line of lovers and begged him to come over to help her drive away the monsters. Normally, he would have been willing enough to come to her rescue, but it just happened that he was recovering from a severe cold that day and did not want to risk going out in the icy streets.

Besides (although he did not overly stress this point) Miriam *had* called him over to her place only a week previously, because she had heard some noises which she attributed to rats—and which later turned out to be the knocking of her radiator pipes. And he had probably got his bad cold by coming over to see her that time. So this time he flatly refused to budge. She could if she wished, he said, come over to stay at his place (which was a long subway ride away) until she became sufficiently unafraid to return to her own; but come to her apartment that night he definitely would not.

Miriam felt crushed by his refusal. Immediately, she retaliated with accusations of his never having really loved her very much, and his certainly not giving a damn for her now, and what good was a guy to a woman, anyway, when he couldn't go a little out of his way in her dire hour of need? He still refused to budge from his warm bed. Whereupon Miriam told him that she never wanted to see him again, gulped down several sleeping pills, and soon blacked out the monsters in a sleep that was so deep and prolonged that she never got to work the next day.

That evening, when she came to group therapy, she was not only still upset about the monsters she had been seeing, but was even more disturbed about the way her boyfriend had treated her, and the angry manner in which she had told him off and broken up their relationship.

The group was not particularly sympathetic. "Look," said Sandra (who herself was so direly in need of the love of others that she could easily recognize it in Miriam), "let's suppose that your friend, when you called him to come chase away your monsters, had actually come over. What could he have done for you?"

"Yes," asked Lionel (who had been going with his own partner for several years now, without being able to decide whether to marry her or leave her), "what *would* he have done for you if he had come over?"

"Oh," said Miriam. "He would have chased away those monsters."

"He would . . . ?"

"How would he . . . ?"

"What do you mean he would . . . ?"

Questions and exclamations came from all sides of the room: all of them skeptical, all of them indicating that Miriam was feeding herself nonsense.

"Well," said Miriam, somewhat abashed, "why wouldn't he? After all, he was able to help me in things like that before."

"Crap!" said Sandra.

"Yes, pure crap!" echoed Lionel, in an even more definite, almost angry tone.

"What do you mean?" asked Miriam, somewhat bewildered.

"Can't you see?" asked Claire (one of the saner and less love-needful members of the group). "Can't you see that your friend, or anyone else for that matter, really can't do *anything* for you like you're asking?"

Miriam, still bewildered, obviously could not see.

"Let's put it this way," said Sandra. "You wanted him to come over to chase away *your* monsters—right?"

"Yes," answered Miriam. "If he came over, he'd show that he loved me. And that sort of love would chase away my monsters."

"*It,* the love, *it* would chase away your monsters?" Sandra persisted. "But how could it? They're *your* monsters— and *you,* of course, made them up. How, then, can anything outside you, such as your man-friend's love, do something to remove what's *in* you. Can't you see that because *you* made up the monsters, you're the only one, really, who can do anything about them, who can possibly remove them?"

"You mean," said Miriam, who was really a bright person, and who had some familiarity from previous group sessions with the ideas Sandra and the others were presenting, "that the monsters really aren't there? I made them up? And if *I* make them up, then *I'm* the only one who can remove them? And Ray's love, or anything like that, can't really do anything for me? Is that what you mean?"

"Exactly!" said Claire. "That's what we all seem to be trying to tell you. Nothing that you make up, in your own head, can be changed except by something else that you do in that same head. What anyone else, such as Ray does, is completely irrelevant—except in so far as you *make* it relevant by, again, what goes on in your own head."

"Only *I* can control my monsters, then."

"Right!" I, as the therapist who was leading the group, finally joined in. "Just as the members of the group have been telling you, only *you* can make up monsters—and only *you* can make them vanish again. And the bitter irony here is that you, and millions of people like you, keep going to such ridiculous lengths both to make up and then destroy, but unfortunately only very temporarily to destroy, the monsters of your own making."

"Do you mean," asked still another group member, Jack, who up to this time had been thoughtfully silent, "that Miriam, like so many of the rest of us in the group, keeps going to great lengths to make up one set of monsters, on the one hand, and then to make up still another set of angels to sort of cancel out the first set? And that she then goes on that way practically forever?"

"That's precisely it," I replied. "Just to put it a little differently: you first go to the movies, Miriam, see a lovely set of ready-made monsters there, and decide—unconsciously, no doubt, but still quite definitely—to use them for your own nefarious purposes. So, later that night, you bring out these ready-made monsters and start to give yourself a real hard time with them. Then, because you are having a hard time of it, you think about a possible antidote, and you quickly and rather cleverly concoct an anti-monster, a sort of anti-missile missile.

"This anti-monster you call 'love' or 'acceptance' or 'help for my hour of need.' Normally, now, you find that this anti-monster works beautifully, at least temporarily, to chase away the horrible monsters. You needlessly upset yourself, that is; then you look for and find some love and approval, particularly from your current lover and lo and behold! you are, at least for the nonce, no longer upset.

"In fact, after a while you come to derive such great satisfaction from unupsetting yourself when once you have knocked yourself off your own pins, that you even sometimes get in the habit of dreaming up the monsters deliberately, with the thought in the back of your mind that you then will have an excellent excuse to dream up and use, for that day at least, the great anti-monster, Love. That is probably what happened to you last night. You had nothing to do, wanted to be with Ray, for some reason decided not to try to see him—"

"—I had seen him until very late at his place the day before," Miriam interjected.

"All right: you had seen him until very late the day before, and felt that it wouldn't be right to go see him again; or maybe, knowing he had a cold and couldn't very well come to see you, you wanted to see him but didn't want to go to the trouble of taking a subway ride to his place. Anyway, for some reason you at first decided not to try to see him again. So, for lack of anything better to do, you went to see the movie.

"The movie, perhaps, scared you a little, since you do find such kind of things generally scary. But then, quite unconsciously, you may have thought to yourself: 'Ah, maybe I can use this scariness to some purpose. Maybe I can somehow employ it to get what I really want tonight—the presence of my boyfriend.'

With this thought in mind, you managed to bring on the monsters, when you got home; and then, of course, it was most logical for you to call Ray and to plead with him to come over. Usually, as I said before, this would have worked very well: and even though you paid a kind of penalty—scaring yourself by your own monsters—you would have got what you most want, nay demand, out of life: love, approval, acceptance."

"Yes, I think I even thought of that when I was calling Ray," said Miriam. "I sort of knew that I could handle the monsters myself. But I didn't *want* to do so. I wanted *him* to come drive them away for me."

"Yes," I continued. "That's the way it often becomes—or, rather, the way we *make* it become. But the real irony is, of course, that there aren't any monsters *or* anti-monsters. We make up *both* of them. In your case, as you well know—since you are not *that* crazy!—the original monsters you saw do not exist. *You* (with the help of the film-makers) dreamed them up. But what you do not see very clearly is that the anti-monsters do not exist either. You make *them* up, too. Not love and acceptance themselves—you don't create them, since they do exist in their own right. But the power that they have over you: that's what you make up. It's pleasant being loved and accepted, particularly when you are in trouble. But instead of just feeling pleasant when you are accepted, you feel positively, absolutely *great*—by which you really mean no longer worthless, but a genuinely worthwhile person.

"Oh, I do, I do!" interjected Miriam.

"Yes—unfortunately you do. From a louse of the lowest sort you lift yourself, when you feel accepted or loved, to temporary heights of power and worth. And *that* is your anti-monster: your *belief* that you cannot truly like yourself and enjoy life unless you are thoroughly approved by others who are important to you. That belief is what drives you to try to coax Ray out of his sickbed, and what even, as I said before, unconsciously drives you to make up some of your monsters at the start."

"Yes," said Miriam, very thoughtfully, wrinkling her brow and curling up her nose in a serious effort to comprehend.

"And what will you do to keep seeing it clearer?" asked Claire.

"I'll keep working at it," Miriam answered, with some real conviction.

And Miriam did continue to work on her problem of needing

rather than just wanting to be loved and accepted, and kept making significant progress.

Overcoming fear of what people think

Much of the desperate need to be loved—which so ironically is the greatest soboteur of loving and mating that exists in our society—stems from the terrible fear of what other people would think of you if you were not ideally doted upon and mated. What, for example, would your parents think if you never presented them with the right kind of mate and several perfect grandchildren? What would your women friends think if they knew that you spent most Saturday evenings alone? What would the world think if it knew that you were so shy and graceless that no outstanding man would ever dream of becoming deeply involved with you?

Let them think!

Life, as anyone who is sensible can quickly see, surely has enough *real* hassles without our creating half a billion false ones that infinitely multiply and complicate the real ones. Making a living, for example, can be a downright nuisance; and keeping physically healthy; and finding, among all the men who may be attracted to you, a single one who, after a few weeks of intimacy, doesn't bore you to death.

Life also includes some very difficult people whom you had better please, whether you care to or not. Like, for instance, your curmudgeon of a boss; or the alcoholic doorman who misdirects your guests; or the cop on the beat who suspects that a good-looking woman like you, with so many prosperous-appearing men friends, must surely be a whore.

O.K.: so life is rough. And for many practical reasons you have often to be nice to people you wish would quickly drop dead. But precisely because this is true it seems thoroughly idiotic for you to kowtow endlessly to strangers and acquaintances to whom you *don't* have to be overly civil, and who actually have little or no effect on your life.

Take, by way of illustration, your neighbors. Suppose they *don't* like the fact that your lover sometimes stays over in your apartment all night; and suppose they *do* think you're a hopeless loser, seeing that you're past twenty-five and are still far from married. Probably, having their own (self-created) problems, they don't even give you and your friend or you and your spinsterhood a single thought more than once a year. But let us suppose the worst: let us suppose that they do (as, of course, grandiosely, you *think* they do) cogitate about you and your ways forty-four times each day, and that they always come up with the same negative evaluation: "My! what a horrible trollop (or bitch, or nincompoop, or ugly old hen) she is! How can anyone stand her? No wonder she's still alone."

Well? Suppose they *do*. Are these neighbors, by their under-the-skull or overtly outspoken estimations of you, going to skin you alive? To rape you? To burn down your apartment? To kill you dead dead dead?

And your parents? And your relatives? And your other friends? And your associates at work? Are any of them, assuming that they watch your *every* move and criticize your *every* man-hunting effort, going to beat you with a whip? Twist your arms out of their sockets? Fry you in the electric chair? Come, now: let's be honest. *Are* they?

"Well, no," you reply. "I know that they're not going to hurt me or kill me, at least not physically. But what about the *mental* anguish they cause me when they look at me and talk to me disapprovingly?"

Well, what about it? Or, more precisely: anguish that *they* cause you? *What* anguish?

"Oh, you know, the anguish I feel when I know that they think I'm wrong, and when I know that they're blaming me severely for being wrong."

Oh, *that!* That crap.

"Crap? What do you mean, crap? I certainly *feel* it!"

Yes, unfortunately you certainly do. And it is anguish, real, live anguish that you feel. But how do *they* make you feel it?

"Well, uh, by criticizing me. By telling me that I'm doing the wrong things, and am just no damned good for doing these things."

That's right. That's just what they tell you. You're doing what in their *eyes* is actually wrong; and you are a double-dyed, hopeless no-goodnik for doing it.

"Well, isn't *that* sufficient cause for me to feel anguish?"

No, not at all. That is only a sufficient cause for you to ask yourself: "Let me see, now. Maybe they're right. Maybe I am wrong. *Am I?*"

If you are, then you had better go about changing your ways and try to be less wrong in the future. But that's not the point in regard to what we're talking about at the moment. We're talking about—remember—their thinking you wrong for letting your lover stay all night, and their thinking you criminal for reaching the horribly late age of the mid-twenties and still being unmated. Honestly, now: do *you* think you're wrong about those kinds of things?

"No. I'm sure I don't. I have a perfect right, the way I live, to let whomever I want to stay over all night. And I guess I have a perfect right, too, to be over twenty-five and unmated. What am I even saying 'I guess' for? Of course I do!"

That's what I thought you were thinking. *When* you actually bother to think for yourself. Now back to our main point.

If you live your life according to what I call the A-B-C method of personality development, instead of the A-C method which you now employ, you need never get hurt—or, rather, hurt yourself—by being called names; and then you can calmly go about your business of mate hunting, or anything else, with maximum security and effectiveness.

"What is the A-B-C method of personality development?"

Simply the acknowledgment of what the Roman philosopher, Epictetus, pointed out some two thousand years ago: that it is never the event, A, which makes us mentally or emotionally upset at point C; rather, it is the nonsense, B, which we tell ourselves about A.

"You mean that it is not people criticizing me, at point A, which makes me miserable at C; but my telling myself, at B, 'Oh, my God! I can't stand their criticism,' or something like that, which really upsets me at C?"

Correct! Whenever you get hurt, depressed, anxious, angry, guilty, or otherwise emotionally disturbed at point C, it is not what someone else did to you at point A that caused you to be disturbed, but your idiotic, senseless, illogical *interpretation* of A that causes you your disturbance at C.

"But why do you call my interpretation 'idiotic, senseless, and illogical'?"

Because it *is*. Otherwise, if it were a sensible interpretation, you would never get emotionally upset at point C. For what you are essentially saying, at point B, when you hurt yourself at point C, is a groundless sentence like "I can't *stand* their criticism of me!" when you really mean that you don't *like* it but you definitely *can* stand it—if you stop telling yourself that you can't.

Or else you are saying to yourself, at point B, an irrational sentence like "They are hurting me horribly with their critical words!" when you really mean that they may be *trying* to hurt you verbally, but that they cannot possibly do so—unless *you*, by taking these words overseriously (by convincing yourself, that is, that you are a worthless slob if their criticisms of you happen to include some truth), destroy yourself with them. So on two major counts, your inner interpretations, or internalized sentences, at point B are nonsense: first, because they just do not make any logical sense, but are a string of non sequiturs; and second, because they cause you needless pain, where other sentences, said under the same circumstances, would leave you, at most, regretful and frustrated, but not horribly pained.

"So, according to your way of looking at things, I *never* have to feel terribly hurt—if I don't take other people too seriously and don't think that their low estimation of me means that I have to deprecate myself?"

Right!

"Sounds easy. When can I start to use your A-B-C system of personality development? I sure can use it fast!"

It sounds *easy*, but it isn't. It takes much work and practice: much *stopping and thinking,* instead of unthinkingly accepting the irrational premises that you now believe, at point B, and that you keep belaboring your life with. But it can be done. And you can start immediately. In fact, seeing the dire love straits you're usually in, you'd better!

Overcoming other forms of self-downing

Worry and overconcern about what others may think of you are important forms of self-downing. But they are hardly the only forms! Other serious modes of self-condemnation include feelings of inadequacy or worthlessness, states of shyness and inhibition, many kinds of phobias (such as fears of social gatherings or of speaking in public), dire need for love, and various kinds of compulsions and obsessions (such as the compulsion to be the life of the party or to make sexual conquests).

You can best understand all these forms of self-castigation by placing them within the A-B-C model of human disturbance.

This model is explained in detail in many of my writings on psychotherapy, such as *Reason and Emotion in Psychotherapy, Growth Through Reason, Humanistic Psychotherapy: The Rational-Emotive Approach,* and *A Handbook of Rational-Emotive Therapy.* Let me now apply it to a typical form of self-downing: feelings of inadequacy or depression after you have been rejected in love.

At point A, an Activating Experience or Activating Event, you go with a highly attractive and brilliant man for some period of time and finally get rejected by him. He tells you that he likes you, all right, and wants to be friends, but that he has no real sex or love interest in you.

At point C, your emotional Consequence, you feel inadequate and depressed. You also may strongly feel, quite wrongly, that A has caused or led to C—that his rejection has *made you* depressed.

Actually, your depression directly or more concretely stems from B—your Belief system. First, after getting rejected, you tend to have a set of rational Beliefs (rB's): namely, "I don't like getting rejected! How unpleasant! Perhaps I acted poorly (such as unlovingly or hostile) and thereby encouraged him to reject me. And if I did, that is most unfortunate!" This set of Beliefs is rational or sensible, since your goal, obviously, was to win this man's approval, and perhaps to have a long-term relationship. And if you did act somewhat poorly with him, and you thereby encouraged him to reject you, you are not fulfilling that goal; and, therefore, that *is* unpleasant and unfortunate. Anytime you wish for or prefer almost anything, and act so as to sabotage that wish or preference, it is rational to evaluate your behavior as unfortunate. For, obviously, you can hardly sensibly evaluate it is fortunate or great!

But having the rational Belief—at point rB—that your getting yourself rejected by a man you distinctly prefer is highly unfortunate or sad would hardly make you feel inadequate or depressed. It would make you feel, at point C, sorry or regretful—but NOT self-downing. Feelings of worthlessness, self-deprecation, or depression would tend to stem, instead, from a second, or highly irrational set of Beliefs (iB's): namely, "I MUST not act poorly with this man that I want to accept me! I absolutely SHOULD NOT, OUGHT NOT get rejected by him!"

For rational-emotive therapy (RET) hypothesizes that virtually every time that you feel seriously upset (as distinguished from your feeling appropriately sorry or regretful) about some loss or about some poor behavior that has led to this loss, you magically jump from desiring, preferring, or wishing to *MUST*urbating about it and, through this irrational kind of MUSTurbation, demanding and commanding that the loss, or the poor behavior that led to it, absolutely SHOULD not happen.

Moreover, the theory and practice of RET says, once you insist and command that you MUST not behave poorly and encourage the man you want to reject you, you almost invariably wind up with three crazy derivatives of your MUSTurbation:

1. "It's AWFUL that I behaved in this bad way that I MUST not act! It's HORRIBLE, it's TERRIBLE that I acted this way and that I therefore got rejected by the man I want!"

2. "I CAN'T STAND my behaving in this AWFUL manner! And I CAN'T BEAR my losing him by acting in this HORRIBLE way!"

3. "Because I behaved in this TERRIBLE manner, and because I idiotically lost the man that I most wanted to mate with, I am a totally ROTTEN PERSON (R.P.) who doesn't really deserve to win virtually any suitable mate; and a ROTTEN PERSON like me will NEVER get the kind of man that I want and is doomed to lovelessness FOREVER!"

Your abysmal self-downing, then, does NOT, definitely NOT, stem from the loss of the man you wanted to mate with (at Point A). Nor does it stem from your desire to win him and from your rational Beliefs (at point rB) that it is highly unpleasant and obnoxious to lose him. No, A (your losing this individual) and rB (your rational Belief that it is exceptionally sad to lose him) would only result in an *appropriate* feeling or emotional Consequence (at point C). And this appropriate feeling, we would call sorrow, regret, frustration, annoyance, or irritation. This feeling is appropriate because it logically follows from your desiring to win this man and your getting the opposite of what you desire—rejection. And it is appropriate because if you stay with, and *only* stay with this feeling, it will help you go back to A (your Activating Experience of rejection) and change it. Thus, the sorrier and more frustrated you feel about being rejected, the more you will tend to try to win this man back or to seek for another, somewhat equivalent man and to attempt to win his love instead of that of the one you have just lost.

Your self-downing, instead, stems from a radically different set of Beliefs (at B): namely, your irrational Beliefs (iB's): that you MUST win the love of this man who has rejected you; and that it is AWFUL, that you CAN'T STAND IT, and that you are a ROTTEN PERSON if you don't.

Assuming that these ABC's of RET are accurate, and that they truly explain exactly how *you* (and not what has happened to you at point A) are responsible for your feelings of inadequacy, worthlessness, or slobhood, you can then forthrightly solve your problem of feeling like a worm about rejection by going on to the D's and E's of RET. Thus:

At point D (Disputing) you dispute, question, and challenge your irrational Beliefs (iB's) about being rejected at A. Disputing consists of using the scientific method and of asking yourself: *"Where is the evidence* that my irrational Beliefs (iB's) are true? *Prove* that they are logically or empirically confirmable? *How* do they have any real validity? *Where is it writ* that they are substantial?" More concretely, you can Dispute your irrational Beliefs as follows:

Disputing: *"Where is the evidence* that I MUST not act poorly toward this man that I want to accept me? *Why* SHOULD I NOT or OUGHT I NOT get rejected by him?" Answer: "There is no evidence whatever that I MUST not act poorly with the man I care for, nor with anyone else I might want to mate with. There is considerable evidence that it is unfortunate and undesirable if I act poorly with him and help turn him away from me. But there is no reason why I absolutely SHOULD NOT, OUGHT NOT act in a way that brings me unfortunate and undesirable results. And there is some good evidence that I SHOULD or MUST act undesirably, in the sense that, as a fallible, screwed-up human, I frequently do!"

Disputing: *"Prove* that it's AWFUL that I behaved badly with the man whom I wanted to love me and who actually rejected me. *Why* is it TERRIBLE that I acted that badly and that I therefore got rejected by him?" Answer: "I cannot prove that my behavior in this (or any other) respect was (or is) AWFUL or TERRIBLE. Because (1) AWFUL BEHAVIOR would be that kind of behavior that is not only bad or very bad but TOTALLY or COMPLETELY bad. Because (2) AWFUL BEHAVIOR would be behavior that is MORE THAN BAD or at least 101% BAD; and nothing of course can be *that* bad! (3) Because (3) AWFUL BEHAVIOR would be behavior that is the WORST POSSIBLE behavior that I could perform; and an AWFUL EVENT would be the WORST POSSIBLE event that could occur. And being rejected by the man whom I want to love me is certainly not in that category. Because (4) AWFUL BEHAVIOR would mean behavior that is worse than any that SHOULD or MUST exist; and if my behavior exists, it MUST right now exist."

Disputing: *"Where is it writ* that I CAN'T STAND my behaving in this AWFUL manner and losing the man I care for? *In what way* can't I BEAR my losing him by behaving HORRIBLY?" Answer: "It is nowhere writ that I CAN'T STAND my behaving in this manner and losing the man I care for. I can STAND anything that happens to me, up to the time I die. No matter how I DON'T LIKE behaving that way and losing him, I probably WON'T die of this loss; and, if I survive, I can still have SOME kind of happiness without him. I can always BEAR things, including my own poor behavior, that I don't LIKE! Now, let me see how I can CHANGE that behavior, so that I can live more happily in the future!"

Disputing: "Where is the data to support the hypothesis that because I behaved badly with the man I love and because I idiotically lost his approval, I am a totally ROTTEN PERSON who doesn't really deserve to win virtually any suitable mate? How does it follow that a ROTTEN PERSON like me will NEVER get the kind of man that I want and is doomed to lovelessness FOREVER?" Answer: "There is no data to show that because I behaved badly and lost the approval of the man I love that I am a totally ROTTEN PERSON, nor that I don't DESERVE to win any suitable mate. There are only facts to show that I probably behaved badly THIS TIME, and that I ACTED rottenly on this occasion. But this present behavior hardly makes me a completely ROTTEN PERSON; and there is a good chance that I will ultimately get into the kind of relationship I want with a man, even if I keep acting badly: since the universe doesn't include DESERVINGNESS. Even though I may well have behaved badly THIS TIME and acted ROTTENLY on this occasion, I distinctly have the ability to do better on future occasions. If I were truly a ROTTEN PERSON, I would (1) ONLY perform rotten acts; (2) behave rottenly ALL THE TIME: (3) behave completely rottenly in the future as well as the present; (4) have a rotten SOUL or ESSENCE; and (5) be damnable, and only worthy of getting rotten results, and ultimately of roasting in hell, if there is a hell. None of these possibilities is likely; and all of them are most improbable. A ROTTEN PERSON would really be a subhuman individual; and, as far as I can tell, there are only HUMANS on this earth and no SUPERHUMANS or SUBHUMANS. Rotten or self-defeating ACTS seem to clearly exist; but not rotten PEOPLE."

When you do this kind of Disputing (at D) and get the kind of answers just listed, you come to point E—a new Effect or new philosophy. This is a restatement of your rational Belief (rB) but in a more general and future-oriented form. Thus, your final conclusion at E (Effect of Disputing) might well be: "Yes, I certainly acted badly with the man I loved and probably helped ruin the relationship with him this time. And, being a fallible fouled-up human (FFH), I most probably will often act badly in the future. Too bad! Most unfortunate! But his is hardly the end of the world. I definitely do not NEED the love that I WANT; and I can be quite happy, though not *as* happy, without it. Now let me see what I can do in the future to behave better, to seek out the kind of a relationship with a man that I truly desire, and to probably get better results than I achieved this time."

In other words, once you arrive at E, a new philosophic Effect, you attempt to go gack to the unfortunate Activating Events or Activating Experiences at A; and you do your best to change them so that you will have better or more desirable experiences in the future. If there is really nothing that you can do to change A (if, for example, you lived on a desert island only with this one man who rejected you), you then conclude: "That really *is* too bad! I'll never get some of things that I really or most want. Tough! Now how can I manage to be as happy as I can be without these things? Let me work on this!"

Overcoming low frustration tolerance

What we have just said leads us logically on to the major, and perhaps most pervasive and epidemic form of disturbance known to man—and to woman! What form? Low frustration tolerance. Although the psychoanalysts, with their frequent wrongheadedness, have emphasized self-downing and have most probably overemphasized hostility as major sources of depression and self-pity, they have usually neglected one of the most common causes of all: LFT (also known as short-range hedonism or whining about the inequities and injustices of the world).

Not that such injustices and needless hassles do not exist. Indeed they do! Especially in the area of enjoying the single life, it is highly probable that you have been unfairly saddled with almost innumerable personal, social, economic, and even political handicaps. First, because various kinds of injustice seem to be the normal human condition; and second, because you are a woman living in a society that is still largely sexist and that tends to place extra, gratuitous difficulties in your way.

In the course of your searching for a suitable love partner you may (for example!)—

Be less well endowed physically than Ms. America or Ms. Universe.

Have one or more children to take care of, left over from your previous marriages or relationships.

Feel so exhausted from the usual routines of earning a living that you often have little energy for socializing—and, especially, for looking for enjoyable socializing.

Be too poor to afford to do many of the things you would like to do in the course of seeking a mate.

Have available too little time and energy for favored social pursuits.

Be afflicted with one or more interfering health conditions.

Live in a community where virtually no appropriate lovers are available.

Happen to be of the "wrong" age, religious conviction, ethnic background, or social status.

Have distinct, and sometimes virtually unremediable, educational handicaps.

Etc., etc., etc.!

Whatever your afflictions and disabilities, you may be pretty certain that you can find a good many other women—and men!—in your community who, often by sheer luck, are considerably less burdened. And even if you have, through sheer luck again, several talents and charms that most women of your age don't have, you can always find a number of others who have still more. Inequity and unfairness are still, by and large, the human condition. If you haven't discovered that yet, I am really surprised!

Because life conditions are so frequently hard and interfering with your basic sex-love goals, you will probably tend to subscribe to the third major form of human irrationality or *must*urbation that is practically pandemic in all cultures: "The world MUST be better than it is and HAS TO be filled with more favorable conditions, so that I can easily and quickly gratify my natural and normal NEEDS. When it is not, that is *horrible!* I *can't bear* it! And I might as well curl up and die (or actively kill myself), rather than suffer an endless insufferable and too painful existence!"

This third major irrational Belief—following (1) "I MUST do well and manage to get myself approved by all significant others!" and (2) "You MUST treat me kindly and considerately and never unduly balk me!"—leads to another form of desperation or depression (or anger) that notably blocks human progress, especially sex-love progress. For when you feel desperately depressed and despairing about the possibilities of your achieving a steady love relationship with a suitable partner, you tend to do worse than desperately strive to get one: you desperately *give up.* You sit on your ass (or lie on your back); mope at work and or home; avoid socializing; fail to follow up on good amative leads; and otherwise passively and inertly view life—and also hopelessly view getting rid of your own "moodiness."

To add to your woes in this regard, your underactive mode of desperation is fairly easily *seen* by potential mates. People who are depressed, despairing, hopeless, and self-pitying almost always give themselves away; and who wants to mate, permanently or even temporarily, with *that* kind of individual?

How can you, if so afflicted, rid yourself of low frustration tolerance (LFT), self-pity, depressed inertia, and other forms of whining that lead to desperation and block love relationships? By, again, using the A-B-C-D-E's of RET and very persistently and vigorous Disputing (at D) your irrational Beliefs (iB's) about the world HAVING TO provide better conditions and your NEEDING life to give you fewer handicaps.

Where—using the Disputing techniques of RET — is the evidence that the world MUST be better than it is for you? Prove that it HAS TO be filled with more favorable conditions? Why have your "normal NEEDS" GOT TO be fulfilled? How can you substantiate the HORROR of not getting what you immediately want in the sex-love arena? In what manner can't you BEAR your present frustration? Where is it writ that you will be afflicted with ENDLESS suffering and TOO painful an existence?

If you ask these questions, and really keep asking them of yourself till you figure out sensible, fact-based answers, you will get to a new philosophy or cognitive Effect (at point E) that will by no means necessarily change the world or remove your real handicaps but that will greatly enable you to live more comfortably with hassles and to do much more about removing them. If you wind up with answers that are still mistaken, and consequently prolong your self-pity, you'd better perhaps go for some professional help, with a good, sensible therapist, and thereby get to more useful, happiness-producing answers.

4

How to Become
Assertive Without Being
Aggressive

Assuming that you are not in desperate need of a man, and that you can settle back more leisurely to find one and to win him, one of your main steps (as we briefly mentioned in the first two chapters of this book) is to show him, and yourself, that you can be healthfully assertive without being angrily aggressive. We shall consider some techniques for managing this fortunate state of being.

Overcoming hostility

Anger is the root of almost all evil in love. "A soft word turneth away wrath," sayeth the Bible. And a harsh word turneth away love, sayeth the psychologist. Just keep being angry and carping with your beloved and, no matter how righteously based your rage may be, it will soon shred your affectional relationship. But good!

Isn't anger often justified? Isn't righteous indignation perfectly proper? Isn't it sometimes appropriate to show how irate you are, in order to get things done well and to get what you want out of life?

No, never. N-e-v-e-r. Not, at least, with your beloved.

Even with children, servants, employees, and other underlings a show of red-hot anger is rarely justified. Sure, it will often scare the living daylights out of them and get them to do things your way. But at what a cost! Children at whom you are angry may tend, while jumping to your verbal whip, to hate themselves forever. Employees will also jump—temporarily. They may also hate your guts and spend much of the rest of the time soldiering on the job. Friends likewise. And almost everyone else you can name.

When you do get the results you want to get from people by cursing your head off, you almost invariably get other results that you very likely don't want: Their internalizing of your angry words, which makes them feel utterly incompetent and worthless; or their defensive externalizing of your angry words, so that they somehow feel that *you* wrongly yelled at them and that you're a no good skunk who doesn't deserve cooperation or devotion.

With people with whom you are in love relationships, the situation is ten times worsened. Not only do they hate you and/or themselves when you are angry with them; but, far worse, your angry words may have a slow-burning insidious effect long after you have said them. For most kinds of enduring love are based primarily on trust. We keep loving not only because people are nice to us or because they have certain lovable traits, but because we predict that they will *continue* to be nice to us, will *keep* having these traits.

Love, then, is *future-* as well as *present-*oriented. If, when you start falling in love with a man because he has beautiful features and a gorgeous build, you discover that he is a leper and that his physical beauty is shortly doomed, you will be surprised how quickly you will forget him as a serious love object.

So with anger and nagging. If you love a man for his sweet disposition and his fine responsiveness to you, and then you begin noting that on many occasions he completely loses his temper, roundly excoriates you for the slightest mistakes, and is thoroughly incapable of sympathizing with you or understanding your side of things, how long will you maintain any high level of feeling for this man? Try as you may to forgive and forget, the cumulative effect of his steady nagging and backbiting will sink in; and before you know it, you will find your love-filled thoughts turning in other directions, toward those who are less angry and more forgiving. Love begets love; and hate begets lovelessness.

What, then? If hostility is the foe of amour, how can you stem the tides of your hatreds and preserve your loving relationships?

By looking at, thinking about, challenging, and changing the internalized sentences of which your hostility essentially consists. For hostility, like all other sustained emotions, is not, as it at first blush seems to be, an instantaneous, automatic reaction to another's behavior; it is, rather, a swift reaction to your own philosophy *about* that behavior. It is not your lover's *actions* that make you mad at him. No, it is your *beliefs* about his actions that really start you feeling that he is a cad and a numbskull, and treating him accordingly.

One of my clients, Marylou S., was a particularly good example of what in common parlance is called an angry bitch. And not without, in the eyes of her close friends and relatives, some reason. For her friend, Robbie, with whom she had gone steadily for a year, was admittedly a difficult customer. He pedantically caught her up on every other sentence and lambasted her for her grammatical errors. He insisted that she subscribe to all the rules of his conservative church group. And he himself, after exacting the highest possible standards of conduct from her, was hardly angelic. In fact, he regularly got drunk every other week or so, and raised the roof for a couple of days before he sobered up.

Feeling so unjustly penned in by Robbie, Marylou took excellent advantage of his own lapses from sobriety and excoriated him unmercifully, both privately and publicly, whenever he fell from grace. "You!" she would scream at him. "You, who are so high and mighty about what I and what others should do. Look, just look, at what you did now! Totally wrecked the car, this time, so that it's only good for the junk heap. And it's hardly half paid up, too! Oh, you big plaster saint! Telling other people what to do—hah!" And on and on like this she would go.

"Why bother to screech at him?" I would quietly ask Marylou, whenever she came for another session of violent complaining. "Why not, if he's as bad as you say he is, leave him forever, and let it go at that?"

"What!" she would scream, almost as if *I* were Robbie and *I* had done her in again. "After all that time, a full year out of my life, that I've spent with that no-good louse? Why should I leave him? And how would *that* get me into a steady relationship?

"It might not," I replied. "But it would get you a little peace of mind. Wouldn't you rather be happy than mated?"

Apparently she wouldn't. Or, more to the point, she was

determined to be happy *and* mated; and if that rat, Robbie, thought he was going to prevent her from achieving this blissful state, well he had better think again. For he wasn't going to get away with this one!

I finally calmed Marylou down a bit—mainly by convincing her that just one more heated fight between her and Robbie would undoubtedly do the trick. Either he'd get drunk, after their fight, and really kill her or himself this time; or he'd go off, perhaps even to another town, and never return again. Is *that* what she truly wanted, I rhetorically asked: his or her sudden demise or Robbie's point-of-no-return leave-taking? No, she replied, she didn't; but what could she do to *stop* haranguing and fighting with an impossible (though at times admittedly lovable) sonofagun like that?

"Do you really want to stop feeling terribly angry toward Robbie?" I asked.

"Yes," said Marylou, "I think I finally do. I've been thinking over what you've been telling me during these last few weeks, and I have to admit you're right. Fighting with Robbie isn't going to change him a bit—except for the worse. And it's got so that it's doing me in, too. My insides have been bouncing around like a basketball for the last month so that I don't enjoy eating anymore—me, who used to be the plate-licker of my entire family! I guess I've had it. Either I stop feeling angry all the time or I'm going to have a real breakdown. I think I see that now."

"Fine," I said. "Now let's see if we can help you to admit just one more thing. And that is that you *can* stop feeling angry. No matter what Robbie or anyone else does—including all the wrong things in the world—*you* are in your own saddle seat, and *you* don't have to anger yourself."

"Sounds great. But *how?*"

"By giving up your grandiosity."

"My *grandiosity?* Oh, that's rich! I thought, as even you have agreed, that Robbie was the one of us with the grandiosity, the see-how-great-I-am-ness. *He's* the one that thinks he's God, and that I'm sort of one of his minor prophets, who should do his every bidding. Why, do you remember that time he—"

"Uh-uh," I interjected. "Temper, temper! You're all set to go off again now. Cut the crap! Sure I remember the time when Robbie did this and Robbie did that. And sure I agree that he's one of the rip-roaringest, most grandiose bastards that ever resided this side of heaven. But that's not the point. However omnipotent Robbie may be it's *your* grandiloquence we're talking about right now. Let's, please, get back to that—and let the reformation of Robbie, if it occurs at all, be the subject for *his* therapeutic agenda, not yours."

"You're right. Let's get back to me. Now what is my grandiloquence?"

"It's your basic stock in trade. Grandiloquence means empty, bombastic talk. And, that's exactly what you're saying to yourself—empty, bombastic talk. Not only you, but every person who, like you, makes herself terribly angry at people like Robbie."

"I know what you're trying to help me to see," said Marylou, "but I'm afraid that it still escapes me. You say that I, with what you now call my grandiosity, keep making myself angry. But doesn't Robbie, or anyone else like him, have *something* to do with it. *Would* I become—make myself, as you say—angry if he did *not* act the way he does?"

"No, you probably wouldn't. If Robbie were a perfect angel, and never did anything to annoy you, you probably would not make yourself angry—at *him.* But just as soon as someone else came along who wasn't such a blasted angel, or as soon as Robbie temporarily fell off his heavenly perch, you would then revert to angering yourself just as much as, perhaps even more than, you do now. For your bombastic philosophy is: "If the world goes exactly the way I want it to go, then I can be calm and happy. But as soon as it goes a little, or especially a lot, worse than I demand that it go, then it's totally unfair to me, this world; it *shouldn't* be the way it is; and I can't *help* being miserable in such a horribly unjust, anti-me universe.""

"And that philosophy, assuming that I have it, is what you call grandiose?"

"*Isn't* it? It puts you right in the dead-center of the entire cosmos, and assumes that, if things don't go the way you want them to go, this entire cosmos is unfair and unethical: that it *shouldn't* be the way it is."

"But why *should* it? If I want things to be in a certain way, why *shouldn't* they be that way?"

"Why *should* they? Besides you're not really expressing any wants; instead, you're making *demands.* For every time you tell yourself that things *shouldn't* be the way they are—when, of course, they *are* the way they are—you are tacitly commanding that they not be."

But isn't it true that *some* things shouldn't be the way they are—like murder and theft, for example?"

"No. It's true that it would be lovely if murder and theft didn't exist. But that hardly proves that they *shouldn't. Shoulds, oughts,* and *musts* tend to be absolutist perfectionist demands on life and the universe. Behind them is the assumption that because *I* don't want a thing so, it *shouldn't* be; and the whole cosmos is centered around me, agrees that what *I* think is right actually is right, and arranges things so that everyone will agree and will set about acting in the manner that I want them to act."

"Yes, but don't many other people, besides myself, think that it is right to be honest and not to commit murders?"

"Sure, many of them do. But many others, also, don't. There is never one hundred per cent agreement on what is right and what is wrong; and even if there were, how long would it last? All absolutist *shoulds, oughts,* and *musts,* however, assume that there is such one hundred per cent agreement—and they assume, moreover, that the universe stands ready to back up that agreement."

"In other words, when I say that Robbie *shouldn't* behave the way he does, I am really saying that *every* single person would agree with me that he shouldn't act that way, and that the universe itself, well, wouldn't *allow* him to act any differently, and would fall apart in, uh, complete disorder if he did do what I and it and *everyone* feels that he *shouldn't* do."

"You've put it unusually well. That's often what your *shouldn't* means: that everyone who disobeys that *shouldn't* is indubitably, *absolutely* wrong; and that they are disrupting the perfect, invariant order of the world by doing what they supposedly *shouldn't.* While, on the other hand, if you say that Robbie is doing what you consider to be wrong and that it would be better for you and for himself if he changed his behavior, then you are stating an opinion rather than an absolute dogma, and you may be able to induce him to follow it."

"Now I'm beginning to see. I show my grandiosity, whenever I feel angry at Robbie because my anger really means that I am utterly convinced that he *shouldn't* be the way he is, when I really mean there is an excellent likelihood, for both his and my sake, that it would be better if he were otherwise. But, by being angry, I blow up that likelihood into an absolute certainty, and there really is no such certainty in the world, and I am grandiose for believing, for foolishly convincing myself, that there is."

"You've hit it right on the nose again. What we call anger is almost always a demand for certainty. It insists that Robbie *must* behave differently, for otherwise he puts an element of chance into the universe that you cannot tolerate. Anger, in other words, is a subtle confession of your own weakness and your own seeking for thorough assurance—which you cannot command into existence.

"The angrier I get, the more bigoted I really am—for I refuse to let Robbie make the mistakes that he's almost certain to make anyway."

"Yes, anger—or blaming others for being the way they are— essentially is a form of fascism. For just as Hitler and Mussolini blamed people for having traits they personally abhorred—such as being Jewish or being gypsies—the angry individual damns others for having traits that they personally do not like. And although it is perfectly proper to *dislike* the behavior of others it is hardly proper to condemn them, and think that they should be annihilated, for having traits you dislike."

"My anger at Robbie, then, is grandiose because I am *demanding* that he be the way I would *like* him to be?"

"Correct. You are insisting that because you want him to change—which is quite legitimate—he *must* do so. Once you stop that grandiose insistence, then he may listen to you more open-mindedly; and there is a greater chance that he actually will change. But if he doesn't—tough! You still, for your own good and the sake of your own blood pressure, had better accept Robbie and the world the way they are—even when you don't *like* them that way."

"I see."

And Marylou did see. She almost immediately began to act more acceptingly with Robbie: to show him that she *wanted* him to change but that she didn't *need* him to do so. As it happened, he didn't change very much; so that, finally, concluding that he was too emotionally disturbed, she broke off with him. But she managed to do so without seriously hurting either him or herself.

A year later, after she had unfrantically got into a relationship

with another man, Marylou did mate, and has since had no
reason to regret her choice. Moreover, what she learned from
failing with Robbie helped her greatly in her later relationship.

Raising your level of frustration tolerance

One of the very best ways to sabotage your romantic life is to be
a spoiled brat or a cry-baby—or to have what we psychologists
frequently call low frustration tolerance. For a woman who won't
bear frustration will not only demand that she have exactly what
she wants, but demand it precisely when she wants it—meaning,
right now, pronto, immediately! And her unreasonable demands
will be communicated to the men whe wants—who, if they are
even moderately sane, will soon conclude: "She's a very nice
person, bright enough, sufficiently attractive and all that sort of
thing. But who needs her kind of childishness? Who wants to live
with *that?*"

Low frustration tolerance, moreover, is one of the chief
sources of goading aggressiveness, as distinguished from healthy
self-assertion. The self-assertive woman asks herself: "What do I
truly *want* in life, and how can I go about getting it?" The
obnoxiously aggressive woman asks: "What must I, right this
very second, absolutely have? And how, by hook or crook, no
matter how many toes I may have to step upon, can I get it?"

If the self-assertive woman is temporarily blocked from getting
what she desires, she tells herself: "Too bad. I can't get what I
want right now. Let's see what I can do to get it later. Or let's see,
if this is going to be impossible, how I can still enjoy life without
getting this thing I want." The highly aggressive woman tells
herself, when she cannot quickly get her heart's desire: "How
awful! I simply *can't stand* this frustration! I'll fix those people
who are blocking me! I'll show them! How can I hurt them as
much as possible, so that they'll simply *have* to give me this thing
that I need?"

Low frustration tolerance, then, leads to anger at the world
and the people in it—including, often, one's best beloved. It also
leads to self-pity; a most unloving and unlovable state!

Alice R. was a charming, vivacious woman of twenty-seven,
who had been married at the age of eighteen and divorced two
years later, mainly because, as she put it, she couldn't stand her

"goddam selfish sonofabitch" husband. For the last seven years, before I started to see her as a client, she had gone with innumerable men, most of them quite eligible as mates, and several of them more than willing to live with her. But they, too, were almost always found to be "too goddam selfish" or "too wrapped up in their work" or something like that; so that she always ended up by rejecting them. But she did, however, very much want to mate and to give her eight-year-old daughter a strong, kindly man to relate to.

"What do you mean," I asked Alice during one of the early therapy sessions, "that all the men you meet are, as you put it, 'too goddam selfish'?"

"Oh, you know. They only think of their own pleasures or their own work. Never think of what *I* really want to do. Won't go out of their way to help me when I need them. You know."

"How often do you generally 'need' them?" I asked. "From what you have told me, you're a pretty competent person in your own right, and do very well at the office, without feeling that anyone around there has to help you in your hour of need."

"Oh, that's different. That's the office. And you just *can't* expect people to help you much there. But in my social life it's quite another thing. I *am* a woman, don't forget. And women should be waited on in many little ways, shouldn't they? Otherwise, we all might as well be one sex and stay away from each other!"

"You mean that whenever you want something, even if you can easily get it yourself, some man should be around to wait on you and get it for you?"

"Well, no. I'm not as bad as *that!* But—well, take what happened the other evening, when I was seeing John. I wanted to go to dinner early, since I hadn't eaten much all day and I was practically starving. And he wanted to go to dinner, too, but he said that he really ought to make some calls first, some business calls that he just had to get through that night, and that if he waited to make them later he probably wouldn't be able to get the people. So he asked if he could use my phone, make the calls, and then we'd go to eat. I didn't like the idea, but I naturally said yes. Then—would you believe it?—he spent the next damned forty-five minutes on my phone, calling god knows who, and leaving me there to twiddle my thumbs and practically starve to death until he had finished. Now, don't you call that terribly selfish? Do you think I should even consider living with someone like *that?*"

"But he *did* have important calls to make, didn't he?" I asked. "He wasn't going out of his way to make unnecessary ones, just to keep you waiting, was he?"

"Oh, no. I guess he did have to make them. But for forty-five minutes! And me just about starving!"

"Now, look," I said. "Let's stop the nonsense! You were hungry, yes. So, probably, was he. But forty-five minutes longer to get around to eating wasn't going to cause your demise. And, if it was, you could have gotten *something* to nibble on before you actually went out to dinner. Now how is it that you always convince yourself, in cases like this, that you're absolutely starving, and will perish any moment, when you really mean that it's somewhat inconvenient for you not to eat immediately, but that you could damned well stand the inconvenience?"

"Are you trying to say that most of my hunger was actually put on—that I didn't really have to eat that quickly?"

"I'm not trying to say this; I'm saying it. And you know I'm right in saying it. Most—not all, but most—of your hunger *was* put on. Suppose, for example, that John, instead of having to make those telephone calls, had brought you a beautiful new dress that night, and wanted you to wear it to dinner. And suppose that putting on the dress and its accessories would have taken you forty-five minutes, and that you'd therefore have to keep *him* waiting before you went to dinner. Would you *then* have been 'starving' so violently that you couldn't possibly wait?"

"Well—well, no, I guess not."

"You *could*, under those circumstances, have waited a bit more patiently and gracefully?"

"Yes, I suppose I could."

"Well? Isn't it obvious, then, that it wasn't your hunger that got you all upset and angry about waiting, but your *attitude?* Isn't it clear that it wasn't the internalized sentence, 'My! my stomach's growling, I simply must eat,' but, rather, the sentences, 'That selfish sonofabitch! How could he make those telephone calls when I'm so hungry?'—isn't it clear that *these* latter sentences were the real ones that were making you so frustrated—and even so hungry?"

"You're saying, then, that I wasn't even actually *that* hungry, as I made myself out to be, but that both my hunger and my frustration were highly exaggerated by the angry sentences I kept telling myself."

"Yes, that's exactly what I'm saying. Not that you weren't hungry at all—for it's most likely that you were. And you really would have *liked* to eat quite soon. But, unfortunately, you translated that liking into a *demand* to eat immediately. And when your demand was not acceded to, you *then* convinced yourself how hungry you were, how you absolutely could not stand being frustrated, and what a horrible sonofabitch he was for not feeding you immediately."

"My very demand to eat made me much hungrier than I really was?"

"Yes. Isn't that so? Think about it, now. Isn't that what happened?"

"Hmmm. You may well be right. In fact, now that you make me think about it, I do remember something, something that kind of proves that you *are* right."

"Oh?"

"Yes. It was a little before six when he came to call for me to take me to dinner, and I really was hungry. But I remember thinking to myself, right after he came: 'Good! Now we can eat. Let's see: if we go to the restaurant next door, we will probably be waited upon right away, and that will be fine. But I'm rather sick of that place, and the food's not really that good there. Why don't I suggest that we go to Mario's instead. It will take us fifteen minutes or twenty minutes until we're seated and served. But it's a much better place, and I think it's worth the wait.' "

"Ah! See! So you weren't exactly starving! And you could, by your own decision, afford to wait awhile to eat—when there was some good incentive to do so. But his telephone calls weren't just that good enough incentive for you. So you *insisted* to yourself that you were starving, and that he was a sonofabitch for keeping you waiting. Just as I thought!"

"Yes, I'll have to admit you're right."

"O.K.: but the point is not that I'm right, but that you're wrong. And not merely this time, since this is unimportant. But so many of those other times you've told me about. You want something from your male companion, such as to take you to dinner promptly. Then he balks, for some reason, and doesn't get you precisely what you want at the split-second that you want it. Then you give *yourself* a real pain in the neck by insisting that you *must have* what you want.

"Then, finally, you beat him unmercifully over the head, and blame him interminably for not getting you what you, by this time, are utterly convinced that you must immediately have. By this kind of childish lack of frustration tolerance, therefore, you are not only frustrating *yourself* much more than you are *being* frustrated by outside events; but you are also winding up with hostility toward your, whomever he may be, current partner. No wonder you feel that all of these partners, including your ex-husband, have been 'too goddam selfish'!"

"I see what you mean. I'm seeing these men as much more selfish than they actually are—because I am making myself much more frustrated than I actually need be. And my low frustration tolerance is getting in the way of my accepting men more tolerantly and seeing them in a truer and more kindly light."

"Exactly."

"But what can I do about this, if this is so? How can I lower my frustration, or raise my tolerance of frustration?"

"Isn't it obvious, from what we have been saying, how you can do this? Think about it for a moment. How do you suppose you could increase your frustration tolerance?"

"Hmm. By—by, I guess, showing myself that I *don't* have to have everything I want the very moment that I want it. By convincing myself that I won't starve to death, or otherwise die, if I don't get what I want in the next half-second."

"Right. By changing your sentence, 'I absolutely, positively must have what I want right now, this second!' to 'I wish I could have what I want right away, but I can, if necessary, wait awhile, and even if I never get everything I want, it won't kill me.' "

"How about the sentence, 'I must have what I want right away, and if he doesn't give it to me, he's no damned good, and I hate him!' Mustn't I change that one, too?"

"By all means! For even if he *can* give you what you want right away, and even if for some reason he does *not* do so, he is not a louse. He is simply a man who is not giving you what you want. And your problem is to get him to change his mind and to give it to you. But calling him a louse or a skunk will hardly, in most instances, help him change his mind or give you what you want."

"How right you are! After I got angry at John, and made such a fuss about his making those calls for forty-five minutes, he threatened to leave entirely, and let me have dinner by myself. I had a job calming him down. And I guess we wasted another forty-five minutes arguing!"

"See? That's what usually happens. The more you demand that you must have your piece of taffy *right now*, the less you tend to get it right then—and sometimes ever to get it. So isn't it worth working on your low frustration tolerance?"

"I see. I guess I have a lot of work to do."

It would be nice to report that Alice immediately did begin to buckle down to work against her own low frustration tolerance and her consequent anger at men, but unfortunately she didn't. She *saw* the problem clearly, but refused to do much about solving it. She calmed herself down sufficiently to get along better with John, and soon after to marry him. But she quit psychotherapy long before she had actually worked through her underlying carping against frustration and she has not, to my knowledge, had a very smooth marital relationship. Too bad; but that is *her* problem.

Your problem, if your level of frustration tolerance is low, is to do the work that Alice mainly refused to do: namely, clearly to see that you are upsetting yourself when things go badly, and then to *work against* this kind of self-upsetment by persistently observing your own angry sentences and vigorously challenging and questioning them until you begin to replace them with more reasonable (but still realistic) assessments of what is happening.

Rational assertion training

Since I wrote the first edition of this book, assertion training has become something of a fad in Western civilization. And, as Arnold Lazarus has pointed out, it is sometimes taken to ridiculous extremes. For assertion does not mean that you *have to* get what you want and that you will go to almost any length to get it. This, again, is largely aggression—and will often lead to poor or self-defeating results. If you think that you *must* do your thing, and express to others exactly how you feel at precisely the moment you feel it, you will tend to antagonize them and consequently *not* get what you wish.

Assertion mainly means that you try to get—not *insist* on

getting—what you want; and that you also endeavor to avoid getting what you don't want. Even with people you love, and in some ways especially with the people you love and live with, you try to discover what you would like them to do and not to do; and then you unhostilely communicate these wishes to them and hope that they agree with a good proportion of them.

In rational-emotive therapy (RET), we do a great deal of assertion training, but we invariably do it within a philosophical framework. For the main reasons why people do not properly and actively assert themselves consist of their three outstanding irrational Beliefs. We have largely, in this chapter, so far discussed the second of these major irrationalities: "You *must* do what I want you to do, and never block me in any notable way; and it's *awful* and *I can't bear* it when you don't, you *worm!*" This irrational Belief (iB) about others and their behavior makes you feel and act angrily rather than assertively; or else it encourages you to be *over*assertive, hence uncooperative with others.

At the same time, as I point out in *How to Live With—and Without—Anger*, lack of assertiveness, or bottled up assertiveness, may well encourage you to feel hostile. For if you consistently want your partner to do something (such as have steady sex with you) or do not want him to do something else (such as be uncommunicative about his feelings), and you fail to assert these desires, you will frequently blame him for not fulfilling them and mightily condemn yourself (or be angry at yourself) for not being assertive. You will therefore wind up feeling quite angry at this partner.

A suitable degree of assertiveness, consequently, wards off potential anger; and, as I keep noting throughout this book, it also helps your efforts to seek out and put your best foot forward with a partner with whom you would like to mate. We speak, in our culture, of an "aggressive" salesperson. But, really, we mean an assertive rather than an angry one. For to be assertive in going after what you want is a good, productive trait; and without this kind of assertion, you will normally get fewer and less suitable people with whom you can potentially mate.

How, then, can you train yourself to become more assertive without concomitantly making yourself angrier? By first minimizing the two other irrational Beliefs that tend to interfere with healthy assertion. Take, for example, irrational premise No. 1: "I *must* not have anyone disapprove of me or be angry with me."

As long as you hold this premise, you will "naturally" conclude, "It would be *horrible* if these people did not like me! I *can't tolerate* their possible disapproval! What a *bad person* I would be if they didn't like me!" Just hold this assumption to any considerable degree, and whoof!—there goes your assertiveness down the drain!

Similarly with anti-assertiveness premise No. 3: "The conditions of my life must *easily* and *quickly* present me with what I want and prevent me from getting what I don't want! It's *terrible* when I have *trouble* asserting myself. I *can't stand* this kind of difficulty! It's not *worth* being assertive if I have to go through so much pain and discomfort!" Firmly hold to this kind of nonsense, and just see how assertive you will be!

In rational-emotive assertion training, then, we first get you to clearly see these interfering philosophies and premises; and, of course, to firmly and strongly dispute them. That is, to ask yourself such questions as: "Why *must* I act quite nicely and win the approval of the people with whom I would like to assert myself?" "Where is the evidence that it is horrible, rather than merely inconvenient, if I do go after what I want and these people do not like me?" "Prove that the conditions of my life *have to* easily and quickly present me with what I want and prevent me from getting what I don't want." "Where is it writ that I *can't stand* asserting myself with some difficulty?"

If you will first Dispute (at point D, in RET) these groundless assumptions or premises, until you really think them through and give them up, you will then be much better prepared to act assertively—and often to do so naturally, easily, and spontaneously. For you will then acquire a philosophy along these lines: "It would certainly be lovely if I won the approval of the people with whom I would like to assert myself; but I don't *have to* win it! And it would be highly convenient if the conditions of my life easily and quickly presented me with what I want and prevented me from getting what I don't want. But it would only be moderately inconvenient, and never *awful* or *horrible*, if I had to keep striving with difficulty to achieve some of my most desired goals."

As Arthur Lange and Patricia Jakubowski show in their book, *Responsible Assertive Behavior*, you can use the A-B-C-D-E's of RET to first get yourself in the philosophic mood to assert yourself more directly and productively. Once you employ this kind of cognitive restructuring, and see that you don't *have to* get your way and that you also don't *have to* be approved by others in case they oppose your asserting yourself, you can then feel much freer to express your thoughts and feelings more directly and more persuasively.

The actual technique of assertion largely consists of forcing yourself to take various kinds of risks: such as the risk of doing things you would like to do (e.g., sending back a poorly cooked dish in a restaurant) but have so far refused to do; the risk of asking for something you want but might easily get refused; the risk of saying no to someone when you really want to say it; the risk of doing something ridiculous or "shameful" (such as singing at the top of your lungs on the street) in public; and the risk of deliberately failing at an important task (like making a speech) when you would prefer to succeed at it.

If you force yourself to do these kinds of "risky" things, while at the same time convincing yourself that failure is *only* inconvenient and disapproval is *only* disadvantageous, and that neither is unbearable or horrible, you will eventually get practiced at this kind of assertion, and begin to do it much more easily and spontaneously. You will then be in a much better position to truly go after what you want and to refuse to do what you don't want to do.

Specific methods of acting assertively have been outlined in detail in many articles and books, including those by Andrew Salter, Joseph Wolpe and Arnold Lazarus, Robert Alberti and Michael Emmons, Manuel Smith, Herbert Fensterheim and Jean Baer, Arthur Lange and Patricia Jakubowski, and Janet L. Wolfe. Go over some of this material and practice using it on many occasions. A few good rules that you can follow in this respect are these:

1. Speak in an audible, firm tone of voice. Avoid angry, harsh, whiney, and accusatory statements.

2. Attempt to have others treat you with fairness and justice, and determinedly point out to them when they don't. But, again, anger is not assertion!

3. When expressing disapproval of someone's actions or stating your desire not to do something, use a decided no. Don't act apologetically, hedge, or leave the decision up to the other person.

4. When refusing to do something, give as prompt and brief a reply as feasible, without using unduly long pauses or interruptions.

5. When someone asks you to do something you consider unreasonable, ask for an explanation and listen to it carefully. After listening, sometimes suggest an alternative solution that you would prefer.

6. Where appropriate—meaning, where you do not expect any severe penalty—honestly express your feelings. Do so with friends and relatives more than with bosses or supervisors; and do so without using evasion, attacking others, or trying to defensively justify yourself.

7. When expressing displeasure or annoyance, try to tell others the aspects of their behavior that you don't like. Don't attack them, name-call, or imply that they deserve to be damned for disagreeing with you.

8. Recognize the usefulness of I-messages instead of you-messages. Thus, instead of saying, "You are wrong about that," you can say, "I feel that that is wrong because—." But watch the manner in which you put even I-messages, for they can include a good deal of self-defeating rage. Thus, an I-message like "I feel put off by you when your sex requirements are so high" may be said in a tone that may lead a lover to think that you are much more aggressive than assertive.

As ever, the main thing to keep in mind in regard to almost all assertion is that you want what you want but those with whom you relate often have quite different desires. And they are as entitled to their preferences as you are to yours. Even when their wishes seem to mask commands, they are *still* entitled to be commanding. As ever, try to use the RET philosophy of giving others the right to be wrong. You can then assert yourself in an unhostile manner that is less likely to engender return hostility and more likely to get you what you want while maintaining cooperative relationships with them. Assertion and aggression frequently overlap. Try to minimize this overlapping!

5

What to Look for in a Man

Let's assume, now that you have been seriously chewing on this book for several chapters, and have begun to be more assertive, more permissive, less anxious, and less hostile in regard to the problem of meeting and winning a man, that you are faced with the concrete problem of having few or no males around with whom you would even care to get deeply involved. What kind of man should you then look for? And where had you better look for him?

Let us consider the first of these questions before, in the next chapter, we go on to the second. The man you will probably want to have, especially if you are considering a long-term mating arrangement, would best have the following kind of traits.

Emotional stability

Let's face it at the start: most men are nutty. Most women are, too; but that, unless you are an eagerly seeking lesbian, is probably not too much your problem. So let's, for the nonce, stick to the nuttiness of men.

Like many neurotics, an emotionally unstable man can be most stimulating and fascinating. His moods may be of the never-a-dull-moment kind. His very inconsistencies may be charming. Because he is undisciplined, he may have plenty of time to devote to you instead of to his work. And, best of all, he may be more interested in love—not sex, but real, honest-to-goodness love—than any other man you have ever met. For neurotics *need* love: violently, incessantly. And they are often obsessively-compulsively seeking it and plumbing its depths when even a bare smidgeon of it is around. So your half-crazy lover may be, in some respects, the most satisfactory man you ever had.

But don't be fooled! Screwballs are essentially, especially in the final analysis, bores. On a once-a-week or even a twice-a-week basis they may be highly tolerable, even more than a bit exciting. But for heaven's sake, think seriously before you try to *live* with one! They are obsessive-compulsive, at bottom, mainly about themselves: and not even, in one sense, about that. For they are really worried almost all the time, about what others (including you) think of them, and not about what they would truly like to do to make themselves vibrant and happy.

Neurotics, in other words, strive for what Helmuth Kaiser called *fusion*. They are not really interested in talking *to* you but in fusing *with* you—that is, in getting your complete, undivided attention, and meriting your undying devotion no matter how badly they behave toward you. Consequently, they carry on two conversations at once: one, a fairly objective conversation, in which they appropriately respond to what you say, and sensibly discuss politics, the weather, your trip to Europe, or whatnot; the second, a most subjective conversation, which essentially goes on with *themselves*, in which they ceaselessly debate: "Was that the correct thing I said? Will she like me any more, now that I've said it? Does she really care for me, or is it just my money she's after? I know that she's smiling, but I'm sure that she actually hates me, and thinks I'm a dunce for talking like this." Etcetera, etcetera!

Emotionally disturbed men, you'd better see and admit, often *seem* to be keenly interested in you; but actually they are mainly interested in what you think of *them*. And they go on incessantly, interminably trying to get you to think well of them—and hating your guts when they even slightly imagine that you don't. What is more, the way in which they try to get you to love them is hardly a sane or sensible one—such as the technique of being so nice to you that you will just have to love them in return—but is often a nastily testing, negative way: such as being unkind and inconsiderate to you, to *see* whether you still accept and love them.

Because disturbed males (exactly like disturbed females) are self-centered (that is, centered on others loving them) instead of self-interested (that is, interested in what *they* really want to do in life), they actually do not give that much of a fig for you; do not see your side of a story; often cannot be reached, no matter how hard you try to communicate with them; and frequently dive into defensive shells such as oversleeping, refusing to see anyone socially, being hostile at work and at home, gambling, drinking, etc. And, having one-track minds ("What, oh what, does So-and-So think of me?"), they are generally bores to be with and are not truly interested in *living* in this infinitely variegated and absorbing world.

Neurotics, to make matters still worse, are usually unsatisfactory fathers, inadequate sex partners, poor providers or savers, inept at facing crises, and otherwise lacking in many traits which are exceptionally important in a good mate. They have so many self-sabotaging symptoms and defenses that, in *How To Live With A "Neurotic"* I have taken thirty-six pages to list them. A seriously neurotic person is about as nice to live with as is a cobra—only not so easily caged.

Should you, therefore, swiftly eliminate every emotionally unstable member of the other sex whom you meet, and rigorously date and try to mate only those who are completely stable and sane? No: for there aren't any such animals, apparently, in our society. All of us are more or less kooky; and if you keep looking for a thoroughly non-neurotic mate, you will have to outdo Diogenes before you find one. Unless spinsterhood is your devotedly chosen lot, please be reasonable and make *some* compromises in this respect.

"But look here!" you may with some justification be saying by this time. "What the devil kind of a choice do you offer me? First you tell me not to mate with a nut. Then you tell me that nothing but candidates for the looney-bin are actually available for mating. What kind of a box are you putting me in?"

Not as tight a box as you might think. In the first place, I have only been telling you not to *mate with* or *marry* a neurotic. But I didn't, remember, say that you couldn't love one, have an affair with one, or even live for awhile with one. Go right ahead: enjoy yourself. Just don't delude yourself that screwballs are permanently delightful; for they practically never are.

In the second place, there are nuts and nuts. Although just about everyone in our society (as well as, probably, in all other human societies) is *more or less* crazy, some are certainly crazier than others. So you can, if you are sensible, look for a man who is not *too* looney—even while frankly admitting that he is not likely to be completely sane. You can often find, for example, someone who is compartmentally screwed up: who is, say, pretty daffy at work but not hard to get along with at home. Or you can find a man who is cracked in a limited and relatively unimportant kind of way: who is, for instance, a rabid butterfly collector, but who in other respects is reasonably on the ball. Or you can find a mate who is zany, all right, but who just happens to be zany in a similar manner to you: say, one who would rather play bridge than eat, and who is a great partner for a bridge fiend like you.

Better yet, perhaps (since it is not easy to find the particular kind of lunatic whom you would enjoy living with), you can look for a man who is just about as neurotic as everyone else are, but who at least *knows* and *fully admits* that he is. Living with a queer duck is bad enough; but staying with one who thinks that he is the sanest of the sane (and that perhaps you and everyone else are balmy) is next to impossible.

So you *can* consider an *admitted* neurotic—especially if he is working on his problem, perhaps going for psychotherapy, and is well on the way to eventually becoming *less* disturbed. In fact, you can frankly tell any potential lover, if you find him too kooky for your domestic tastes, that just as soon as he does admit that he is somewhat off his rocker, and just as soon as he begins to *do* something about his emotional upsets, you will *then* be glad to consider him seriously as a mate.

Suppose that the love of your life either does not know that he is batty or admits that he is but refuses to do anything about it—should you then mate with him and try to be a therapist to him? Yes and no. Yes, as we show in a later chapter of this book, there is often much that can be done to help a disturbed partner overcome some of his worst emotional difficulties. But no, it isn't too wise to commit yourself fully until you are pretty certain that you *will* be able to help him. How can you make pretty certain? By living with him for a fair period of time before you marry him;

or seeing so much of him, even though you do not live with him, that you are able to work with him on his problems and actually *see* that he is making some progress.

Suppose, though, nothing works in this respect. Your dream man is a real nut; he won't admit it or go for help; and none of your own efforts to get him saner are taking any effect. But you still love him, find him fascinating, and are most loath to leave him. What then?

Leave! Love him, if you will. But if you are at all interested in a permanent affair with someone with whom you have at least a fair chance to live happily, love him from a distance. Every once in a while—say, about one in a thousand cases—a woman lives satisfactorily with a severe neurotic or a psychotic. Don't fool yourself that you are going to be the lucky (and infinitely hard-working!) exception. Insist that your disturbed lover be professionally treated. Accept nothing but real tries on his part to get over his disturbance: don't swallow any pious resolutions or promises about changing tomorrow. If he won't, even for the love of you, do anything to help himself change, what makes you think that he *ever* will do so? Stop kidding yourself, lady. *Leave!*

Willingness to mate

Mating is by no means the only legitimate or worthwhile sex-love relationship. Many individuals, especially those who have been mated and have separated, thrive on living alone for the rest of their lives—but also thrive on love affairs along with their domestic privacy. Other individuals remain solidly tied to one mate—but also carry on romances with other partners. Still others follow different kinds of nonsharing patterns and end up with surprisingly good love relations. So let us not assume that everyone *must* mate in order to enjoy love and sex; nor that *you* must be among the majority who do.

If, however, you do want to live with the best man you can find —then you'd better be concerned with his willingness to mate. By this, I do not only mean that you should ascertain at the start whether or not he is already mated. For even if he is, that does not mean that he must *continue* to be; and he of course *can* separate from his current partner and live with you.

This, though, is definitely *not* to be counted upon. Innumerable married men go for long periods of time with women who *think* they are going to leave their partners and then the men just don't. Not that they necessarily love the women with whom they stay; often, in fact, they loathe them. But there is many a slip between a man's having an affair with another woman and his leaving his mate for her. Money—yes, m-o-n-e-y—matters may easily keep him tied up. Or his relatives. Or his children. Or his job. Or his feelings of guilt. Or Lord know what else.

Does that means that you should never, under any circumstances, go with a mated man if you yourself want a permanent relationship? No, not never; but hardly ever. Or, at the very least, it means that you'd better not go with one *too long*. For a few months, yes: since he may well leave his current partner at the end of that time. For a year or so, occasionally: since it still may take him some time to get up the guts, the money, the drive to leave her. At anything over a year, however: watch your step!

Certainly, there *may* be extenuating circumstances. In one case I know about, a married man went with his secretary for five years, until his children became old enough to go away to school. Then, just as he said he would, he divorced his wife and went to live with the secretary. In another case, a married woman stayed with her mate for three years, until he got on his feet financially; and then she left him for the man with whom she had been having a clandestine affair during the entire period.

These, however, are the exceptions. Most of the time, if a man does not leave his current mate for your board as well as your bed after you have been intimate with him for a year or more, he will never do so. He may say he will, and may think he will; but he probably won't. And I have rarely seen women unhappier than those who consulted me after they stayed three, five, and more years in a sex-love relationship with an already mated man and *then,* finally, discovered he definitely was not going to leave his partner. So beware of relating to a man who takes a long time to separate from another woman. Unless, of course, you really *don't* want to mate.

Many unmateable men are not living with someone else and are technically "single." Nonetheless they just aren't—or at least *believe* they aren't—up for a domestic partnership. Some of them—in fact, a large number of them—would probably like to live with a woman but are afraid to do so. Some are scared of women; some of sex failure; some of financial responsibilities; some of rearing children.

These fearful men aren't necessarily hopeless—since it is *possible* for them to overcome their fears, especially if they go for therapeutic help. But they are certainly not the best mating prospects! Coaxing or trapping them into living with you, moreover, will only help them overcome their fears in a certain percentage of cases. In many instances, in fact, cajoling them into doing so will serve only to enhance their fears, and only a separation will calm them down.

Usually, the best tack for you to take with a man who is terribly fearful of mating is flight. The quickest and farthest that you get away from him, the better. Let him live "happily" ever after with his mother. If he won't go for psychological help, you'd better seek it yourself: in order to help you get over him.

If fearful men are poor bets, hostile men are even worse. The male who hates women; or who loathes people; or who abhors anyone who balks him in any way—this man you need like you need cancer. There seem to be, in general, two kinds of people: acceptors and malcontents. Acceptors graciously go along with reality, even when it is notably unpleasant; malcontents inwardly or outwardly seethe and rage at even the slightest of life's inconveniences. If the man you dearly love is a malcontent and is not willing to do anything about changing his unusually low level of frustration tolerance, mate with him as readily as you would with a rattlesnake.

Many other men, who are neither overly fearful nor too hostile, are still essentially unmarriageable; for instance, males who are highly dedicated to some cause and who therefore never have the time nor energy truly to be absorbed with a woman. Or men who have nomadic occupations (such as that of being a sailor or a big game hunter). Or men who are unhappy staying at home, and have to be out doing something literally every night of the week.

Many of these individuals might make good partners *if* they weren't so absorbed in various anti-domestic pursuits. But since they are so absorbed, and most probably will not change in the next fifty years, you'd be far wiser to let them be what they most want to be, and to look elsewhere for someone who is really *interested* in a long-term relationship.

In sum: in looking for a man to live with focus not only on his good qualities but his advantageous mating traits. Always remember the words of the English poet, George Wither, who (to paraphrase a little) said of any of his potential women friends, "What care I how fair she be, if she be not fair to me?" Wonderful and fine, indeed, may your would-be partner be; but how wonderful and fine, really, is he *to you?* And how long is he likely to remain so after the two of you pledge your troth and actually go to *live* together? Let me repeat again what I so often tell my clients. Don't, normally, mate with any man you don't love; but don't, also, commit yourself to every man you *do*.

Permissiveness

Just as you yourself, as we noted in Chapter 2, had better strive to be permissive with the man you want to win as your mate, so you'd better look for a husband who himself is reasonably permissive, and who doesn't equate womanhood with servility. Good-looking and strong your chosen male may be; bright as a whip, and with a substantial bank account. But if he is any substantial kind of bigot, moralist, or male supremacist, leave him be: poison is his name and Ms. Dead Duck yours if you are crazy enough to live with him.

"Well suppose," you ask, "the next man I meet is unusually fine in most respects, but he happens to have been conservatively or orthodoxly raised, thinks that women's place is in the home, and has several similar ideas. In most ways, he's great, but he just happens to be conventional in regard to women and mating. What then?"

What do you mean, I counter, *he just happens to be?* Rubbish! People—except in naive Freudian and behavioristic thinking—just don't happen to be anything. They *make* themselves, for the most part, into what they are; or they fail to make themselves what they are not.

Granted that your unusually fine man was raised by tradition-bound parents, or reared as a Holy Roller or a Seventh Day Adventist. That's no excuse for his *maintaining* bigoted, anti-female sentiments. All of us, practically, are raised with considerable religious, socio-economic, political, and other bushwah. But those of us who are sufficiently sane and self-accepting *re-think* the nonsense with which we were inculcated, and discard at least a great deal of it before we reach our majority.

So ignorance is no excuse. Any man who is raised by some orthodox group which will not accept women as people and who *still*, by the time you meet him as a mating prospect, believes the hogwash with which he was reared, is distinctly suspect. The chances are at least nine out of ten that he really *wants* to believe the nonsense—that he *prefers* to see women as second-class citizens and feels happy (because of his own deep-seated feelings of inadequacy) to think of them in this category.

Instead, look for a partner who is truly permissive: who will, without necessarily liking much of what you do, nonetheless give you gracious permission to do it; and who, when he disagrees violently with you, will firmly attempt to persuade rather than coerce you into seeing and doing things his way.

This does not mean that you should avidly seek out a man who is so meek and weak that he will gladly let you do anything you want, including walk all over him, because he doesn't think himself worthy of trying to get you to desist. Such a man is as spineless, in his own way, as the dogmatic fascist is in his. The midway male, who is firm enough to know what he wants and to go after it, but kind enough to allow you, too, to know what you want and to go after this, is the sort of male you would be wise to seek. Is such a male rare? Indeed, he is. Which is no reason why you shouldn't keep looking until you find him.

Communicativeness

Marriage or mating is a *social* institution. If you really don't care for social discourse, and would rather go live in a modern version of a cave, by all means hop to it. *Everyone* shouldn't marry; and mayhap the mating game is just not your malted milk. If you do want to mate, however, it is to be assumed that you want some reasonable measure of companionship, of clear-cut communication with your mate.

O.K.: look for just that—*before* you make a serious move toward the altar. However, the world, you might as well know from the start, is literally full of uncommunicative mates. Some read the newspaper all night. Some dote on television. Some sit glumly quiet, doing nothing, just nothing. Some sleep practically all the time they're home. Some communicate beautifully—with neighbors, friends, relatives, children: in fact, with everyone except you. Some are always opening their big mouths—at the office, at the Elks Club, at cocktail parties; but almost never at home.

This is not quite so unusual as it may at first sound. For men and women, after they have lived together for a period of time, often *don't* have very much to say to each other; while, when strangers are present, things quickly become much more interesting and novel, and considerably more may be said. Domestic sharing—let us face it squarely and honestly—is *not* the most charming, exciting relationship ever invented. It has its distinct limitations as a communicative institution. So do not, please, unrealistically expect constant stimulation and interchange from your poor human, strictly limited and fallible partner.

Nonetheless!—there are extremes of uncommunicativeness in man-woman relationships; and, if your would-be mate is at one of these extremes, you'd better recognize the bright red danger signals and do something about his buttoned-lip tendency. Such as? Well, you might see if he has any distinct blocks to communication—e.g., his fear that you will put your foot in his mouth if he dares open it, or his fear that he will give himself (meaning his underlying feelings of worthlessness) away if he talks too much. And if he has such blocks, you might try to help him remove them by taking the initial brunt of the talking on your own shoulders; by showing him that you will not pounce on him cruelly when he says the wrong things; by frankly discussing with him why he is verbally blocked; or by insisting that he get professional help in unblocking himself.

And if such techniques as these do not work? Run, woman, run! Bright and handsome and rich indeed your man may be. But there *are* others equally endowed; and some of them *are* less tied up in uncommunicative knots. The essence of mating is talking (and sometimes copulating). If you haven't got at least that to begin with, you might as well not start!

Sexual drive

Sex isn't everything. But a man-woman relationship completely without it usually isn't very much of anything. If your partner does not like to play tennis, go to the movies, or go out socially with you, your relationship may possibly still survive on an amicable plane. But if he hates going to bed with you, your chances of having a good relationship are not merely low, they are often nonexistent.

How can you tell, before mating, whether your chosen man

really cares for you sexually, and is likely to keep caring for you in that manner for years to come? Obviously, there is one obvious test: try sex with him and see. This does not mean, now, that you should merely try kissing him passionately goodnight, or pet with him in the car, or even go away for a single weekend in a motel before you start living together. Almost anyone can pass *that* namby-pamby kind of sex test, and the great majority of males usually do. Including, alas, those who later turn out to be the world's worst bedmates.

Should you, then, actually try to live with a man before marrying him: live, that is to say, under the same roof, and at night in the same bed, for a considerable period of time before you legally wed? You certainly had better!

If I had my way, in fact—which seems most unlikely, at the moment—we would pass a special law in this country, requiring couples to live together for at least a year before a marriage license is issued.

Why so long? Because most couples can easily fool themselves and each other for a few months, and remain sufficiently in love during that time to make themselves genuinely believe that they are well suited for each other for a lifetime. But very few couples can keep up such a pretense for a full year. Sooner or later, their real nasty little selves begin to show through, especially when they have to be with each other day and night, through sickness and through health, for 365 full days. And until they actually see the other's nasty little self, and see their own honest reaction to it, they rarely have the foggiest idea of whether they would like to stay married forever.

Sex, in particular, is a tricky business. In our society, where many people are pretty sex-starved before mating, few couples have low sex drives when going together. On the contrary, they tend to become sexually obsessed, to think that they want to spend all their time in bed together, and to adore almost every minute of their petting and their fornicating—even when (as more than infrequently happens) they are far from liking many nonsexual aspects of their relationship.

Sex desire, as any expert in the field knows, thrives on novelty, newness, variety, and abstinence. In a few instances, as most of the prissy sex manuals are apt to say with considerable exaggeration, it gets better and better as the years go by. But this is often because it was so bad at the start, in some inhibited couples, that it couldn't possibly get any worse, and had to improve as their inhibitions finally decreased. Where, however, a man and a woman are not notably repressed to begin with, their sex interest in each other usually wanes rather than waxes as they go through years of steady monogamous congress.

If they are both sufficiently high-sexed creatures, they can greatly enjoy each other in bed in spite of the relative monotony of their persistent relations. Even then, they rarely get *maximum* satisfaction from this one-track diet. And if, as frequently occurs, one or both of them are moderately or low-sexed, it is almost incredible how seldom, after a few years of marriage, they actually have intercourse with each other and how little they miss it.

The average American female is brought up to avoid masturbation, to be guilty about even relatively light kissing and petting before marriage, and to remain a technical virgin until the night of her wedding. She learns little about how best to bring herself and her male partner to maximum pitches of arousal and fulfillment; and in her own blundering way, aided by the repressiveness of her society, she generally manages to bring both him and herself to high peaks of desire—and to leave either or both of them hanging there dangerously, often ending up with genital congestion and sexual indigestion.

In consequence, she frequently becomes relatively anaesthetized while her date often becomes afflicted with premature ejaculation, erectile incapacity, overdelayed orgasm, or other varieties of impotence.

When, with this kind of sexual heritage, people mate, they are likely to have a frustrating honeymoon. Alternatively they may have a honeymoon that is the one, and practically the only, highlight in their domestic history.

Even healthy individuals have a hard time continuing to come fresh to sex within monogamous mating, since our biological urges are *not* particularly monogamous. But unhealthy individuals, who because of their allegiance to their sexually repressive upbringing have never had steady sex before marriage, and who are overeager and overinhibited at one and the same time, have even less of a chance to reach their maximum fulfillment after the glamour of first discovery has given way to the dull routines of everyday domesticity.

The more you overcome your unhealthy sexual upbringing *before* you mate, the better you are likely to get along sexually within the confines of monogamy. Which means? Something, preferably, along the following lines:

1. Gather ye rosebuds while you may and start your sex life as early rather than as late as possible. Learn the ins and outs of your own genital apparatus when you are still in your teens, and don't hesitate, not for one guilty moment, to satisfy yourself sexually when no suitable partner is around. Females, in particular, often require certain special kinds of strokings, massagings, and manipulations of their clitoral and vulval areas if they are to achieve maximum orgasmic satisfaction; and unless you yourself discover, through your own straightforward experimentation, exactly what most satisfies you, it is unlikely that you are going to be able to show your male partners what is your particular cup of erotic tea.

2. If, you are young and vulnerable to censure, and terribly afraid of coitus, do not hesitate to pet—and to pet up to and including full climax. Petting that is prolonged and that does not lead to orgasm may possibly result in overstimulation, genital engorgement, and consequent physical and psychological ills. Petting that leads to climax is good, clean fun, and has virtually no disadvantages. Both you and your partners can be satisfied with this kind of sex; while complete or partial refraining from petting is likely to be quite disruptive and unenlightening.

3. If you have and want to avoid pregnancy, learn proper methods of contraception and use them. Do not rely on the so-called "safe period," since it is not that safe. And don't leave responsibility for birth control up to the male, since he can be careless about those things and rarely has the incentive that you do to avoid pregnancy. Consult with a reputable gynecologist, and carefully follow the procedures that he or she outlines. If you have any super-romantic notions in this respect, get rid of them fast! Having intercourse under safe and secure conditions can be infinitely more ''romantic'' than having it spontaneously and carelessly.

4. Syphilis, gonorrhea, trichomoniasis, Herpes 2, and other unpleasant venereal diseases are still prevalent, and are

especially so among promiscuous individuals. If you restrict your sex relations to relatively mature, sensible, responsible males who, you are reasonably sure, are not copulating with every woman in town, you will be less likely to become infected. When you don't know a man very well and want to have sex with him, don't hesitate to insist on his wearing a condom—not merely for contraceptive purposes but as a disease preventive. If he whines and wails about having to protect you in this manner, recognize that he is something of a baby and seriously consider finding a more grownup partner.

5. Forget, except for practical purposes, about your sexual reputation. If you live in an uptight community where you may be distinctly penalized for having sex, you had better think of moving somewhere else—or of to some extent obeying your community's idiotic rules, since the possible penalties may not be worth the sexual gain. But if all that is going to happen to you if you have sex is that some of your acquaintances or friends are going to censure you or boycott you for being "loose," then hurry, hurry, hurry to have it, in order thereby to rid yourself of "friends" who are hardly worth knowing anyway.

Your main goal, remember, is not that of liking yourself and feeling yourself to be respectable only when other people happen to approve your behavior, but that of accepting yourself *whether or not other people approve of you.*

6. When you have sex be as honest and straightforward as you can possibly be about your own urges and what you require to satisfy them. Don't shut your mouth and groan to yourself while your partner clumsily tweaks you in the wrong spot or carelessly leaves you unfulfilled. Tell him— yes, in plain damned English tell him—what you want and how he can do what you want. Guide his hands and his body. Teach him how to kiss properly. Show him the positions you have previously discovered to be best. If he thinks you are terrible for knowing so much, or feels that you are imposing on him by asking him to do what most satisfies you, good—you'll know better than to try sex with him next time.

7. Try a reasonably large variety of sex partners before you settle down to one. Don't be cowed by the term "promiscuity"—which, rightly defined, means indiscriminate sexual congress. Almost no woman, except a prostitute, is truly promiscuous, since most women get hundreds of sex offers from men every year, and even if they accepted a score of these offers they would be far from indiscriminate in their selection. So don't surrender to the promiscuity bugaboo.

Experimental variety—or what Rey Anthony has called selective promiscuity—is the cornerstone of sane sexual choice. For one man, you will find, has a touch like none of the others you have ever known. Another can prolong intercourse for an hour or more. Still another can show you things you never dreamed existed and make you enjoy manipulations you never thought you could possibly like. And how would you *know* which one of these lovers was good—or, for that matter, bad—if you had never, never tried?

Even having poor sex relations can be most instructive. The calm, unromantic, good technician that you can rely on having a good time in bed with may, after awhile, seem rather boring and uninteresting. But when you have had, in between his biweekly visits, a couple of romantic cats who declaim the most high-flown love spiels imaginable, but whose manual dexterity equals that of a polar bear, you may decide that the technician's skills are not so dull after all and that love is more than pretty words.

The main point is that you and your partners are always distinct individuals, and all the good intentions and best training in the world will not make a concert virtuoso out of a tone-deaf person. Unless you try several partners before you settle down to an exclusive sex-love contract, you will never, in all probability, know what you do or you do not want when the chips are down and the bed clothes are flying.

Moreover, unless you often discover with A, B, and C what really sends you, you will not too easily induce D, with whom you may want to end up for the rest of your days, to do the special things that split your guts and make your goose pimples swirl. Would you, if you were aiming to become a first-class gourmet, rely on a single cook or a narrow batch of recipes? Why, then, limit your sexual education to a partner or two who are most unlikely to have been specially born for the total assuagement of your own inimitable libido?

8. Don't spend too much time trying to "cure" homosexuals, fetishists, impotent males, and other kinds of sexual queer ducks. If any man keeps taking you out steadily but never makes any serious passes, don't assume that it's his great love or consideration for you that holds him strongly in check. Assume, rather, that he has some kind of sexual problem; and, if possible, try to get him to talk about it.

If he seems to be only moderately inhibited—as in the case of a male virgin who just hasn't the courage to try to break the ice—help him along as much as you can, and do not hesitate to lay your lustful hands on him. But if his sexual evasiveness persists, don't start seeing yourself as the Florence Nightingale of the boudoir, who is absolutely determined to help this poor soul achieve a virility that surpasses all understanding. After several unsuccessful tries that leave you still totally frustrated and him as lily white as when first you met, insist that he go for professional aid—or else!

It's hard enough, in this world, to mate permanently with even the most physically healthy of lovers—since, Beelzebub knows, he's likely to have many *nonsexual* peculiarities. So don't add an extra handicap, to your potential relation with a man, of his being a real sexual screwball and refusing to do anything psychotherapeutically about it. If he won't see a therapist, you go for your own kind of sex therapy—with someone who knows a sexy woman when he sees one, and is more than willing to look.

Basic compatibility

Almost any two highly intelligent and fairly sensible human beings can have a pretty good steady relationship if they really want to adjust to each other. But an excellent question that is too little asked about most men and women who are contemplating living together is: Why the devil should they *want* to?

You can, in other words, dote on a man who loves to stay at home while you love to go out a great deal; who wants to have sex every day when you want it once a week; who is wholly absorbed with music and science while you only care for art and literature. You can love such a man, live with him for forty years, and somehow manage to make innumerable adjustments to his likes and dislikes, so that neither of you is too miserable staying together. But why on earth *should* you—when in all probability you could fairly easily find another lovable man who dovetails much more closely with you in regard to staying at home, having sex and being absorbed in art and literature?

Are, then, all truly compatible relationships made in heaven? Must one be *born* to live easily with one's mate, instead of having enormous difficulty endlessly and mutually adjusting?

Largely, frankly, yes. All of us have many highly individualistic styles of living—such as our sleeping and eating habits, our biological rhythms, our energy levels, our exercise patterns, our physical handicaps and health deficiencies.

Obviously, therefore, when it comes to mating, you'd better damned well try to find someone who rather *naturally* goes along with many of your ways of doing things and who *innately* seems to be attuned to many of your own basic likes and dislikes.

This particularly applies to what may be termed your vital or main interests. In *Creative Marriage* (which happens to have been written by Robert A. Harper and myself) the authors point out:

"Every marital relationship . . . consists of something of a compromise, and includes some sacrifices of interest. If many of your minor interests—such as eating Chinese food or looking at the late late show on television—have to go by the board because your mate won't share them and object to your participating in them very often, that may be too bad, but your relationship will probably survive. If, however, even a single one of your most vital interests must be sacrificed to living together, beware! If, for example, you do not merely enjoy Chinese food, but are an outstanding authority on it, and are compiling a massive tome on Chinese cooking; or if your one main enjoyment in life is viewing the late late television show—then you really have a serious problem if your spouse objects to these pursuits."

The moral seems clear: Consider, what your own and your would-be partner's vital interests are. If these mesh, or at least are not in serious conflict, fine!—consider the possibilities of mating with this person; and, as we noted previously, think seriously of living under the same roof with him for several months, to see if the meshing of major interests that seems to exist is as much a truth as a hope.

If it becomes obvious that, in spite of the fact that you love each other you have several important incompatibilities, then consider establishing every kind of sex-love relationship that you might possibly share together—except living together. For the chances are that *that* particular kind of monogamous, domestic, two-for-all-and-all-for-two relationships is just not going to work.

6

Where and How to Look
for a Man

Assume that you are emotionally ready to look for a suitable man and that you pretty well know what to look for. How, now, do you actually go about looking?

I am fond, in this connection, of quoting Sinclair Lewis's famous definition of the art of writing. "What," he was asked one day by an aspiring young writer, "have you found, in all your experience as a novelist, to be the art of writing?" "The art of writing," Lewis is reputed to have said, "is very simple. It consists of putting the seat of the pants to the seat of the chair—and writing!"

So with the art of looking for a man. It largely consists of putting the balls of your eyes to the front of your head—and looking! *Where* should you look? Anywhere, naturally, that you happen to be: in the office, on the street, at a party, on a bus, at a museum or art gallery, in a classroom, on the beach, at a dance, around your own neighborhood, on a trip, at a picnic, at a meeting, etc. As long as you keep actively, assertively looking, you are fairly sure to find several good prospects within a reasonable period of time. But you'd better *keep looking*.

This isn't as easy as it sounds. Millions of women don't really look at all for the man they want. Or look very half-heartedly. Or look in theory—with their eyes, at a distance—but not in practice—with their whole being, at close range. Or they look in the places where they obviously have only a small chance of finding the kind of man that they want.

Let us suppose, for example, that you have decided to take up painting, or to collect antiques, or to take some courses at a nearby university. Normally, in order to carry out your intent, you will do quite a bit of research. Thus, in regard to painting, you will read some material on the subject, look in the classified directory for art schools or private teachers, send away for catalogues of several schools, discuss with your friends what experiences they may have had with painting teachers, have an interview at an art school, perhaps sit in on a few trial classes, and do a score of other things to discover which teacher or group is best for you.

You will carry on these activities in regard to picking an art school or getting involved in some hobby because, in most instances, you feel thoroughly unashamed—in fact, even proud—of what you are doing and because you desire to do it as promptly and efficiently as possible.

Not so, alas, with the gentle art of manhunting! For some of the most idiotic reasons imaginable, we have encased this art in an aura of hesitation and shame, and we have particulary brought up our females so that they are unusually reticent about looking for what is often the most important thing in their whole lives—a suitable mate—while at the same time we have raised them to be quite bold and shameless about seeking many far less important things—such as a hobby, a sport, or a new dress.

Today, we are somewhat more liberal about a female's taking the initiative in various aspects of life, and especially in male-female relations. But we are far from being truly equalitarian and it is still regarded as a little shameful for a woman to be unhesitating and forthright about going out to get what she wants.

This anti-feminist, male-supremacist attitude is what you'd better fight. For if you willingly go along with it, you will almost certainly reduce your chances of finding the kind of man you want just as you would reduce your chances of finding the kind of job you wanted if you shyly stayed in the first job you happened to get and let the males in your office take the initiative in pushing forward or looking for more suitable and better-paying work elsewhere.

Before, then, I make any attempt to give you specific directions on where and how to look for the man of your choice, let us spend a little time trying to get you over some of the emotional blocks that you may well have in this connection.

Overcoming emotional blocks against looking

Linda Q. was an attractive, bright woman of twenty-six, who had graduated with honors from college and had worked for six years, first as an assistant, then an associate, and recently as a full buyer for one of New York's largest department stores. She did exceptionally well on her job, was liked by her bosses and her co-workers, and got along swimmingly, at least in a superficial sort of way, in her social relations. Women friends she had galore—except that, in recent years, almost all of them began mating and having children, while Linda, who at first seemed to be the real princess of them all, never seemed to form any long-term relationships. Her friends and her parents kept wondering about this, and finally induced her to come for psychotherapeutic aid.

"Where do you look for suitable male companions?" I asked Linda the first time I saw her.

"Oh, the usual places. I go to dances all the time. And weekends at resorts. And cocktail parties, when I can get to them. But I never seem to find what I want at any of these places. I'm sure that the kind of fellow I would like rarely goes to these kinds of affairs—though Lord knows I meet many men all the time, and even have difficulty getting rid of some of them who just aren't my type."

"Well, what do you think *is* your type? Is there something special in a man that you are looking for, and that you are not likely to meet in the places in which you have been looking?"

"Well, I guess there is. You'd probably never think it of me, since I'm not exactly the shy, retiring type myself; but that's what I kind of want in a man. A—well, a very sensitive person; not in the least brash, nor with a lot of gall, like my father has, and like I've always hated him for having; and definitely not cruel or cold or well armored and insensitive, again like my father is. Someone, I guess—yes, I guess that's it, like my mother, whom I've always been very close to, and who is soft and buttery."

"Did you *ever* actually meet a man like the one you describe? Do you think one actually exists?"

"Oh, yes; I know he does. I had one just like this, five years ago. He was almost just like my mother, and he got along beautifully with her, incidentally—would have made the perfect son-in-law. I think, in fact, he almost liked her more than he did me. Not that we didn't get along well, the two of us, for we did, and had a lovely relationship. I've never known anything like it before or since."

"And—what happened? Why didn't you stay with him?"

"He was a foreigner—an Indian. Over here on a diplomatic mission for the U.N. And he had to go back to his own country. Besides, it just couldn't have worked out, there were such great cultural differences between us. He was Mohammedan, and though I don't think he really believed in it, his religion was tied to his political career. He couldn't give it up without ruining himself politically. And I could never have become a Mohammedan, or anything like that. So we had to break up the relationship, before it became too involved. But he was so *sweet.* Yes, that's what I really want: a *sweet* man. And there are so few in this country—or anywhere!"

"But there are *some.* In a metropolitan area like New York, where there are some tens of thousands of men to choose from, surely there are a *few* of the kind of men you'd like."

"Oh, there are. I'm sure there are. Every once in a while I meet one, when I'm waiting for a bus, or sitting in a restaurant. And I'm sure, just by looking at him, that he's the type I would like. But what can I do—go up to him and say, 'Look: you seem to be such a sweet man, just like Armandi was. Don't you think we could, well, get together?' You certainly couldn't expect me to do a thing like that, could you?"

"Why not? If that really is the only way you could meet such a man, and you are not likely to find one at the usual dances and cocktail parties you go to—"

"—Oh, I'm not! I assure you. I just *never* do!"

"All right, then: what's *wrong* with accosting one in the street, if necessary, and telling him that he looks just like the lost Armandi? Or wasn't he once in your class at Columbia University? Or does he happen to know where the New York Public Library is? Or something like that?"

"Oh, I couldn't! Not that kind of thing. I just couldn't!"

"Why *couldn't* you? According to what you've said, this type of sweet, gentle man you're looking for, and who is so rare apparently in these parts—he's not going to accost *you* on the street, is he?"

"Oh, no. I'm sure he wouldn't. And I know that people like that rarely even *go* to the sort of places I usually go to, the resorts and the dances and things like that."

"O.K., then. A man like that is not likely to be at the regular places you go to meet males. And he's also not likely to be bold enough to pick you up if you do happen to meet him at a bus stop. Obviously, you've boxed yourself in, and narrowed down your possible prospects to practically zero. Unless, of course, *you* are willing to be more assertive and to make overtures when you do happen to meet one of these rare creatures in a situation where he's not likely to be formally introduced to you."

"But I couldn't! How could I? I've never done a thing like that in my life."

"No, you haven't. And where has *not* doing a thing like that in your life got you? Where you want to be? With the kind of man you crave?"

"No, it hasn't. But—well, you really don't think I could go out and, well, you know, actually, that is, *pick up* this kind of man, do you? You really wouldn't expect me to do *that?*"

"*I wouldn't expect* it—not with your crummy, inhibiting upbringing in this silly society. But I'd certainly *advise* it."

"You're *serious* about that? You really *are?*"

"I damned well am. For what have you got to lose? If you continue to operate your way, you're not likely to get any closer to your goal. You could, of course, change this goal: go for a different kind of man, one like your father, for instance; and that might well solve your problem. But if you don't want to change the goal then you'll have to change your tactics."

"Do I have to do either? Can't I keep looking for the kind I like and not change my tactics?"

"Sure you can. But as we just noted, what are your chances, under those circumstances, of succeeding—of getting what you want?"

"Hmmm. Pretty slim, I guess."

"All right: that's the point. The shyer the man you want, the unshyer, usually, you'd better act. The logical way to increase your chances, if you keep going after your desired type, is to do *more* looking than the average woman would do—and to be more forward when you finally find what you seem to be looking for."

"Meaning—exactly what?"

"Meaning, that you can go where your sensitive men would most likely go—to museums, for example, or art galleries, or concerts—and then approach the good candidates and try to engage them in conversation."

"Like asking them for a match, you mean? Or making a comment on the painting we are both watching at the museum?"

"Exactly. I see you know *what* to do. Now, how can we get you to do it?"

"But how *can* I do it?"

"How *can't* you, if you want to get what you want?"

"But I just never *have.*"

"You probably have never eaten whale steak, either. But that doesn't mean that you can't order one and eat it."

"Oh, but this is different! I wouldn't—well, feel ashamed about that."

"And you would feel ashamed approaching a sweet, shy man, and asking him a question or two, or making a comment on a painting?"

"Why, yes. Wouldn't almost any woman?"

"I'm afraid you're right: almost any woman in this idiotic society of ours would. But that's *her* problem. Let's get you out of her class and on the way to solving *yours.* What are *you* telling yourself, when you see a desirable man and think wouldn't it be nice to meet him, and then you make no efforts whatever to do so?"

"What am I telling myself? Nothing, as far as I know. I just *feel* it's not, well, the right thing to do, to approach him. I wasn't brought up that way."

"Sure you *feel* it's not the right thing to do—*after* you tell yourself that it's not. Without convincing yourself, very forcefully and vigorously, that you just couldn't, no you just *couldn't,* approach a strange man, you never would *feel* the way you do. Now just look at the nonsense you're telling yourself to *make* yourself feel that you couldn't."

"You mean, I'm saying to myself, 'Oh, nice women just *don't* approach strange men,' or something like that?"

"*Aren't* you? And: 'What would my mother ever think if she knew that I did a thing like that?' And: 'What would my women friends think?' And, even more: 'What would *he* think of me, if I approached him so boldly?' Aren't *these* the sentences you keep telling yourself, as you're standing there drooling about him—

and then walking off and making no contact? Aren't they?''

"I'm sure you're right. Those *are* the sentences I'm saying to myself. But shouldn't I be saying them? Wouldn't my mother be shocked? And my women friends? And *would* he think well of me if I did speak to him like you're telling me to do?''

"Suppose that's true? What have you got to lose? This way, by not trying to go after what you want, your mother and friends don't think ill of you—and what does *that* get you? Let us even suppose that you meet the kind of man you want, and you boldly approach him, and *he* thinks badly of you—thinks you're a whore, or something like that. Have you *still* lost anything? The chances are, of course, that he won't think poorly of you at all— that he'll be delighted that you are making the overtures, since he's afraid to make them himself. But even if he does think you're a tramp—what have you lost? For if you *don't* make any approach, what chance have you got *then*?''

"I can see what you mean. This way, I'm *sure* not to get what I want. That way, I *might*.''

"Right. And even if your mother, friends, and the man you pick up at the museum *all* think badly of you at first—which isn't very likely, but let's suppose, at the worst, they all do think badly of you. What are they going to *do* with their poor thoughts of you: kill you with them? Maim you? And how *long* are they going to think badly of you?''

"They'll get over what they first think? Is that what you're saying?''

"*Won't* they? Take, even, a man whom you might pick up. Let us assume, again, the worst: that he thinks you're a pushover who's only interested in going to bed with him, and that he has no respect for you at first. Will he, after he speaks to you for a half hour, and actually tries to plop you right into the nearest bed, will he *then* think you're such a pushover?''

"Not unless I act like one.''

"Exactly. If, after you have coffee or a drink with him, as he's most likely to ask you to do, you behave normally, show him you're not just interested in sex, but looking for a permanent companion, will he then think it awful that you picked him up?''

"No, I guess he won't.''

"You know damned well he won't. And your mother and your friends? Suppose you do get a man in this highly 'improper' way, and he turns out to be a fine mate for you? Do you think that they'll *still* think it was terrible that you picked him up?''

"I can see what you're getting at. No, they'll probably be telling the story of my famous pickup, in a sort of merry, joking, but still favorable manner, for the rest of their lives."

"I'll bet you're right. That's exactly what'll happen."

"But suppose it doesn't work. I pick up a man, or a dozen of them, and none of them quite work out. Won't my mother be quite upset by what I'm doing?"

"I'm sure she will. And your women friends, too. Just because *they* haven't got the guts to do what you're doing, they'll probably jealously pick on you and think how awful it is, you're doing what they would so like to do themselves. All right: let's suppose that they will be upset. So?"

"You mean *I* don't have to be upset just because they are?"

"Well, *do* you? If you enjoy reading the Marquis de Sade or wearing a skimpy bikini, and they think that kind of thing is perfectly awful—do you let *their* views stop you? Do you always live exactly the way *they* think you should?"

"No. Sometimes I let them stop me, of course. And then I hate myself for it. But not usually."

"Right: you hate yourself when you sell your soul for their approval. And don't you think that's just about what you're doing now, when you refrain from going after the kind of man *you* really want because *they* wouldn't approve of the way you go about finding him?"

"You think I really do? I hate myself for following what they think I ought to do?"

"Well? Don't most people who play the patsy role, and refuse to do what they really want to do because someone *else* wouldn't like it, tend to hate themselves?"

"Hmmm. I guess you've got something there. I can see, now, why I've tended to become so depressed recently. Not just because I wasn't getting the men I want. But because I *knew,* I guess, that I wouldn't get one if I continued to look in the way my mother and friends think I should look, and I *knew* I couldn't bring myself to go against them and to do things the way *I* thought they should be done."

"Evidently, then, you've given some thought, on your own, to what I have been pointing out this session."

"Oh, yes. Everything you've just told me, I've thought of before. Because I could *see* that I wasn't getting anywhere. I could tell that the man I'm looking for practically will *never* show up at the kinds of gatherings I've been attending. I knew I had to do something else to find him. And I sort of knew what it was, just as you've been pointing out. But I couldn't see myself doing it, against the criticism of my friends, and particularly of my mother. But I see it all even more clearly now."

It took several more sessions of therapy before Linda not only theoretically but actively convinced herself to do anything. She used every excuse to keep following her mother's and her friends' views. And I used every rational-emotive procedure to help her to formulate and to act on her own philosophy of life.

At one point, she almost lost out completely, when she started to become attached to a man pretty much like her father, whom she had met through one of her friends, and when she began convincing herself that, after all, maybe she was just prejudiced: maybe she *could* make it with this kind of insensitive, typical businessman-type person. Fortunately, she found that she just couldn't—or, rather, really didn't want to.

In desperation, she did go to an art gallery one day and started a conversation with an Indian-looking man (who actually turned out to be from Iran, and who was nothing like her lost Armandi, as she thought he might be). Though nothing came of this, she was surprised at the ease with which she carried off the pickup, and began to see that there really *was* nothing to be afraid of.

After that, there was almost no stopping her. Nearly every nook, particularly each highly cultured nook, in New York City became a potential place for her to find and actively work at getting the kind of a man she wanted. She still, at this writing, has not quite made it. But she most definitely will, I am willing to bet. In the last six months, she has come fairly close three times—and each time with males whom she never would have met had she not gone out of her way to introduce herself. It is only a matter of time, if she continues to do what she has been doing recently, for her to strike real pay dirt.

Must *every* woman, then, go out and literally pick up men if she is to find the male of her choice? No, not literally: since some women manage, without such activity, to meet as many men as they can handle, and to find, among the males that easily come their way, one or more who are to their tastes. But the more selective you are, the more you will probably have to look and look and look—and act and act and act—to find what you really want.

If you were looking for an unusually interesting, well-paying job with a very kindly boss and with lovely associates with whom to work, you would expect to have to go through many, many job possibilities before you actually found such an opening. Similarly, if you are looking for an unusually interesting, fascinating man who will truly love you and introduce you to stimulating friends and adventures, you can expect to go up many, many blind alleys before you find your way home.

Let's assume that you have been preparing yourself to go out to look actively for men, and that, whatever people may think of your tactics, you are determined to open your big mouth and go after what you want. Where shall you look? What are some of the best—and the worst—places? Let us look at some of the possibilities.

Friends

By all means, if you can, use your friends as a source of new dates. But if they are good friends, really *use* them, rather than passively let them, in a sense, use you.

Tell them exactly what you want—and don't want—in a male. Don't merely say, "I'm desperate for a date, please fix me up," or "Any suitable guy that you happen to meet, be sure to give him my phone number." This kind of promiscuous date-making will probably pay off badly and often leave you stuck with a horse's ass.

Say, rather, to your married cousin, or to your co-workers at the office, or your ex-love who insists on staying with his wife: "Look, I really want to get attached to someone. But *not* anyone. I just don't like sloppy (or greasy, or stupid, or sports-mad, or overly dedicated) men. Sure, they're great guys. But not for me. Now, what I really want is—" And detail, as accurately as you can, what it is you truly want.

Don't feel ashamed to be precise. Don't think that they think you a dope for being so choosy. Or even if they *do* think you such a dope—so what? If you have fetishes and anti-fetishes, name your poisons. And when one of your friends finally does come up with a fellow who just seems to be for you, don't hesitate to ask "embarrassing" questions about him before you actually make the date. Such as: "Does he still, at 38, live with his mother?" "Why hasn't he been involved up to now?" "What kind of work does he do?" "What is his financial condition?"

Questions such as these, if you can get good answers to them, not only help you decide whether to go out with a prospect, but also give you leads as to what to talk about when you do decide to date such an individual. You can, of course, use such information in a defensive manner: to convince yourself that you should *not* see a man, ostensibly for good reasons, but actually because you yourself are afraid of dating.

So the general rule is: When in doubt, date. You have nothing to lose but a little time and energy. And even if your date turns out be a dud, you can usually get some experience (about yourself and others) that will serve you well on future dating. If, however, you really do have sufficient experience, and are not afraid of seeing anyone, prior information obtained about him may well be a good reason for not seeing him at all.

The decision as to whether or not to see a friend of a friend can often be taken not merely with the immediate prospect in mind, but with a longer-range view. If you feel that a man someone wants to introduce you to is a poor prospect, but you also feel that he has a wide circle of friends to whom he will probably introduce you, dating him (at least for a few times) may have some value. Short-range hedonism in meeting males can be just as self-destructive as in other aspects of living. The date of the moment may be of little interest or value; but the future prospects that it offers may be considerable.

In general, there are certain rules of the dating game when you enlist the services of friends. If your woman friend gets you a date and you double date with her and her lover, don't try to make eyes at her lover or date him yourself. Once he stops seeing her, you may then (especially, with her permission) see him; but while he is seeing her, you keep your eager little hands off! Although dating is a competitive sport, you normally do not compete with your friends and relatives—else you are likely to end up sans dates *and* friends.

Although some amount of caution is wise in dating people who have been introduced to you by friends, don't think that you must entirely walk on eggs. If you date your cousin's neighbor, you naturally do not tell him how awful you think your cousin's taste in clothes, furnishings, and friends. At the same time, you do not necessarily act like the Duchess of Bloomsbury, because you are terribly afraid that, through your date, your cousin will learn something bad about *you*. Try to let your cousin know, in advance, those "bad" things about yourself—and then you can to relax and be yourself with your date.

Double dates arranged by your friends (or by yourself in conjunction with your friends) are perfectly fine forms of entertainments—but don't abuse them and use them for self-protective devices. It's relatively easy to get along with a man, especially a strange one, when there is another couple or two present to help carry the burden of conversation. But any date that begins and ends with another couple present is almost certain to be lacking in intimacy, and will not help you really to know a man and how you feel about him.

Moreover, double dates normally exclude sex intimacy, and are particularly frustrating to a male—if he is a true male! If you must have double dates regularly at least see that they usually end up with an hour of being by yourselves. Otherwise, you are likely to have a pleasant time for months and end up mating with a man you hardly know.

Blind dates are fine—as long as you manage, as noted above, to find something out about the man before you actually make the date. Blind dates, also, are safer if you make them for cocktails, lunch, or some other relatively brief meeting, so that you do not have to spend a whole evening with someone that you can see, practically at first glance, will not suit you at all.

Blind dates are particularly good if you have any trepidation about meeting new males. For if you have such fears, and you use them as excuses not to date, you will protect your fears forever; while if you throw yourself into having blind dates, in spite of your fears, you can use them as excellent therapeutic homework assignments for working through these worries. As ever, it is not the blind date itself that you fear, but some assumed catastophe you are constructing about it. And it is your own constructions—your demand that something connected with the date MUST or MUST NOT exist—rather than the date itself that you'd better become aware of and then start attacking and attacking and attacking.

Thus, if you are terribly worried about what will happen when you finally meet a blind date, you are almost certainly starting with assumptions such as: "I MUST do well on this date! I HAVE TO meet a suitable man and get along beautifully with him! I've GOT TO do the right things on this date and MAKE SURE that everything turns out well!"

Starting with these assumptions, these MUSTurbatory ideas, you then go through the A-B-C's of blind dating as follows:

A (Activating Experience)—a friend of yours, usually one of your woman friends, arranges a blind date for you, presumably with a partner that she thinks you will like.

rB (rational Beliefs)—"I hope that this blind date turns out to be with a suitable person and that I make out well with this individual and we end up by having a serious, ongoing kind of affair. I hope that things do not get botched up; because I definitely wouldn't like it if that occurred."

iB (irrational Beliefs)—"I MUST do well on this date! I HAVE to meet a suitable man and get along beautifully with him! If the man turns out to be the wrong one for me or, worse! if he turns out to be the right one and I muck things up with him, that would be *awful;* I couldn't *stand* it; and I would be a *lousy lover* and a *rotten person!"*

aC (appropriate Consequence or feeling)—concern that the blind date turn out well.

iC (inappropriate Consequence or feeling)—severe feelings of anxiety about the date.

Once you acknowledge that you're not only concerned about the blind date—which is appropriate, since otherwise you would approach it in an *overly* relaxed manner—but that you are also *over*concerned or *anxious* about it and that this anxiety is created by you and not by the date, you then go on to the D-E part of rational-emotive self-help therapy. Thus:

D (Disputing your irrational Beliefs): "Where is the evidence that I MUST do well on his date? Why do I HAVE TO meet a suitable man and get along beautifully with him? If the man turns out to be the wrong one for me or, if he turns out to be the right one and I muck things up with him, in what way would that be AWFUL? Where is it writ that I COULDN'T STAND IT? How would I be a LOUSY LOVER or a ROTTEN PERSON?"

E (Effect of Disputing your irrational Beliefs): (1) There is no evidence that I MUST do well on this date, though it would be highly preferable if I did. I of course could do poorly on it—and that alone proves that there is no reason why I MUST do well. There don't seem to be any absolute MUSTS in the universe; and I am merely inventing this one—which, if I follow it, will only keep me overconcerned and anxious!

(2) I obviously don't HAVE TO meet a suitable man and get along beautifully with him—though it would be great if I did! But this doesn't prove that it SHOULD occur. And if it doesn't, I certainly won't die; and it is highly possible that I shall have some subsequent happiness in life!

(3) If the man I meet on the blind date turns out to be the wrong one for me; or if, worse, he turns out to be the right one and I muck things up with him, that would not be AWFUL because (a) it is hardly *totally* bad if I muck up things; (b) it is certainly not *more than* bad or *101* × bad; and (c) it is hardly *as bad as it could possibly be,* since I always can have other dates and sometimes not muck them up!

(4) It is not written anywhere that I CAN'T STAND having a lousy date with this person I don't know. I may never like it; but I definitely CAN stand what I don't like! I could even, if necessary, stand real torture; and having a crummy blind date is somewhat less than tortuous!

(5) It will not make me a LOUSY LOVER if I muck up this blind date—but only a person who has loved lousily *this time.* And I certainly won't amount to a ROTTEN PERSON, since such an individual, if one truly existed, would be totally, only, and for all times and occasions rotten; and there is no evidence that I am *that* bad!

If you go through the A-B-C-D-E's of RET in this fashion, you will not only end up with a new, rational philosophy—namely, that you will always be human and fallible and quite forgivable no matter how many blind dates you louse up—but you will feel concerned rather than anxious and will probably do something about preparing adequately for the date and making it as good as it is likely to be.

Blind dates, then, are hardly the best way to meet suitable males. But they are often worth trying, if you overcome your needless anxiety about them.

Parties and dances

Among the easier places to meet new men, are parties or dances. Particularly at a dance, etiquette states that the male normally approaches the female. Which means that you, as a female, have to do little but look approachable.

Not that there is a law against doing more. There isn't. And if you *really* want to make out well at a dance or a party, you'd be wise to do some of the approaching yourself. For men, especially after they have been rejected by several women, are often loath to keep plunging in and risking more rejections. And if you can make the overtures, or at least indicate by a smile or a gesture that you are most willing for the male to make them, you will improve your chances of meeting a greater number of men.

When a male does approach you, watch your own self-repeated nonsense! Yes, he may be ungainly looking, or a little too forward, or dressed peculiarly, or awkward in his speech. But are these the *real* reasons why you remain aloof, give him no help, and finally reject him? Or is it not, rather, that *you* feel so afraid that he will find out the depths of *your* inadequacy, that you would rather find almost *any* excuse to reject him than wait for him to discard you later?

Watch, particularly, the garbage you tend to feed yourself when you talk with the most attractive males you find at a party or dance. Are you telling yourself that they're too superficial? Or conceited? Or cold?

Don't you really mean at a deeper level, that they could never possibly be interested in drab, shy, unexciting you? And have you any factual evidence, really, that they couldn't be? None of that crap, now! What have you got to lose? You know you came to this affair precisely because you might meet such an attractive man. Now why don't you barge in and try? If you can siphon him off from the crowd of other women who are probably interested in him, fine. If you cannot, and he never gives you another nod or takes your phone number and fails to call, what does that mean about you? That you're a worthless slob, a hopeless fool? Rot! It merely means that you have made a good effort and unfortunately failed.

Not that dances and parties need be the best hunting grounds for you, for they may definitely not be. The easiest place to meet a male is not necessarily the most satisfactory. Perhaps the crowd that attends these kinds of affairs is too young for you; or too unintellectual; or too crude. Even then, you still may find *one* man who happens to be your special cup of tea. Unless your dream man is truly impossible to find, there is *some* place where he hangs out. Find it and go *there*.

Organized groups

Another of the easy places to meet suitable members of the other sex is in an organized group; such as a political organization, a religious group, a poetry reading society, a school class or a country club. Groups of this kind meet regularly, not merely for a single session; and if you keep attending them, you will probably become friendly, at least in a superficial way, with most of their male members. This is fine: particularly if the group tends to include people of your own kind.

The trouble with most groups is that they are too limited in number. A class, for example, usually only has thirty or forty students, and half of these are likely to be of your own sex. Of the other half, a good number will be mated, or otherwise taken; and several will be too homely, too stupid, too disturbed, or too something else for your tastes. Consequently, you will be lucky to find even three or four eligibles and during the four or five months that you may stay in this class, this number will remain exactly the same or even decrease, if some of the members drop out of the class.

In terms of numbers, therefore, organized groups tend to be distinctly limited; and for the amount of time that you spend in such groups—perhaps thirty or forty hours a term, for example, in a class—you will not be getting very many choices. The same amount of time spent actively looking for men in more public places—in the school cafeteria, say, or in the library—will bring you in contact with a greater number of prospects, even though it may not be as easy to talk to them as it would be in an organized group.

Organized groups also are often sexually or amatively constrictive. In a church group, for instance, you will naturally meet church-interested people: who in many instances will be puritanical, not very sophisticated, and perhaps fanatic individuals who may make great church members—but hardly great lovers. In a political group—especially an extreme right-wing or left-wing group—you may largely encounter dedicated men who are much more interested in the Cause than they are in you and a potential family life. In a ballet or modern dance class, you may meet many males who are homosexual.

If, therefore, you choose to join a group pick one where you will be most likely to meet the types of males that you would be interested in—and will meet them in sufficient numbers to make your participation worthwhile.

To make out well in a group try to follow some of the same bold and assertive patterns that work in less protective environments. For even in a class, where you see the same people over and over again, you can quietly stick to yourself, get into few intimate discussions with others, and remain so afraid of direct contact that others will hardly know you are there.

Even when you get to know the members of a group well enough, the eligible males (particularly the brightest and most alert ones) are not going to look upon you with favor if you are shy and withdrawn. The more you speak up; the more you courageously jump in where others fear to tread; the more you frankly try to be intimate with certain males, the more you are likely to impress them with the idea that you are actually *worth* knowing.

So again: watch your internalized crummy sentences! Are you continually saying to yourself: "Oh, well, if I speak up, the members of the group won't like me, anyway, and they'll just see what a dunce I am!" Or: "They'll think I'm too forward, and hate me for that?" If you are, then look for your underlying MUSTurbatory assumptions, which are really the premises for these self-downing beliefs. Such as: "I MUST be outstandingly bright and forward in any group that I join; and if I am not the way that I MUST be, it is AWFUL and I am an INCOMPETENT CLOD!" With perfectionistic premises like this, how can you *not* down yourself when you participate in a group?

Also: watch your rationalizations! You may well find yourself saying: "What's the use of getting to know the members of this group: they're really not my type?" Or; "If I join this group, I would only keep myself from doing other more worthwhile activities; so I won't join." These rationalizations or defenses frequently are derivatives of your MUSTurbatory assumptions. For if you think you HAVE TO do well when you join a group and that you are a COMPLETE NO-GOODNIK if you don't, you will then feel so hurt at the mere thought of being rejected by this group that you will invent rationalizations of the above sort. Then you will be safe—and withdrawn!

Are *these,* then, your conversations with yourself? If so, look for the perfectionistic SHOULDS, OUGHTS, and MUSTS behind them, and give these up. Then you will best be able to make valuable relationships in almost any group you join.

Business contacts

Making sex-love contacts through your job has its disadvantages: since if they fail to work out well (which, statistically speaking, *most* social-sexual contacts do) you may lose your job, have to work closely with an ex-lover for whom you now have no love or even liking, or otherwise get into career difficulties. It is often wise, therefore, not to get closely entangled with those with whom you work.

Nonetheless, your job can still serve as a good source of eligible males. If, for example, you work as an airline stewardess, travel agent, receptionist, or any one of a number of jobs that puts you into contact with many people you may well meet a lover or mate. If, on the other hand, you are cooped up in an office by yourself, or only working with a group of cantankerous females, your job is not likely to be any asset to your social life.

This does not mean that you should rush to take the first job that comes along that offers you some man-hunting possibilities. You probably could attract quite a few men if you worked as a ditch-digger or a road-mender; but I wouldn't exactly advise such occupations. Where, however, one job is pretty much the same as another, and one offers man-meeting potentialities while the other does not, carefully consider the former even though it may pay a little less money or have other disadvantages. If you are a working woman you will not have a great deal of time in your leisure hours to look for males. If you can do a good bit of your hunting while being paid for working, so much the better!

The fine art of the pickup

Let's face it squarely: the quickest, easiest, and in many respects best way to meet a man, if you are a resident of or work in a metropolitan area, is by the spontaneous pickup techniques— yes, I said by picking him up right where you first see him: on the street, in a restaurant, at the library, on a bus, or wherever else he happens to be. Why is this often the best method? For several reasons:

1. It is the fastest technique ever invented. Going to dances, parties, lectures, group discussions, etc., all are fairly time-con- suming: since, at the very least, you must dress, go out, get to where you are going, and then usually spend some time there

before you find any man-grabbing opportunities. But picking a man up on the street corner or at a bar where you just happen, anyway, to be is not at all time-consuming: in fact, it is instant companionship.

2. If you actively (rather than passively) pick up strange men, you are employing probably the most selective technique known. For when you are formally introduced to a man, or arrange through friends to go out on a blind date, or even meet a man at a dance, you are being relatively unselective: since your field of choice is strictly limited, and you can only select someone from within this restricted field. On a blind date or a formal inroduction, you have only one man out of one to choose from; and if he is not exactly your style, that's too bad, you are simply stuck with him, at least for the evening. At a party or a dance, you may have fifteen or twenty eligible males to choose from—but rarely more than that.

If, however, you go out on the streets of almost any sizable town with the intent of picking up a strange man, you have hundreds, even thousands of men to select from, and it is extremely unlikely, if you persist in your attempt, that within a short period of time you will not find one who is more to your taste than the one you are likely to get from a much smaller pool. The more highly selective you are, in fact, the better off you'll be picking up strange men: since you will have a wider selection to choose from.

3. If you pick up men correctly, your chances of getting the kind of person with the calibre of looks, brains, character, etc. that *you* want are much better than if you use more passive techniques of encountering males. What do we mean by picking up men "correctly"? *Actively* seeking them out and *boldly* making the first overtures youself.

Passive pickup techniques are much inferior. If, for example, you walk along the street, or sit around a museum waiting for some man to pick *you* up, you are first of all not easily going to get the person whose looks and attributes you especially want. Secondly, you may only get, this way, the brash, truckdriver types who specialize in picking up females. Thirdly, the man who picks you up may possibly be a murderer, a sex fiend, or some other kind of unpleasant character who is not really interested in your companionship, but who only has ideas that you aren't enthusiastic about. Getting the idea out of his head that you just *have* to sleep with him that night may be difficult.

If, on the other hand, *you* are the one to do the active selecting and to make the first overtures, there is much less of a chance that the man you choose will be too peculiar or be looking for a murder victim; and if you decide that you definitely don't want to go to bed with him that night, you will have much greater ease, in most instances, convincing him that a longer friendship is desirable before you do decide to do so. Men who pick you, in other words, may be out for no good; while men whom *you* pick are likely to be healthier and more easily handled.

Aren't you *still* likely to get into some trouble if you go around promiscuously talking to strange men? Not if you handle yourself correctly. For there is no law that says that just because you pick up a man you *must* go to his apartment or take him to yours. All you have to do, usually, is go somewhere with him, some public place like a restaurant or a bar, where you can sit and talk for hours, and find out various things about each other.

If, after several hours of conversation you *then* feel you know him well enough to go to his place or ask him to yours, fine. But again: you don't *have* to. In fact, if you find, after being with a man for a short length of time, you just do not like him as you thought you would, there is no reason why you can't plead a previous engagement or say that you're not feeling too well, and insist on going off by yourself. If necessary, you can even give your nonwanted acquaintance a false telephone number and address, just before you fondly bid him adieu.

4. The art of picking up men gives you, of course, something to do almost any single minute that you want to do it. Even at three in the morning, if you are bored, you can always go out and find a man to pick up somewhere. And talk about an antidote to loneliness—what could be better? Naturally, some of the men that you pick up will hardly be the most exciting or most fascinating creatures you ever met. But they will always be *new;* will tend to be somewhat *different* from the last man you were entangled with; can teach you *something* you haven't learned before; and can certainly fill up your time far better than your filling it up by moping around, feeling that you never can get anywhere in your love life, and wishing you were dead.

5. If the law of averages works—which it invariably, in the

long run, does—then the pickup technique is the one best calculated to work. For if you stick to the usual sources of supply, you will be lucky if you meet, every year, twenty new males; and, on the law of averages, you will be damned fortunate if even one of these is your particular cupcake. But if you resort to the pickup technique, you should easily be able to encounter a dozen or more males every single month, or a hundred and fifty or more a year. Out of *that* supply you really do have a good chance to pick and be picked by at least a couple who are good prospects.

6. The pickup method, of course, need not be used exclusively. There is no reason why, while you are employing it, you cannot use all the more "regular" methods, too—such as friends, parties, organized groups, and the rest. But when these are not working too well, when you have no good prospect in sight, and when you just happen to be out on the street, sitting in a park, or eating a sandwhich at a lunch counter, and there just happens to be an attractive, intelligent-looking male within reach, what is the point in your *not* asking him the time, or commenting on the weather or asking for a match, or otherwise making an innocuous overture to him?

"All right!" you say, "you've convinced me that if I did resort to the highly unorthodox method of selecting my own prospects in public places, and making some kind of verbal and gestural overtures to them, I would have a better chance to find the kind of man I want than if I go along sticking to more formal means of meeting men. But I just *know* that I won't do it that way. I just *can't*."

You mean you *haven't;* and that you *think* you can't. But, of course, you can. *If* you stop telling yourself the dreadful nonsense that you've been telling yourself for the last decade or more: that what would people think if you picked up men? And what would the men think? And wouldn't it be terrible if, after putting yourself out to meet males like this, the males kept rejecting you?

Bosh—pure bosh! You keep telling yourself this nonsense: that the men you would try to pick up would think it terrible for you to assertively go after them. Drivel! Some of them would, of course—and those would be exactly the kind of bigots that you wouldn't want anyway! At my workshops for singles, that I regularly give at the Institute for Rational Living in New York City (and in various other places throughout the country), I almost always ask the men in the workshop how they would feel about any ordinary woman's approaching them in public to try to talk to them, and about 99 per cent of them honestly say that they would be delighted. For, as they note, such an approach is entirely unrisky to them, the men; and they know at the start that the least the woman is really *interested* in meeting them.

So it's not what the *men* would think about you for trying to pick them up—it's what *you* think about yourself for doing so. *You* think this is "terrible" and you, especially, think it's "awful" if you get rejected in the process. Society, admittedly, teaches you *part* of this: teaches you, for example, that it's good to get accepted and bad to get rejected by someone you prefer. But society—including, even, your sainted mother—hardly teaches you that you *must* be accepted by *every* male you would like to encounter; and that you are a worm if a single one of them rejects you.

Even, moreover, when social rules state that the male, normally, in our culture approaches the female, and that it's not quite "proper" for you, as a female, to approach a male, it is not this rule that bothers you but your *listening* to and your *agreeing* with it. For society teaches you lots of rules—such as, "Vote Republican," or "Never work if you have a young child"—which you may decide to ignore. And rules about whether to try to pick up a man or allow yourself to be picked up by one only control your life if you *agree* to abide by them.

"All I have to do then," you ask, "is to *un*convince myself that the conventional rules of mate hunting are the right ones, and then I shall fairly easily be able to talk to strangers in public places? Is that right?"

Almost right. Not *all* you have to do—but *mostly*. Just like with the political rule, with which your family and community may have raised you, "Vote Republican." You *first* better *un*convince yourself that this rule has to be followed. Then you also better go to the polls and vote for various non-Republicans. Similarly with various other political, economic, religious, or social views that you were taught—or that were willy-nilly crammed down your throat—when you were young and foolish. You now can *un*convince yourself of the truth of these beliefs and then actively work against them—in different political, economic, religious, or social groups that you care to join today.

So with choosing a mate. What you'd mostly better do, but

not have to do, is to *un*convince yourself that your mother and friends have the right ideas about mate hunting. Then you can become active—and I mean active—in employing techniques different from the ones they would recommend or approve. After just a few weeks of this kind of vigorous, activity-directed *un*convincing, you will probably become so convinced of the *new* line of approach that you will tend to find it second-nature, just as the old, conventional, more inhibited line of approach has been up to now.

In other words: to break virtually any self-defeating habit, and especially one you have had for a long period of time, you had better make a tripartite, cognitive, emotive, and action-oriented attack on it—as I show in *A New Guide to Rational Living, Humanistic Psychotherapy: the Rational-Emotive Approach,* and my various other books on self-help therapy. First, you think about and challenge the ideas, particularly the MUSTurbatory ideas, behind this habit. Then you forcefully, dramatically make yourself feel differently about the habit. Finally, you actively work and practice, on new and conflicting habits, until you finally make them easy and "natural" for you to follow.

"But it's not easy. it's very hard to do what you are encouraging me to do."

You're right, it's not easy. It's hard—at least for the few weeks that you're first working at it. But it's much harder *not* to change a self-destructive, inhabiting habit; and it's much harder that way *forever.* So go back to your ultra-conventional ways of meeting men, if you inist that the unconventional ones are too hard. Continue to be the ninny you were encouraged to be by your early teachers and models. Keep being that way for the rest of your life. You won't die of it. But you won't live very much, either.

7

How to Get Along with
the Men You Meet

Let us suppose that somehow or other, by hook or by crook, you have met a suitable man, and you want to get along with him well, so that he will think you a suitable companion and will be interested in prolonging the relationship with you. How can you help yourself in this respect?

The art of conversation

"But when I do meet a man, I have absolutely nothing to say."

"I just lose all my wits, when I am with a man whom I really like. I sit there like a high school freshman, and can't think of a thing that's intelligent."

"I know that men like witty girls, those with snappy answers and bons mots. But even though I have a good sense of humor when I'm with my friends, I'm as dull and unwitty as I can be when I'm with a date."

These are remarks that, as a psychotherapist, I hear all the time. Almost every unmarried female I see believes that she must be utterly clever and inordinately wise every moment she is with a potential lover or mate, and that she will most certainly lose him if she is not.

Like Ida R., who said to her psychotherapy group members one evening: "I don't know. I'm just out of it. I keep going away to resorts on weekends and during the summer, in order to meet new men, and I just can't seem to get anywhere. The other women stand around chatting gaily and talking ever so wittily to the guys they meet, whilte I just stand there saying nothing. I can't get out a clever remark to save my life. So naturally I don't get anywhere with those I want to like me."

"What does that have to do with it?" asked Tom, another group member. "Since when do men want terribly witty and clever females?"

"Don't they?" asked Ida.

"Not me!" said Tom. "When I see a very clever woman, always the one with a bright grip, I run like hell. Who needs it?"

"Me, too," chimed in Fred (the one male member of the group who had no mating problems, but who was pretty messed up in his business affairs). "I think I can say that I've had many good relationships during the past several years. But of all of the women I really liked and got along with well I can't remember a single one who was exceptionally good at repartee. Oh, yes: there was one. But she was such a nut, who just *had* to be cleverer than anyone around her, that I just couldn't take it, and I soon had to break off with her. Hell, I couldn't open my mouth for a minute, without her making a joke of something I said. As Tom just said: Who needs it?"

"But *don't* men like witty women? Ida persisted. "From what I've always seen, they do."

"Sure they do," said Grace (who also had few difficulties with members of the other sex, but enough parental problems to fill a case book). "They *like* witty women, especially right at the beginning, when a clever remark will help put off or cover up some of the embarrassment that usually goes with meeting a new person. But it's hardly as *necessary* as you think it is. And some of the best operators I know, the women who get further with the men in the briefest period of time, aren't witty at all. They just barge in, say whatever is on their mind—things that to me often sound very stupid, in fact—but the boys seem to love it. As long as they *keep* talking. *That* seems to be the thing."

"That's what I've found, too," agreed Marilyn (a group member who had been very shy several months previously, but was now improving in this respect). "I used to feel just the way you do, Ida. I sounded so darned *stupid,* whenever I opened my mouth in front of men, that I said just as little as I possibly could. Of course, *they* then had a hard time talking to me, too. And soon there were long periods of almost dead silence, while I anxiously racked my brain for something brilliant to say. Naturally, the more I racked, the less it came."

"Yes, that's just what happens to me!" said Ida. "I know just what you mean."

"Yes," continued Marilyn. "I'm sure you do. Anyway, no more! I gave up, a few months ago, right after we spent the entire group session speaking about my problems; gave up trying to be so sparkling, and settled down to being me, just me. You should see what a difference it has been making! I'm probably even *less* scintillating, now, than I ever was in my life. But men seem to find me more *interesting.*"

"But what exactly do you do?" asked Ida.

"Do? I just listen carefully to what *they,* the men, are saying. And I think I listen for the first time in my life, this way, since before I was listening only, really, to myself, and the junk *I* was saying to me. Now I listen carefully to them and when I respond I respond the way I feel like responding. If I have another point of view I express it and we talk about it back and forth for a while. The men seem to like it. And *I* actually enjoy myself much more, because I am really being much more *me.*"

"Do the rest of you men seem to feel the same way, too?" asked Ida of the males in the group. "Do you feel, as Fred and Tom do, that clever women are not necessarily the best to be with? Or, as Grace does, that to be bright and wise-cracking has its advantages, but that one can easily get along without it?"

We took an informal poll of the male members of the group. Much to Ida's surprise, *every single one of them* said that he preferred a woman who was less brilliant but more interested in him and more honest about her own responses. In fact, the consensus seemed to be that the cleverer, at least at incessant repartee, a female was, the less likely was she going to turn out to be a nice enough or stable enough person for the male to get along with on a more permanent basis.

Ida finally began to be convinced that her problem was not her inability to be a supremely clever conversationalist with the males she met—but her worry *about* her lack of brilliance. She defined herself as heterosexually adequate in terms of her excellence at repartee and because she defined herself in this manner, she actually became hesitant at dialogue. This is what normally happens to people who define themselves as worthwhile in terms of some outside criterion: they then usually become worse at fulfilling that criterion. They are so focused upon "How am I doing at this thing?" that they fail to focus on *"What* am I doing?" and they lose instead of gain competence. When Ida, prodded by the group, started to follow Marilyn's example and to try to *enjoy herself* with her male companions, instead of striving mightily to *impress them* with her cleverness, she began to do much better in her dating relationships.

The art of conversation, then does not necessarily depend upon the knack of being brilliant or scintillating. Most of all, you can be *interested* in your partner—rather than obsessed with what he is thinking of *you.* Ask him questions about himself: where was he raised?—how did he grow up?—what are his likes and dislikes?—how does he feel about intimacy—how does he react to your ideas?

As he responds to your questions, respond back. Don't merely say: "Oh, that's fascinating!" or "How nice!"Tell him what *you* feel about your parents, your hobbies, your work, friends, marriage, sex, etc. If you want to become intimate with anyone, the best rule usually is: confide in him. The more of your own deep and dark secrets you let out, the more he is likely to tell you how many people he has killed and stolen from. The more precise you are about your sexual religious, political, and other views, the more he will tend to tell you the gory details of his.

Conversation, in other words, largely consists of drawing out others and expressing yourself. If, in the process, you can get in a bon mot or two, and indicate that you have a sense of humor and some verve, fine. But don't overdo the glib line! And don't crack so many jokes that there's no time for serious interchange. Remember that if you really do get along well with this particular guy and he in turn is favorably struck by you, you are likely to be spending hours, days, even years together. And who can keep up a series of gags for *that* long? Or who would want to, if she could?

Accepting the male viewpoint

For both biological and social reasons there *is* a definite difference between males and females. And if you are going to get along wondrously well with men, at least gracefully accept this difference, even though you may never get highly enthusiastic about it.

This means, in plain English, that you'd better fully accept the fact that most males are much more interested in sex than love, that they love *after* being sexually satisfied rather than (as females often do) in order to be, and that even their loving (or vital absorption in some person or thing) tends to be considerably less romantic and monogamous than is, in our culture, female loving. This also means that there is nothing *insulting* or intrinsically *nasty* about how the male feels about sex, you, and his outside interests. You may never greatly *like* the way he is in these respects; but it is pointless for you not to accept the fact that he is the way he is, and at best you're probably only going to be able to change him slightly.

You may, then, be right if you find yourself saying, "Men are interested in only one thing—sex," or "Men are mainly interested in their work and not in their home or family," or "Men are all selfish." To a considerable degree, if not entirely, these statements are true. So they're true! What's the *horror* of men being interested in sex, in their work, or in themselves? It might, perhaps, be a much better world if this were not so (though it might be a much worse world, too!). But it *is* so. And all the wishing on your part and all the bitter demanding that men be different from the way they are, are not going to change things very much. Except for the worse!

If, then, you are interested in finding a man for your true, true love, seek exactly for that: a *man*. Not a mouse; not an angel; not a female; not a little boy; but a man. And fully expect, if you find such a man, that he will have, for better *and* for worse, some distinctly *manly* traits. For the most part, in all likelihood, he *will* be more sexually demanding, less devoted to the children, more fickle, more absorbed in outside affairs, less warm and romantic, less sociable, and more interested in some silly sporting events than you. Tough! That's the way the sonofagun is. After all, he's a *man*. And isn't that why you wanted him in the first place?

Treating your man as an individual

The first, and probably most important, psychological principle is that although all human beings are surprisingly alike in many respects—since they are born of the same species and raised in a fairly uniform social atmosphere—they are also significantly different from each other. Even identical twins, who are born from the same neatly divided cell, are never exactly alike, but have some different tastes, desires and ways of responding. And nontwins, even when members of the same family brood, can be so dissimilar as to seem to be the offspring of different families.

Any particular man you choose, therefore, is *not* exactly the same as all other men. Perhaps you intimately knew, before he came along, a father, a brother, a prior lover, or even a now deceased or divorced husband. Fine: you may well have learned some interesting and useful things about men from your association with these others. But he, your present man, is not the same as they were. Nor *should* he be. He is only himself; and if you are to understand him and get along well with him, you had better accept him as such.

All men, in other words, are *not* as protective of you as your father may have been. Nor as sexually disinterested in you as your brothers perhaps were. Nor as neat, nor as sweet-smelling, nor as carefree as the first sixteen-year-old who walked hand in hand with you on the dunes and talked to you endlessly of you and you and you.

Sometimes your present lover is surly. Sometimes he is a bore. Sometimes he is completely indifferent to you. O.K.: that's he. By the same token, he may at other times be maddeningly delightful or the best damned lay you ever had. Whatever he is, he is definitely not your mother's or your best friend's man; he is the unique, good and bad, sugar and spice individual who is *yours.*

So stop the goddam endless comparisons, comparisons. Stop feeling that you are terribly deprived when some lack of his clearly shows up; or horribly hurt when, for the nonce, he insensitively ignores you. A flawless angel, he will never be; a perfect doll, rarely and, at best, intermittently. He is, as you are, an individual; and individuals are always exceptionally sweet—and painfully sour; unusually nice—and awfully nasty. How could they possibly, as individuals, be otherwise?

"But," you may sadly wail, "he is much *too* much of an individual for me. Other men play golf—but he just *lives* on the golf course. Or other men eye every lovely woman who passes—but he actually gets up and follows them to their doorsteps. Who needs *that* kind of individuality?"

If that's the way you feel, I reply, fine. You are certainly entitled to your belief that your particular man is *too* much of an individual, and that you'd rather have someone who is more like the run-of-the-mill lover or husband. But if that's what you want, why don't you stop your silly wailing and go get it? Whatever the man of your choice now is, he is not to be damned for being what he is. You don't have to put up with him, to be sure; but neither is there any necessity for his changing. If you will firmly show him that you won't take him the way he is, and try to get him to improve somewhat, maybe you'll succeed. But not by wailing! Besides, what makes you think that some other man won't have *his own* pain-in-the-neck idiosyncrasies, too?

"Are you saying that I simply must accept the man I have, no matter how badly he behaves? That I must have patience and fortitude?"

No, I am saying that, if you are to act sanely, you'd better accept or reject him. *Agitatedly* staying with him (or whiningly leaving him) will do you little good. If he has too many bad traits leave him. If he has poor traits but is still, all things considered, the man you want, then try without anger to help him change these traits. If he cannot or will not change, but you still do not want to leave him, then accept him with his deficiencies: dislike his disadvantages, but nonetheless continue loving *him*.

Patience and fortitude, then, are in order after you have decided that, in spite of his failings, you still want this particular man. Up to that time, you can afford to be somewhat impatient—since there are presumably plenty of other fish in the sea, and your desperately hanging on to this one may not be an act of wisdom.

Even under these circumstances, however, the general rule still is: Be as patient and as nice as you can be to your chosen partner for a period of two or three months, no matter how badly he behaves during this time. If persistent good behavior on your part still does not induce him to act better, then by all means start to pack your things, or his. If you still, at this time, have great difficulty in leaving, and want to take the risks of living with a seriously deficient or disturbed mate, you've really got a problem. Seek professional help yourself—and read the next chapter.

8

How to Be More
Sexually Enjoying

Good sex relations, as we have been noting throughout this book, are as important before as after marriage. You may mate with a ninny if you insist on preserving your pristine purity or lying like a log and refraining from wriggling your butt when you finally allow your partner to get you between the sheets. But your chances of getting a real, live, swinging Joe this way are infinitesimally small.

Moreover, if you do, by sheer accident, get a good man by dint of avoiding the issue and defending your hymenal tissue, what *then?* Are you *still* going to maintain your ignorance and aspire to copulative bliss? Or are you going to consider sexual aptitude at least as important as cooking and shopping, and take a few lessons in the art of satisfying yourself and your mate?

Although this book does not purport to be much of a sex manual, let me crib a little from some of my other works in that area (particularly from *The Art and Science of Love* and *Sex and the Liberated Man*) and outline some of the main methods by which you may achieve sexual adequacy. If you want to wait to read this chapter until *after* you are safely mated, that is your prerogative. But I have to warn you that what you will read herein is hardly ungermane to the mating process, too. In fact, it could be one whale of a help.

Arousing and satisfying a man

Normally, it is not very difficult to arouse and satisfy a virile man. In fact, it is often a little too easy: any man who is attracted to you is likely to have a vigorous response; and, if you engage in almost any kind of sex activity with him, he may quickly come to orgasm. The younger he is, the more easily this is likely to happen; and the earlier it is in your sexual relationship, when you are still a novelty, the more again he is likely to become quickly aroused and satisfied.

But not always! Many young males have difficulty obtaining full sexual arousal. Either they are fearful, especially of sex failure; or they are diverted by certain conditions (such as the possibility of your parents or your roommate walking in on the two of you any second!); or they are sexually unsophisticated and are not focusing on the proper arousing ideas; or they may not be too highly sexed, and may naturally have some difficulty in responding to your attractions.

What is to be done under such circumstances?

Well, the first thing is: Don't panic! Don't quickly say to yourself: "Oh, my God! What have I done wrong now? It surely must be me. Probably he doesn't really like me. Or I'm not pretty enough for him. Or he finds me less stimulating than the other girls he's known. I might as well give up and get me to a nunnery!"

Balderdash! The chances are nine out of ten that it's not you at all. He's merely got sex problems—as millions upon millions of men have. And that's too bad. But it's hardly catastrophic. Now, if you will only calmly accept the fact that there's a problem and exert more effort at solving it then wailing about it, a fairly simple solution will probably be available.

First of all, ask your man—yes, *ask* him, with no beating around the bush—whether he does not have any kind of sex problem. Is his present state of nonarousal normal? Does it happen under certain specific circumstances? Is he afraid of anything in particular? Does he usually require any special kind of preliminaries or technique of excitation before he starts firing on all cylinders?

In other words: what goes with your friend? Open your trap and find out. Don't *assume* that you know the answer; in fact, don't assume *anything*. Just because your last lover may have needed you to wear black stockings and high-heeled shoes before he could get going does not mean that this one necessarily has the same fetish. Maybe, in fact, he *hates* black stockings and high-heeled shoes. Who knows? Who will ever know, without asking. So ask!

Whatever the reason for your man's unarousability, keep cool. It's neither horrible, nor perhaps even very unusual that he is the way he is. At most, it's a problem. And one that, if it really is too bad, you don't even have to solve: since there are other males, no doubt, with lesser problems. So accept his unaroused sexual state calmly, uncatastrophically. And *think* about how you might go about helping him solve it.

How about, for one thing, his erogenous zones? Almost all human beings have parts of their anatomies which are more susceptible to sexual stimulation than other parts; and these differ widely from person to person. The male of the species, usually, has one main erogenous zone: and it isn't ordinarily his lips, his forehead, or his big right toe. Right: it's generally his male organ, his sacred penis. You can frequently kiss and caress a man from now till doomsday, and very little will happen. But just make a few passes at his membrum virile, and lo! the situation changes rapidly.

What kind of passes? Well, not just any kind. For the easily aroused male, practically a single glance at his main source of delight will do the trick. But for the less easily aroused one, not only the correct touch, but the exact right touch in the exact right spot may be necessary to arouse him. The penis, except in rare instances, is not equally sensitive in all areas. Much of it, especially the back parts which are closest to the body, are relatively deadened in sensitivity. Other parts, such as the glans or front part of the organ, and the underside of it about one inch behind the glans, are usually much more sensitive. Just a small amount of stimulation in these areas will go much further in arousing your man than a considerable amount in other parts of his penile anatomy.

Nor will any kind of touch or caress necessarily serve. Some men require an extremely vigorous kind of massage, and simply do not get aroused at all if they do not have this kind of forceful stimulation. With other men, however, such vigor is merely painful or neutral; and only the lightest strokings or kissings will get them truly raring to go. Since the man you have chosen is a unique individual never assume that what is good for others is also good for him. Find out. Experiment. Try a variety of strokings in a variety of ways. You may well discover something about him and his sexual excitability that he himself never knew before. And if you do, your discovery will be most appreciated, and will do much to help your rapport.

Caresses and kisses, moreover, need not only be genitally oriented. Some men, particularly after they have had one or more orgasms, find that their penises are overly sensitive and cannot pleasurably be stroked or touched. Instead, nongenital manipulations—of the thighs, buttocks, breast, lips, shoulders, or almost any imaginable part of the body—may be the thing when more direct stimulation fails.

Nor is physical contact, of course, the only avenue to arousal. What you *say* to a man—particularly if you are able to employ vigorous, down-to-earth sexual language, or to tell him sincerely how much you *enjoy* making love to him—can be exceptionally exciting. Sometimes stories or verbalized fantasies will help. You can read him erotic literature; or encourage him to use his memory and imagination to review sexually stimulating events.

Don't forget eye-appeal, too. Maybe the black stockings and the high heels *will* work with your present lover. Or clinging negligees. Or nudity in a bright, bright light. Or the reflection of the two of you in a sizable mirror. Or looking at sexy pictures or films. Or the devil knows what! Anyway, exercise your imagination and see if you cannot think up something when arousal becomes difficult.

All sorts of things may help in individual cases. Some men like musky perfumes. Or unusual sex positions. Or copulation under different conditions: such as on a grassy hill, or in the shallow waves of the ocean. Explore. Try. What have you got to lose?

Don't hesitate to take the initiative. If your partner expressly gets upset by your doing so (since he may have some Victorian ideas about its being the male's prerogative, to start things going), then you may at first tone down on priming the sexual pump. But if you calmly keep persisting, and feel no hesitation or shame in doing so (including no false pride about his not caring for you enough to take the initiative himself), you will often gain what you want.

Unless your man is really devoid of sexuality, persistent and patient attempts to arouse him will sooner or later begin to pay off. The very fact that you *want* him (as long as you do not show hostility when you can't have him) will be exciting in most instances; and even though he *thinks* that he is incapable of being aroused—on nights, for example, when he feels tired or believes he has had sex too recently to have it again—he will often be amazed to find Old Roger startlingly at attention and ready to go when just the minute before he felt that he couldn't possibly be sexually interested.

The experiments of Dr. Lester A. Kirkendall are particularly instructive in this connection. Dr. Kirkendall asked many young males what they thought their maximum sexual potency was, and then got them to try to have orgasms more often than they thought they could. In virtually all cases, he found, the male was considerably more capable of arousal and fulfillment than he thought he would be. His sexual *capacity* in other words, was much higher than his actual *activity*.

So it probably is with your man, if he does not have sex with you as often as you would like. Left to his own devices, he may be a once-a-weeker or even a once-a-monther. But why should you leave him to his own devices when you're right there, handy-like, in bed with him? Let's not go to any extremes, now—such as waking him out of a sound sleep each night to begin all over again when you've both been satisfied before you dozed off. Or sucking him as you're driving him to meet the 8:15 in the morning! But, within reasonable limits, you can often show him that he *has* more sexual capacity than he normally thinks he has—and that he can enjoy using some of that extra capacity.

Another point to watch is timing. Just as many women are not particularly aroused at certain times during their menstrual cycles, males may have some degree of periodicity too. Sometimes they are too physically fatigued; or too worried about how things are going at the office; or recovering from a debilitating illness; or on a working schedule that makes it difficult for them to have regular sex. If so, make all due allowances and try to beat these kinds of limitations.

Having intercourse in the morning, for example, instead of always in the evening, is much better for some early-to-bed-and-early-to-rise men. Or massing your sex relations mainly on weekends, while keeping the midweek for more workaday activities. Or getting away from your regular environment (especially if you have children and they are part of this environment). Almost every man has some kind of timing which is best for him and his sexuality. You won't find it too difficult to discover your particular man's pattern and to plan and plot a little so that you can the better cater to it.

Intercourse itself can sometimes be arousing, even though you and your mate are not especially excited when you begin to have it. As long as he is able to effect an even passably good entry in coitus, the continuation of the act may do more, after a while, to get him fully and eagerly aroused than may any other kind of caressive or manipulative foreplay technique.

The more difficult it is to arouse and satisfy your man the more you may find it an advantage to resort to unusual, dramatic, and so-called kinky sex.

"In this modern day and age," as I note in *The Art and Science of Love,* "some of the most sexually arousing and orgasm-producing methods are those which for centuries prior to this have been taboo in our society but are now more widely accepted. Oral-genital contact, anal insertion, mild sado-masochistic forays, and similar acts lead to maximum arousal and satisfaction of millions of individuals in today's world.

"Consequently, any person whose partner is difficult to arouse or satisfy had better be especially unshy about trying all possible techniques, including many of those which were erroneously considered perverted in the past, but which are now commonly accepted as a normal part of human sex behavior."

Don't, under any circumstances, be misled by the propaganda in favor of simultaneous orgasm which is still rife in many of our leading sex manuals. It is indeed nice and convenient when you and your mate can come to climax at exactly the same time; but *nice* doesn't mean *necessary.* If both of you want to achieve orgasm, just see that you do so at some time during the sexual proceedings; and in *some* satisfying manner. You definitely need *not* have your orgasms during intercourse; and if you do have them coitally, you do not need to have them at the same moment.

The goal of striving mightily to achieve orgasm during penile-vaginal copulation and to achieve it simultaneously often defeats its own ends: since both partners are so overconcerned about such a "necessary" achievement that they shift their sexual focus from "What shall I do to enjoy myself?" to "*How* am I doing at what I am doing?" This latter focus clearly implies that if I am not doing well, I am a no-goodnik, a complete failure, and I might as well give up what I'd like to do and dig ditches instead.

The main reason for having sex relations, then, is your own

and your partner's *enjoyment*—and not achievement, "ego-bolstering" or anything of that sort. As a female, you will want to obtain the fullest satisfaction of which you are personally capable—which will differ widely from person to person, and you will want your partner to be as satisfied, generally, as he can be.

This does not mean that either or both of you must have the greatest orgasm under the sun every single time you copulate. Nor does it mean that you should have as intensive or extensive sex gratifications as John or Jim or Sue or Mabel—all of whom may be biologically and psychologically quite different from you. It simply means that you and your mate can learn what satisfies *yourselves,* and then use all the pleasurable approaches that you cooperatively discover.

Arousing and satisfying yourself with your man

If, as noted above, it is relatively easy to arouse and satisfy the average male sexually, it is often hard to achieve the same degree of arousal and release for the average female. Males have such large and easily accessible genitals that they usually can be excited and gratified within a few minutes of active sex play. Females, on the other hand, have genitals that are relatively hidden and inaccessible and that sometimes make it difficult for them to achieve full psycho-sexual release.

This is especially true when women are puritanical or when they pretend to be sexually liberal but actually cover their sexuality with a blanket of stultifying romanticism. Not that romanticism doesn't have its advantages, for it does. Females can sometimes, by focusing on love rather than sex, work themselves up into a high emotional pitch, and thus help themselves to become more sexualized.

But the reverse is probably often just as true. The average female is quite practical and unromantic about her masturbatory practices. She experiments with the various parts of her anatomy, usually finds that her clitoris is the most sensitive part of her genitalia, and then (with considerable further experimentation in a most down-to-earth manner) she discovers exactly what kind of physical manipulation and what kind of mental imagery will bring her to full orgasmic release in a relatively brief period of time.

Often, she tries various sorts of external devices—such as

hairbrushes, running water, electric vibrators, etc.—to heighten her pleasure; and frequently, she indulges in fantasies to help herself become sexually aroused and satisfied. In the course of this procedure, she is usually practical and unromantic and quite properly does not permit any high-flown idealizations to get in the way of her sexual self-expression.

Not so, unfortunately, when this same woman starts to pet or copulate with a male with whom she is enamored. Under these circumstances, she more often than not insists that love conquers all, and expects him telepathically (just *because* he presumably loves her) to divine exactly what she requires sexually and to go about satisfying her in the most approved manner. And, since her romantic conceptions in this connection are almost entirely unmitigated hogwash, she soon finds that she is *not* enjoying heterosexual relations as much as she previously enjoyed masturbatory forays, and she becomes disillusioned with her partner and perhaps with heterosexuality.

What should she do, instead, if she is fully to enjoy sex with her best loved male? Obviously, speak up and *communicate* her wishes. If she requires, for her fullest pleasure, a soft or a hard stroking, a massaging of her clitoris or her vaginal orifice, a copulative or a noncopulative approach to sex, for Pete's sake *let her say so!* No man, no matter how much he may love a woman and be eager to please her, is a mind reader.

Moreover, he has sexual prejudices of his own which tend to make him feel that the woman is pretty much the same way he is. If he, for example, likes vigorous massaging of his penis, he will tend to think that she enjoys equally vigorous stroking of her clitoris. Or if he thinks that intercourse is really the end, brother, yes, really the end, he will tend to believe that she feels exactly the same way about it. Unless she unbuttons her lips and informs him to the contrary, how is he possibly to know exactly how she *does* feel?

Honest, forthright sex talk and shameless positioning of bodies does not destroy human romance—unless you, by senseless definition, happen to *think* that it does. Loving, particularly in the male, frequently stems *from* good, solid sexual enjoyment; and millions of couples throughout the world stay together in unwedded or wedded blessedness mainly or partly *because* they have determined what satisfies each other sexually and are unashamedly doing what works best. Not only do many of these couples merely stay together, but they *lovingly*, even *romantically*, maintain their ties because they have found, in their mates, at least *one* person with whom they can be sexually honest and with whom they can do exactly what they most like to do.

Let's then, not louse up sex with super-romanticism. Sure, it's nice to go to bed with your lover or husband when the moon is on high, violins are singing through the trees, and he is whispering endless sweet nothings of love into your enchanted ears. But do you really *need* this stuff to have a hell of a good roll in the hay? Is he truly a bastard and a boor when at times he *doesn't* behave with romantic ardor, but more matter-of-factly takes twenty minutes of distinctly mechanical maneuvering to bring you to a high ecstatic pitch, and then focuses on his own supreme enjoyment while you go to work on him in an equally "mechanical" manner?

What, in fact, *is* romantic about not bothering to discover precisely what is most satisfying to your mate, or discovering it and then refusing to do what he or she wants because this is "too premeditated" or "too practical"? Is the man who brings his partner a box of chocolates unromantic or unloving because he has made sure, before he buys them for her, that she actually likes chocolates or is not allergic to them? Is the husband who purchases a new car for his wife on their tenth wedding anniversary unromantic because he has determined, beforehand, precisely what kind of a car she wants and what color she prefers? Naturally not. Then why should we look upon a man as unromantic because he bothers, quite lovingly and considerately, to discover what his mate wants and to go to some amount of time and effort to fulfill her particular (or even peculiar) sex preferences?

The mutuality bugaboo works both ways in human sexuality; and it is just as important for the female as the male. First of all, there is no reason why you *must* get an orgasm every time that your lover does. Men tend to be in a sexual mood more often than women do, and to require climax every two or three days. Females, on the other hand, are frequently more episodic in their desires, and can live without fulfillment for a week, or two or even three or four on many occasions, without feeling undue deprivation. Even when they are reasonably well aroused sexually, they still do not require orgasm and may be sometimes content with petting or copulation that does not lead to climax.

If you are this type of female, stand by your guns, and let your partner know that you don't *need* a climax every time he does, and that your not achieving one does not mean that you do not love him, that he is not really a good lover, or any of that other bosh he may be thinking. It merely means that you are different from him. And both you and he can learn to live comfortably with this difference.

On the other side of the fence, you may well have a male partner who only occasionally requires sex, while you lust much more often than he. So—what is wrong with *that?* If he wants to eat oftener than you, you normally feed the brute as often as he wants. Similarly, if you want to come to orgasm more often than he, why should he not be persuaded to help you fulfill your desires as often as *you* want? If either of you is just about insatiable in regard to food, sex, or anything else, that may be truly onerous for the other, and full cooperation in satisfying the insatiable one's wants can hardly be expected. But if one of you wants *somewhat* more food, or sex, or almost anything else that the other can fairly easily supply, why should not this other do, in the spirit of full loving, the supplying?

Recently I had two clients on the same day who had basically the same problem. In the morning, Gerald K. came to see me, to complain that his wife was a great housewife, mother, theater companion, and so on, but that she only wanted to have intercourse about once every two weeks while he was raring to go every single day of the week. He was easily satisfied by almost any kind of sexual stimulation, and he didn't quibble about how his wife gave him an orgasm. He didn't care, moreover, whether she had one herself, or whether she was *even* romantically or sexually involved while she satisfied him. But he did care, and mightily, when he was not satisfied, and found that his unfulfilled desire interfered with his work, his behavior to the children, his recreational activities, and almost everything else in life. Could I, therefore, prevail upon his wife to give him a sexual release about once a day, and no nonsense about it?

That same afternoon Mrs. Nina T. came to see me, with the much more hesitantly presented tale that her husband seemed to be satisfied with having intercourse about two or three times a year—yes, a *year!*—while she had always, up to the time of marrying, masturbated two or three times a day—yes, a *day.* Since marrying, she no longer wanted to resort to masturbation;

so could I—well—er—that is, could I—well—show her husband that—er—just a few minutes petting her each night would please her and—well—make her a much calmer and less irritable wife and mother?

I saw Gerald's wife only once. Although she at first objected that she was just too tired, by the time they got to bed, to satisfy her husband sexually on most occasions, I quickly got her to admit that she did all kinds of household chores, from morning to night, that were much more onerous than the five or ten minutes she would have to spend giving Gerald a daily orgasm. Since this was the only objection she raised, and I soon reduced it to shreds, she said she would see what she could do about giving her husband more regular satisfaction.

Being a woman of her word, she followed up this session by definite action, and when I next saw Gerald, he said that the problem was completely solved, that their marital relationship had never been so good in the eight years they had been together, and that even their two young children seemed to be benefiting greatly by their newly regularized sex acts. Also—as I had half-predicted, his wife was now getting stimulated herself about half the time she started out by just wanting to satisfy him; and her own sex pleasures had increased considerably.

Nina's husband was a much more difficult customer. In the dozen times I saw him, we debated endlessly over why he should satisfy her even though he himself had few sex urges. He used every argument in the book: that only intercourse was the proper sex method, and he wasn't often capable of that; that having sex as often as his wife wanted it would make him a most unspontaneous participant; that he was so tired by the time he went to bed with Nina that he literally couldn't lift a finger to help her; that it was abnormal and unnatural for a woman to be as sexy as his wife was; that sex was largely designed for procreation rather than for mere pleasure; and so on and so forth. I calmly batted down all these arguments, and showed them how illogical and unscientific they were. He would admit most of my points, but still not change his antisexual behavior one jot.

Finally, it became apparent that he was rigidly and compulsively sticking to his guns mainly because he was terribly afraid to be forced to do anything, even to his own advantage, and that he construed such force as a direct impingement on his integrity. Although he would not admit that his fear of being dominated by people and outside forces stemmed from a seriously disturbed state of mind, it became more and more evident to Nina that this was true, and she finally gave him an ultimatum: either try to satisfy her sexually or she would leave him. He still refused to change his ways and they eventually got divorced.

The main point here is that one of two people in an intimate relationship may be sexually deprived because of the other's physical or psychological perculiarities; and that unless some clear-cut adjustments are made so that the deprived mate receives at least a moderate amount of sex satisfaction, their relationship is not likely to last too long or too well. If you, then, are on the nonreceiving end of sexual gratification, do not hesitate to express your dissatisfaction and to try to induce your mate to do everything possible to place you on the receiving end. This does not mean, of course, that you are to *blame* him for not giving you more pleasure. But you'd better call to his attention, politely but firmly, that he is not giving it. Show him, by mental and physical guidance, exactly what it is you require for full gratification; don't accept his easy excuses for not doing what you want.

And don't, under any circumstances, blame yourself for not being easily satisfied! There is nothing great or marvelous about a woman who, after her man looks her steadily in the eye or kisses her softly on the lips, goes into a string of powerful orgasms. This is simply her nature; and she probably would act similarly with almost any man with whom she had some degree of pyschosexual rapport. Even though she may find it highly convenient to be that way—just as you may find it convenient to be tall, or beautiful, or large-breasted or brainy—you are not, in comparison to her, a total loss.

If you never achieve the kind of quick and intense sex pleasure that she achieves, that is too bad—but that's all it is: too bad. And if your man demands that you be in her class, that is too bad, too: for most probably you'll never make it (any more than you'll be as lovely as Helen of Troy or as good a novelist as Jane Austen). But just because you are not the greatest bedmate of the century doesn't mean that you are no good whatsoever in this respect, nor that you can't show your lover or husband a trick or two. You probably can, if you're not too perfectionistic or over-romantic.

If you do find yourself somewhat deficient sexually, in that you do not get easily aroused and have a difficult time achieving climax once you are, you are probably not focusing as well as you might on sexually exciting stimuli. The main art of sexual arousal and satisfaction consists of proper focusing.

Females, for some reason which is not entirely clear but which may be related to their antisexual upbringing in this society, are often poor at sexual focusing. Even when they are actively engaged in intercourse, and presumably enjoying it, they are able to think of a host of nonsexual things, such as cooking, their overdue job promotion, the dress they saw in Macy's window yesterday, and even the kitchen sink.

This kind of nonsexual or antisexual thinking enhances your sex pleasure just about as much as thinking about murdering your neighbor and cutting him up into little pieces is likely to add flavor to the roast beef you are eating. Sexual excitation is largely brought about by (*a*) signals or thoughts from the cerebral cortex of the brain to the sex centers of the body (especially those located in the lower part of the spinal cord), and (*b*) direct and indirect physical manipulation of the sex organs themselves.

If only the second of these two forms of arousal is employed, lots of people can become sexually aroused—but they have the devil of a time experiencing orgasm. And one of the main reasons why women so often become sexually aroused without achieving orgasm is that they are getting the proper kind of physical stimulation of their erogenous zones, but are not using their brain power to give themselves sufficient additional stimulation to propel them to climax.

Matters become much worse in this connection whenever an individual who wants to become aroused and satisfied is worrying mightily over whether she actually will succeed. For the thoughts: "My God! it looks like I'm not going to succeed this time, and then he will think I'm a dud in bed," or: "Will I make it? Will I make it? Will I make it?" are powerfully antisexual. They sometimes seem, these worrisome internalized sentences, to be about sex; but really they are about personal worth: about how am I *doing* at sex? And no matter how close to orgasm a woman may be, if she at the last minute starts thinking, "Will I actually come? Won't it be awful if I don't!" she is likely to stop her sexual processes and to wind up frustrated.

What can you do instead of focusing on nonsexual or antisexual thoughts? Obviously, you can think of whatever most arouses you, and avidly concentrate on that until you impel yourself to climax. You may think, in this connection, of your lover or husband; or the handsome man you saw on the street yesterday; or your favorite actor; of some particular kind of sex act, even a bizarre or peculiar act; or of literally *anything* that excites you. If love and romance work for you, think loving and romantic thoughts. If sheer, unadulterated sexy thoughts work, use them.

"But is this really cricket?" you may ask. "Here I am trying to achieve full satisfaction with George, and you tell me I may have to think of Jim or Donald or Guy. Or of some sado-masochistic fantasy. Isn't that unethical? Isn't that pretty crazy?"

It may be crazy, say I; but that's the way millions of perfectly "normal" human beings are. Even though they madly love George, and are having sex relations with him, thinking of him is no longer exciting while thinking of Jim or Donald or Guy is. It seems a pity that this is so; but it *is* so; and if it is so in your own case, you'd better calmly accept it as the one of the facts of life and use it to your own advantage.

Similarly with other kinds of sex fantasies. Both men and women, I have found in my clinical practice, think of the damnedest things when they want to arouse themselves sexually. If they ever carried some of the things into practice—if, for example, they actually allowed themselves to be beaten with a whip in order to bring on orgasm—they would have weird kinds of sex lives, and we might consider them deviates. But as long as their fantasies remain precisely that, and are not carried into practice, there seems to be nothing unusual about them; and such fantasies are so common among otherwise sane people that it seems fanciful to call them deviant or perverse.

Focus sexually, then, without guilt. It would be nice if you could merely think of your man's wavy blond hair or huge genitals, and thereby bring yourself to a peak of sexual excitement. But suppose he has black hair and small genitals, which just do not send you. Or suppose he has the right kind of physical features that match your own prejudices but you *still* are not enthusiastic about focusing on these features, and you find your mind straying excitedly to someone or something else. Too bad; but hardly catastrophic. Do the best you can with the fantasies that work for you; and your relations with your lover or husband, as well as with yourself, are likely to be much better.

Try hard, then, to discover what satisfies you, physically and mentally; and do not prudishly or romantically hesitate to use the information. Don't, at the same time, *over*-try for perfect orgasm, since there is no such thing; and women (as previously noted) can have very pleasant relations on many occasions without ever coming to climax. If you don't, at certain times, reach the highest summits of sexuality, that is somewhat regrettable but that's all it is—regrettable. It does not mean that you are sexually incompetent; nor that you are personally worthless; nor that your man will quickly leave you; nor that you have missed the only true joy in life. It merely means that on this particular occasion you have not got your piece of taffy; and that next time you'll have another chance to get it.

9

How to Get a Reluctant
Man to Commit Himself

Let us assume that you have been getting your money's worth out of this book and have looked for a man, found a suitable one, and are getting along well with him sexually and otherwise. Unfortunately, however, the particular man you have chosen does not seem eager to mate, but is more than willing to go along forever having an extramarital affair. Perhaps he is now married and balks at divorcing his wife; or perhaps he has had several marriages already, and is not joyful about adding another legal notch to his belt; or perhaps he has never been mated, and just does not see why he should ever be.

What can you do about *these* difficult circumstances? Let us see.

What not to do about a reluctant man

The main thing *not* to do when your chosen man will not, for the present, mate with you is to become exceptionally resentful and vengeful. For one thing, he has a perfect *right* not to do so—no matter how strong your own urge to be mated. Certainly he enjoys your company, your sense of humour, your love-making, and many other aspects of your relationship with him. But how does *this* prove that he therefore *should* marry you and is a bastard if he doesn't? Does a man necessarily have to *pay* for every advantage he gets with a woman? Does he have to be made to *suffer* for the benefits he gains from a heterosexual relation? If *this* is what you think, then you have a deadly, commercialized view of love and mating—and it is highly doubtful whether you can satisfactorily mate if you have that view.

If, moreover, a man does not want to live with you, in spite of the fact that you are getting along splendidly, there is a good chance that he still has some fear of becoming domestically bound. Perhaps he thinks that you're treating him very well right now, but that who knows what you will do after the mating knot is firmly tied. Perhaps he feels that underlying your calm surface you have a nature that is hostile, vengeful and nasty and that mating with you would be too risky.

If this is so his worst fears will be confirmed if you become resentful and backbiting when he balks at a more permanent relationship.

Resenting a man for not mating, moreover, is to tell yourself the sentence, "Because I *want* him to live with me and *dislike* his not doing so, he *should* marry me and I *can't stand* his not doing so." This sentence is both grandiose and anxiety-provoking, and it follows from *your* irrational assumptions rather than from *his* poor behavior. You would be much wiser if you questioned and challenged your *own* nonsense rather than blamed your lover for being the (admittedly regrettable) way that he is.

While you are trying to keep yourself from becoming terribly resentful if your man is not in any mating mood, don't at the same time go to the other extreme and act in an unusually weak, namby-pamby manner. Don't just let your relationship with this man drag on endlessly, without ever bringing up the issue of living together. Let him know, in a frank and direct manner, that you are interested in mating and that you hope that you and he will do so in the not too distant future. Don't pretend that you *like* going on for a long time living apart when you definitely do not. Tell him your real feelings.

This does not mean that at certain times you are not to keep your gentle trap shut about your domestic urges; if, for example, your friend is obviously in a poor financial situation and is therefore in no position to mate; or if he has a vindictive wife who at the moment clearly will not divorce him; or if he is still smarting from the unpleasantness of breaking up with his last mate, it would be wiser in such cases if you kept reasonably quiet about your goals and let him first work out some of his own problems.

If, however, there is no good or special reason why the man you want cannot mate, and if he nonetheless seems to be dilly-dallying as the precious months go by, don't be a coward: tell him, in a very nice way, exactly what's on your mind, and let the chips fall where they may. Perhaps, when you bring up the question of mating, he'll be most surprised, and blurt out that he has no intention of ever living with you (or anyone else). Perhaps he'll quickly lose interest in you, after you raise this issue openly, and stop seeing you again. Perhaps he'll scream and sulk and lament that you don't really love him, but are only selfishly interested in making your own future secure.

Good! If your friend goes on in this kind of way after you have nicely let him know that you aren't getting any younger, that you may well want to raise children, and that in one way or another you intend to end up living with some man, you have done yourself a real favor by bringing his negative attitude into the open so soon. For there is every reason to believe that if you had waited a month or a year or a decade longer, these *still* would have been his basic reactions; and where would you have been *then*?

How long, generally, may you wait until you gently and sweet-ly convey to a man the notion that love and sex are great stuff, honey, but a woman often wants something more than that? That depends partly, of course, on circumstances.

If you are fifteen or sixteen years of age, you can afford to wait quite a few years before you encourage your male to mate. If you yourself have something to do that is most important in life— such as to finish medical school or tour the world with a ballet company—you may also be more than willing to put off domes-tic bliss for months or years to come. If your man is already married, but is making every possible effort to get away from a wife who is reluctant to let him go, you may have to wait until his legal entanglements are sorted out before you persuade him to pop the question.

Suppose, however, that no such impediments to mating exist? Then, as I tell most of my female clients, the general rule of thumb is: If you have intimately known a man you want to live with for from three to six months, *and have spent considerable time with him during this period,* your relationship with him had better be heading in the mating direction; otherwise something is definitely wrong.

This does not mean that every one of your beaux should have formally proposed to you by April Fool's Day, assuming that you met on New Year's Eve. But it does mean that by the time a quarter of a year or more of dining, wining, and monkeyshining has amiably passed, your current friend had better indicate strongly that he cares for you, and would like a prolonged relationship. If he is not even *thinking* along these lines, and you definitely are, then you'd better jog his memory and let him know that you are eagerly awaiting some kind of a decision.

Should you play games to get your friend to do his duty by Our Nell or else get off the pot? You can, if you wish—but not on my advice. I see no particular point in your pretending to have other dates when he wants to see you, refusing to see him very often even though you are just dying to be with him, or keeping him away from you sexually until he asks to move in with you. I am sure—as women have often told me—that these games sometimes work. But they also frequently backfire. Thus, they may win the man, but it may help him hate your guts for the next thirty years just because you have pushed him against his will.

I am seeing at this writing a man who has been married for eight years and who gets along reasonably well with his wife, but who has been carrying on a series of affairs and who keeps wondering whether he should divorce his wife and live with one of his inamoratas. One of his reasons is that he discovered, shortly after marriage, that the man he thought was his greatest rival for his wife's hand, and whom she had been using to make him jealous and to induce him to propose to her, was really her cousin in whom she had never been seriously interested. He has been so resentful of this trickery that he has never really buckled down to trying to make a good relationship with his wife; and it will probably be some time yet before I can help him overcome his childish resentment and rebelliousness.

So forget the coy games and stick pretty much to the truth. Calmly and nicely show your friend that even though you do care only for him, and have no intention of baiting him with other men or seeing him more seldom, you are just, in a self-protective manner, going to *have* to stop being intimate with him and to seek other affairs if he remains adamant about living with you.

If, moreover, you can have this kind of serious, heart-to-heart talk with your man *after* you have, for a period of at least many weeks, been unusually nice to him and have definitely not nastily beaten him over the head for not living with you, you have a much better chance of getting him to say yes. In fact, if this kind of behavior will not work, I doubt whether anything else will.

Mary D., under my guidance, followed this kind of procedure and found that it worked beautifully. Mary, although only twenty-seven, had already been twice-divorced and had two young children when she began going with Roger S. Roger came from a highly conservative, well-to-do family which was loaded with clergymen, army officers, and politicians. Almost no one, least of all Mary, expected Roger to form a permanent partnership with her, and their relationship went on and on, every Wednesday and Saturday, with no sign of Roger's even getting close to moving in with Mary as she would have preferred.

Mary's mother, who was even more eager than Mary to see her daugher settled down, kept pressing her to keep far out of arm's reach of Roger. For Mary was unusually comely of face and figure; and the mother figured that if Roger realized that he could get his sexual due with Mary only after he had moved in with her, he would then be willing to overlook her previous history, as well as the objections of his family, and might even marry her.

When I first saw Mary, she was dutifully trying to carry out her mother's idea—and there was a bit of hell to pay. Roger, though obviously most attracted to Mary, was getting more and more jumpy, complaining that she clearly did not care for him. He was beginning to drink too much and to occupy himself with other women on the nights when he was not seeing Mary. As a result of one of these extracurricular affairs, he had got one of the other women pregnant and, out of a sense of guilt, had come within a hair of living with her. This affair had blown over; but Mary was not sure when a similar crisis might not rise again; so she was just about as jumpy as Roger was.

I quickly put a stop to all that. "Look," I said to Mary during one of our first sessions, "what do you really *want* to do with Roger? Do you want to go to bed with him and enjoy yourself— or do you want to keep as far as possible away from sex relations, because sex is not your particular metier?"

"Oh, no," she replied, "that's not it at all. I *do* like the sex. I liked it even with my first two husbands, neither of whom I got along with too well in other respects. And I almost pop off just from kissing Roger goodnight. So there's no doubt about my wanting it. But my mother keeps insisting that if I do give in that way, that'll kill everything, and he'll never want me permanently."

"Damn your mother!" I said. "She's apparently been pulling that line ever since your father divorced her twenty years ago; and how come, if that approach is so good, that she hasn't got together with a man again?"

"Yes, I can't help wondering about that myself. Mother's had plenty of suitors ever since the divorce. She's one of the most beautiful women I know. And she says she wants to marry again. So I wonder."

"Well, that's her problem, and we aren't here to get her straightened out. But it does look as if her advice doesn't work too well for her, so why should it work that well for you?"

"But *won't* Roger lose most of his incentive to live with me if I have sex with him now? You know the old saw: 'Why buy the cow when milk's so cheap?' "

"Not so. The assumption there is that one *only* wants milk from the cow—and that, of course, is not always true. Some people *like* cows: like their looks, like to raise them, to milk them, to own them. And most men don't *only* try to get sex from a woman. They want other things from her as well—such as steady companionship and family living.

"But how about my handicaps in this case. You know: my two previous marriages, and the children?

"How about them? As you say, they probably are handicaps. Especially from the standpoint of Roger's relatives. But what women *doesn't* have known handicaps to the man with whom she mates?"

"Then you think I should do what I really want to do, and have sex with Roger?"

"I think that you'd better stop playing games and be *yourself* with him. Not only yourself, but your *nicest, warmest* self. Since you do, we know, have those handicaps; and he wants good reasons for mating. If, therefore, you treat him exceptionally well, including sexually well, for the next few months; and if, after treating him in such a manner, you then frankly tell him that you can't very well go on that way forever, since you *do* very much want to live with a man, if that kind of relationship with him doesn't make him want to accept you with all your handicaps, I can't imagine what else will make him want to."

"You are sort of saying that I might possibly get Roger by the kind of game my mother is trying to get me to continue, but that even though he would want me if I played such a game, it isn't exactly *me* he would want. Is that right?"

"Yes, I think that puts it pretty well. If you get him by a cat-and-mouse game, what you are really getting is a game-lover. While if you get him by being exceptionally nice to him—which presumably you will continue to be after you mate—then you get a you-lover rather than a game-lover."

Mary followed my suggestions and began to have a full-blown affair with Roger. Her mother almost had a fit but Mary stuck to her guns and within a few weeks was practically living with her lover. For the next ten weeks she gave him as much of herself as she could; and whenever she began to feel badly again, because he still was not moving in, she strongly reminded herself, as I kept teaching her to do, that he had a perfect right to be the way he was, and that he was not a louse just because his wishes did not coincide with hers. Consequently, she was able to be unresentful toward Roger even when she felt somewhat saddened by her position.

At the end of this time, when Roger had still made no mention of mating, she sat down with him one night and calmly but firmly told him that she loved him very much, and was now more than ever convinced that he would make a fine mate and a good father to her children, but that living separately from her man wasn't her thing.

Therefore, she simply owed it to herself to discontinue their affair, and look for a man who would be interested in mating. She doubted, she said, that she would ever find anyone who was as much to her liking as he was, and she was most sorry to have to end this relationship with him; but what else, under the circumstances, could she sanely do?

Roger was at first taken aback by her sudden confrontation—since apparently he had just put out of his mind the fact that time was passing and that she would not go on this way forever—but he was able to see that she was not merely trying to put him over a barrel, and that she was entitled to her feelings. He told her that he had no doubt whatever about his love feelings for her; but he admitted that he could not see his way to living with her as yet, because of the great to-do that would arise in his family. He hoped that he would be able to do so one day, but was most indefinite when this day would be. He agreed, therefore, that it would be sensible if she did stop seeing him, even though both of them would suffer for awhile.

Roger's answer was most disappointing to Mary, since she had naturally hoped that he would be so averse to giving up the happiness they both had been experiencing that he would simply disregard the opposition of his family and any other objections that there might be to mating with her. She was so torn by the prospect of losing him forever, that she came within an inch of reneging on her position and of agreeing indefinitely to continue their affair. She pulled herself together, however, and steadfastly, if sorrowfully, held her ground. They agreed to part, sadly kissed goodnight for what was supposed to be the last time, and Roger left.

Early the next morning he was on the phone, saying that he hadn't slep a wink that night because, in thinking things over, he couldn't find any objection to moving in with her *other* than the displeasure of his family. And if that was all that was standing in the way of their permanently getting together, to hell with it!—he was not going to be ruled by the opinions—not to mention the bigotries—of even his closest family members. How soon could he arrange to bring over his belongings?

Whether Roger and Mary lived happily ever after, I am not sure—though when I last heard about them, they were still going strong and had no regrets. Nor does their success necessarily prove that Mary's tactics will *always* work as well as they did for her. Many other Rogers will not be tied down. Others will be led to mate, when they are treated as Mary treated Roger, but will only do so with great reluctance, and will never forget the fact that they were forced to mate somewhat against their will. Not all males act alike; and it is foolish to assume that your particular male friend will follow Roger's example—when he may well be quite a different kind of Tom, Dick, or Harry.

Nonetheless, being exceptionally nice and unresentful to a man for a period of a few months before you let him know that you will not carry on a casual affair forever is one of the best ways to put him in a mood to settle down with you. The more you carp and wail the less a man is likely to become inclined to live permanently with you. If, as noted above, you insist on trying various jealousy-arousing and other tricks of the trade to get your man go ahead and try them. But keep in mind that any good kind of realtionship is warm, cooperative, and permissive. I think you will see the wisdom of getting a head start on *this* kind of togetherness.

Sigmund Freud remarked that many people remain married because their revenge against each other, particularly for some of the nasty games they have played on each other during the courtship stage, has not yet been exhausted. Let us hope that your mating relationship never falls into this category.

What to do about a reluctant lover

Is there anything else you can do about a man who presumably loves you but who is reluctant to mate? Yes, several things, such as these:

1. Be permissive. It is safe and secure for you when you know that your man is exclusively devoted to you, never looks at other women, and would never be sexually unfaithful. But to the degree that you demand such security, you may be unduly restricting him, and making him resentful of you. Perhaps, he had better have some time to sow some wild oats before he settles down. Or perhaps you can allow some room for comparisons, to see whether you are really better for him than some of his other women friends. Also: it is by no means a bad idea to give a man sufficient rope with which to hang himself, if he is actually set to do so. If he is really a run-around, or insists on spending most of his time at the office, or keeps refusing to go out with you, it is better that you know these propensities of his beforehand. The more you discover about your potential mate's bad traits the better position you are in to decide whether or not it is worth mating with him.

2. Be sexy. Nine out of ten men mate because they believe that they will have steadier and better sex relations than they have had during their bachelorhood. Most of these men, alas, will be sadly disappointed: since it is almost incredible how *little* sex there is in the average domestic union, particularly during the early years of pregnancy and infant-rearing, which frequently reduce the copulatory urges of the woman (and often of the man

as well) to a minimum. But at the time when they actually mate, males generally do not realize how well off they were with their generally exciting, if also somewhat sporadic, premarital affairs; and they have the highest hopes (or illusions) about what a great ball they will continually have when their partner becomes their spouse.

Don't disillusion your man *before* mating! Try to be, at this time in particular, one of the sexiest women he has yet encountered. For one thing, you will then be able to keep him from being too interested in your competitors—who, let us face it, are many, and some of whom actually *are* mainly interested in his bed prowess. For another thing, he will almost always construe your violent sex interest as interest in *him* rather than in his genital agility. Tell a woman that she is great in bed, and she will frequently be insulted: she thinks that you think she is *only* good for one limited purpose. But show a man that you truly appreciate his copulative ardor, and you indicate that you think him a great guy and a scholar.

So be sexually imaginative. Try to devise, in your spare time, a new coital trick or two. Think, specifically, of how to please your man *sexually*, and not merely conversationally. Almost any woman can sew on his buttons or whip up a souffle when he is hungry. But how many of your competitors can really *swing*?

3. Be loving. If you sit back cautiously, and wait until your man has cast himself at your feet and promised to love you forever, you may possibly intrigue some self-punishing individual who does not love until he is stepped on, or some big-game-hunting male who is mainly out for difficult conquests and will not love any woman who is fairly easily available. But who needs a masochistic man? And who wants one who, being primarily interested in the conquest side of amour, will most probably become supremely disinterested once he has succeeded in warming up an initially cold lady?

Love, more frequently than not, begets love. If you are consistently warm and outgoing—especially when your man is more than a bit cool and reserved himself—you will tend to present a side of life that is more intriguing and exciting than his own uninvolvement and neutrality. If he himself is highly affectionate and ardent, he will feel most comfortable with your own warmheartedness; and if he is somewhat deficient in this respect, he may be most pleasantly surprised to find that, under your thawing rays, he begins to show feelings which he thought he was hardly capable of having before you came along.

Super-romanticism, as we previously pointed out, may defeat its own purposes. But a more moderate degree of romantic passion may call forth a surprising responsiveness in the man of your choice. If you send a card on the anniversary of the day you met, or write him a poem when he is on a business trip, or tell him how much you would like to see him on a weekday night when you usually do not get together, he may quite unconsciously take similar flights of fancy himself; and, before you know it, you may be sailing away on the same romantic carpet.

No nagging, now! Telling your friend that he never sends you roses, like your previous lover or husband used to do, and that therefore how could he possibly, possibly love you, will usually get you nowhere—except out in the cold, looking for a new partner. He will tend to see you as being obnoxiously demanding, and may well think back on *his* last sweetheart, who (with all her faults) at least didn't keep putting pressure upon him to do what he didn't want to do. If, however, *you* send the roses, he may soon find himself *wanting* to respond in kind; and may even start devising original romantic approaches to you.

Moreover: just as the male's persistent sexuality frequently wears down female resistance and eventually induces the female *willingly* to jump into bed, there is no reason why persistent female romanticism cannot encourage the male willingly to jump into romantic courtship and mating. You are obviously not likely to get very far in this respect if you select a distinctly reluctant partner, and then put on a campaign of telephone calls, telegrams, letters, visits, and other means of intimate contact. Very probably, he will think you a royal pain in the gullet, and resist you more and more.

Toward a man, however, who at least seems half-willing to become involved with you, and who continues to seek your sexual and nonsexual companionship when he very well could go elsewhere, your affectionate, romantic overtures are likely to fall on much more fertile soil. So don't, just because he *is* a male, necessarily wait for him to start the loving preludes. The millennium may arrive sooner.

4. Be understanding. Loving a man is often rather easy, since you are not going to select, in the first place, someone for whom you do not have some spontaneous interest or involvement, and

if you do fall in love with this individual you usually will manage to do so unconsciously, unthinkingly, without much effort on your part.

Understanding is much harder to achieve—and I mean *achieve*. For understanding usually involves several acts which are not entirely spontaneous, and which are to some degree self-sacrificing. Thus, in order to understand fully how an individual is behaving and to accept his behavior even when it is not exactly kindly or appropriate or correct, listen carefully to his point of view and forbear jumping to any immediate conclusions.

Whatever your *first* and *spontaneous* reactions to his deeds and misdeeds, stop and take a second or third look—literally hold yourself back, in many instances, from making a quick judgment; and patiently continue to get all the facts of his actions, until you have obtained pretty much the whole story behind them.

Secondly, to understand a person's behavior, you can temporarily be objective and withhold *any* judgment about it until you have given him time and opportunity to offer excuses, extenuating circumstances, and special exceptions to many of the usual rules of living. If, for example, your friend tells you that he has double-crossed his business partner, don't immediately respond: "Oh, that's wrong! How could you have possibly done such a thing?" Instead, give him a chance to explain how his partner previously has double-crossed him; what his special reasons for behaving in this manner toward his partner were; why he thinks his "wrong" deed was really necessary in this particular instance; what unusual stresses he was under when he committed the deed; etc.

Thirdly, understanding—as we have been emphasizing throughout this book—consists of acceptance of the other's behavior even *after* you have finally decided that it is mistaken or immoral. Thus, you may never like the fact that your lover has double-crossed his partner or treated his mother badly—but you can nevertheless understand that he *is* a fallible human, and consequently may be *expected* at times to do distinctly wrong things. Understanding this, you can still fully accept, though not necessarily approve, his behavior, and can concentrate on trying to help him change it for the better next time instead of blaming him for committing it this time.

Understanding another, then, consists of holding back your

immediate responses to his actions, carefully giving him every benefit of the doubt, objectively weighing whether or not he has really done wrong, and accepting him even after it has been clearly proven that he has behaved badly. Understanding is consequently a *highly disciplined* form of responding to another; and, in the short run, it tends to be self-sacrificing, since at the moment of understanding you are considering this other rather than only yourself, and you may even be going along with some of his behavior (such as his nastiness toward you) which is inimical to your own happiness.

In the long run, however, understanding of a lover or husband need not be self-sacrificing, since it is basically to your *own* interest to comprehend and forgive his poor conduct, so that (a) you will not unduly upset yourself about it, and (b) you will eventually get him to see that you are truly on his side and that he would be wise if he similarly understood and loved you. Understanding of another person, in other words, usually leads to long-run rather than to short-run hedonism. It is difficult; but in the end it is often most rewarding.

By way of illustration, let us take the case of one of my clients who was recently invited for a weekend with some charming people; and when she delightedly told her man that he was invited, too, and that she looked forward to their spending the weekend with these people, he suddenly balked and refused to go. She was shocked by his refusal, was certain that he was deliberately punishing her for another occasion when she did not want to meet his boss (who, she had feared, would not approve of their affair) and came close to breaking off their relationship.

As a result of my talking over this incident with her, she began to see things differently and to be more understanding. She realized that her lover did not want to go away for the weekend because he was afraid that the people they would be spending it with were more educated than he, and thought that they would despise him, and also because he was afraid that she would drink too much during the visit and might do something to shame him. Instead of condemning him for having these fears, she calmly accepted that he was fearful, and she tried to help him see that there was nothing to be afraid of. She also indicated that if he still remained fearful and didn't want to go away for the weekend with her, she would be quite willing to go away alone—or, if he wished, to stay at home with him.

Seeing that she had reversed her previous angry stand, and that she was able fully to understand (though not to like) his position, her friend at first agreed that it would be quite all right if she went visiting alone. Then, at the last minute, he thought things over again, decided that there really wasn't that much for him to be afraid of, and went on the weekend visit with her. In the process, he did manage to become less fearful, and their relationship improved.

Understanding, then, usually requires *work*. It does not come spontaneously; is not an inborn gift. It involves creative listening and acting; and, especially when it is added to permissiveness, sexiness, and loving, it is hard to resist. Give a man this combination of acceptance, and even if he is a most difficult customer, and comes to your relationship with no idea of mating, he is very likely to sacrifice his freedom willingly. If he does so, and if you still continue to give him a similar sex-love relational pattern after you are living together, he may even come to enjoy domesticity. And so may you!

10

Overcoming Blocks to Mating: Attachments to Other Persons and Goals

Many women firmly believe that they are vitally interested in forming a stable relationship with a man when, if they really searched their hearts, they would find that they are actually more interested in some other goal or pursuit. This, of course, is their prerogative: since there is no reason why any female, especially in today's world, has to enter a permanent or semi-permanent heterosexual relationship, and several good reasons why many women had better not put this as their prime interest. Quite legitimately, you, as a woman, may be more absorbed in your original family rather than in building one of your own. Or you may simply want to avoid the responsibilities of mating on a fairly permanent basis. Or you may favor lesbian rather than heterosexual relationships. Or you may have other goals and values that would be interfered with by a solid relationship with a man.

If so, fine. Don't be apologetic. Don't think that you *have to* be heterosexual, or monogramous, or raise children, or otherwise do what the vast majority of women in your society tend to do. You are an individual. You have a right to your own decisions. Make them largely (though not necessarily totally) for yourself.

In some cases, however, you really do primarily want a prolonged intimate relationship with a man and yet you foolishly or neurotically let other affairs or other goals interfere with this primary desire. In this chapter, I shall consider some of these interferences that you might well want to overcome, and show how you can—but only if you truly *wish* to do so—minimize them and thereby rid yourself of these kinds of blocks against mating.

Perfectionism

There is a wide gap between selectivity and perfectionism. The selective woman asks herself what she really wants in a male, discovers that there are many traits which she definitely does *not* want, and then carefully excludes nine out of ten possible suitors because they have one or more of these traits. Considering that she will only mate a few times during her lifetime, and that each of her matings is likely to last for a number of years (and one of them, perhaps, for forty or fifty years), she would be *crazy not* to be selective.

The perfectionist woman, while pretending to be selective, is actually impossibly eliminative. She sets up *so many* male traits as being totally undesirable that she leaves herself virtually no one from whom to choose; and winds up as a spinster or a wholly disgruntled mate. Like nearly all perfectionists, she is not merely saying to herself, "I dislike a man who smokes or gambles or works long hours or wants to copulate every night in the week." But she is also convincing herself: "*I can't stand* an imperfect male, who will not thoroughly satisfy me in *every* conceivable way, and who will do things that I may dislike."

The perfectionist, in other words, is only seemingly strong and firm; actually, she is anxious and weak. She refuses to live in a world of probability and chance—where her mate *may* get drunk at times, or be unfaithful to her, or forget their anniversary— and demands an absolutely predictable world in which that there will never be any serious difficulties. Naturally, she can never know such a world—for the simple reason that it doesn't exist—so she lives, usually with a false security, in another, nonrelating part of the universe, where she believes she can control her destiny in a somewhat neater and safer manner.

A special kind of perfectionism in our society is super-romanticism. The ultra-romantic woman (or man) feels that mating must be one long feast of romantic love without the crasser aspects of mating—such as financial hassles, housecleaning schedules, and disciplining of the children. As they cannot help but observe that such super-fanciful relationships are as rare these days as Moorish castles in Kansas, the devotees of super-romance soon withdraw from the field and confine their amours, if any, to sporadic interludes.

How can perfectionism and ultra-romanticism be overcome? By analyzing the irrational ideologies that lie behind and create these attitudes. The perfectionist is telling herself: "Because I dislike certain traits in men, I simply cannot live with such traits. Rather than risk living with a man who has some of them and helping him to change them. I will, if necessary, wait forever until the perfect male, who has no such traits, comes along. If I live with an imperfect man, I shall be completely destroyed. If I find the perfect one, my underlying slobbishness will be compensated for, and I will be able to get along satisfactorily in this terrible, terrible world."

These self-defeating sentences can be vigorously challenged with several pertinent questions, such as: *Why* can't I live with a man who has some traits that I happen to dislike? *What* is really so risky about marrying someone who has some undesirable characteristics? *Why can't* I help a potential mate overcome some of his habits and attitudes that I deplore? *How* would I be destroyed if I lived with an imperfect man? *Where* is the *evidence* that I am such an innate slob that I must mate with a perfect male in order to compensate for my lousehood?

The more you question your own perfectionism, and the so-called horrors of your being an imperfect, fallible wife in this imperfect, fallible world, the less perfectionistic and ultra-romantic you will tend to be. The more you unthinkingly assume that you *must* have a perfect man to make up your own awful deficiencies, the more you will actually need such a paragon of all virtues. Moreover: the more you think you require godliness in a male, the weaker you will keep yourself, the more self-hating you will be—and the less, ironically enough, you are likely to win and keep a reasonably good man if and when he comes your way.

Perfectionism is a self-inflicted vice. Designed to make you feel holier-than-thou, it invariably winds up by making you feel unworthier-than-all. Your one chance of being happily mated when you are perfectionistic is for you to be Ms. Jehovah; and Jehovah, apparently, was so infallible that he never mated at all.

Fears of rejection

Many women who are emotionally blocked against mating have dire fears of rejection. They are afraid to meet males, in the first place, because they cannot guarantee that they will be accepted by these males. Or, sometimes later in the dating and mating game, they feel that they will be thrown over by their lovers, and that that would be disastrous. Some of these women have actually suffered from a previous rejection, and have no wish to suffer so cruelly again. Others have never let themselves get close enough to a man to be finally spurned by him, but they so graphically imagine the horrors of such a possible occurrence that they continue to stay out of the area of serious courtship.

Claudi V. was a real honey of an avoider when it came to meeting males. At dances, she would stand rigidly on the side lines, glaring malevolently at any male who happened to look invitingly in her direction. On trains and buses, even if she was attracted to someone sitting next to her, she never looked his way, and ignored his overtures or grunted back a discouraging retort to any propoosal he might make. Actually, she was dying to meet eligible males and was miserably lonely as she sat home, night after night, waiting for telephone calls that rarely came.

Claudia insisted, when I first saw her for psychotherapy, that she really liked herself. She was sufficiently good-looking, she thought; she had been bright enough to do very well getting her Master's degree (in, of all things, psychology!); and she kept making rapid advances in the job she held. Why should she doubt, therefore, that she was a fine enough person and that she had a good estimation of herself?

"Baloney!" I insisted. "You're obviously scared witless to approach a strange male or even to have one approach you. You clearly are telling yourself that if you became intimate with him and he really found out how weak and inept you are socially, he'd quickly leave you, and that that would be catastrophic. Isn't that so?"

"Yes, but I'm just describing what's true. I *am* socially inept; my whole history proves that I am, doesn't it?"

"It proves," I replied, "that you *have* been inept at talking to males: that you *have been* tongue-tied and uncommunicative."

"Well? Isn't that enough?"

"Yes, it's more than enough. But how does *has been* prove *always will be*?"

"But when I keep trying and failing—doesn't that prove that I simply can't? Like the other day, when I wanted, really wanted, to speak nicely to a man who sat next to me at the lecture I attended, and who tried several times to talk to me. And I just couldn't! I tried, but no matter how hard I tried, I just couldn't. Now doesn't that prove that I *can't?*"

"It proves nothing of the sort. It merely proves that when you *think* you can't do a thing, you can't."

"But why should I think I can't, except that whenever I've tried I haven't been able to? Isn't that why I'm so sure I can't?"

"No, it's really the other way around: you actually haven't tried because you *think* you aren't able to. Then, not trying, but falsely *believing* that you're trying, you conclude: 'I can't!' "

"But how do you know I can? All the evidence points the other way."

"The hell it does! Let me prove to you that it doesn't. Suppose, for example, that the man who sat next to you at the lecture, and whom you say you could not talk to, suppose that you suddenly noticed that smoke was coming out of his pocket. Could you *then* talk to him?"

"Why—uh—yes. I guess I could."

"You could quickly tell him that his pocket seemed to be on fire, and that he'd better investigate and put it out?"

"Yes, I' m sure I could."

"And after telling him that, you could then go on, could you not, to talk further with him—once the ice was broken like that?"

"Yes. I guess so."

"Well? Under *those* circumstances you could open your mouth and talk quite freely. Then why this bosh about 'I can't? Obviously, you can."

"Then why do I keep thinking that I can't?"

"Very simply. For two reasons. First, you keep imagining that it would be horrible, if you did talk to this man, or anyone like him, if he rejected you. *This* is where you are self-hating: for, of course, if you did talk to him and he did throughly disapprove of you, it would only mean that he didn't like you, and not that *you* would have to dislike yourself. But clearly, you would dislike yourself if he rejected you—would you not?"

"I—I suppose I would."

"Which proves what I first said: that in spite of the fact that you like yourself in various ways—for your various good points and efficiencies—you still basically dislike yourself whenever anyone else thinks that you are not good enough for them."

"Doesn't everybody?"

"Almost everybody in our silly society, yes. But we're not talking about everybody now, but about you. The fact is that *you* dislike you. Instead of saying to yourself, 'Too bad; so he rejects me; I can still live happily without his acceptance,' you tell yourself, 'How terrible that he rejects me! How low I am because of his rejection.' And those sentences constitute your essential self-hatred, your low estimation of you."

"But how does that make me think that I *can't* talk to males?"

"That's the second point. After first thinking, quite irrationally, that you are no good if you do speak up with men and get rejected, you naturally withdraw from such speaking up, and practice silence or evasion. Time after time, when you think of speaking up, and when you even want to do so very much—as you did with the man at the lecture—you make yourself so uncomfortable by your fear of rejection that you run away from the situation and force yourself to shut your mouth. In fact, whenever you force yourself to keep still, at these times, you immediately feel relieved, comfortable."

"That's right. I do feel very comfortable as soon as I know that I can't say anything."

"*Can't,* hell! As soon as you *don't* say anything. And that, of course, your feeling comfortable temporarily when you don't say anything, gives you a great incentive for convincing yourself 'I can't, I can't!' For the more you are convinced that you *can't* speak up, the quicker you will give up trying, and the more comfortable you will (temporarily!) tend to be."

"Hmmm. I see. I reduce my conflict by keeping quiet; and because I know I am reducing my conflict, I have an incentive to quiet myself again and again. So I tell myself that I can't talk."

"Right. Moreover, what may be called 'false verification' soon tends to creep in. You keep telling yourself that you can't talk. Consequently you never do talk. Consequently you build up a long history of never talking. Finally, observing this history, but not observing the nuttiness that caused it, you falsely conclude: 'Well, because I never *have* talked, I obviously can't.' This is like saying, 'Well, because I never have eaten carrots, once I became convinced that they would harm my complexion, I can't eat them.' Can't, crap! Of course you can eat the carrots, if you tackled your idiotic fear of eating them; and of course you can talk to males, if you tackle your idiotic fear of talking to them."

"I never saw it that way before. I mean about my fearing to do the talking, and then getting a history of not doing it, and then using the history as a false proof of my not being able to do it."

"Oh, yes. That's very common among human beings. They don't do a thing, for one reason or another—usually a fear of some sort. Then they see that they've never done it. Then they falsely conclude that they can't. But, of course, they can. They just haven't ever tried. And, by convincing themselves that they can't, as we said before, they avoid the pain of trying, the conflict over trying. So they have a kind of double incentive to believe that they can't."

"And by believing that I can't, I've made myself this miserably lonely, haven't I?"

"Yes, that's the real irony. You avoid the conflict and pain of the moment, by not speaking to males, and by convincing yourself that you can't. But then you get the much greater pain of continually being alone at home and desperately wanting the telephone to ring, when of course it won't. So you produce, in the end, a much greater pain than the one you avoid in the beginning.

"That's what I really haven't seen, I guess: I can't afford to avoid the pain at the beginning, since then I'll bring on this loneliness at the end."

"Exactly! You get a very false gain when you avoid the initial pain of making contact with males. And you get a very real pain when you sit home alone, night after night, not doing what you'd most like to do—which is to be with them."

"I never saw that before."

"Are you seeing it very clearly right now? Do you see that there's simply no percentage in avoiding males, no matter how frightening it at first might be to talk to them, when you finally only avoid life itself and bring on the loneliness you desperately do not want?"

"Yes, I think I'm beginning to see it clearly."

"Fine! Now let's see how you can work on it, work on what you're seeing. By forcing yourself, if necessary, to talk to males whom you now say you *can't* possibly talk to."

Claudia, hesitatingly and slowly, did start to work on her new observations and insights, and within the next several months began to force herself to speak to some of the males who were eager to approach her. At first, she had quite a hard time of it; but, as I predicted, it soon became easier and easier, and eventually even enjoyable. And her sitting home alone became rare as she made more and more dates.

Fear of rejection, and the false concept of the impossibility of making involving moves toward males to which it so often leads, can similarly be tackled by anyone. The basic philosophy of the woman who fears social disapproval is that she will be downed as a person, proved to be a worthless individual, if she actually makes a social move and is rejected. This philosophy is obviously definitional: since her rejection by *others* hardly means that she has to reject *herself*. Nor does her refusal by A, B, and C, if it actually occurs, mean that she must inevitably be refused by X, Y, Z and everyone else in the world.

This does not mean that being rejected is a good thing, nor that you are not to feel sorry or sad when you lose out with a male to whom you would very much like to relate. Rejection is *bad,* normally; and it is highly appropriate for you to feel sorry about it (just as it is inappropriate, meaning self-defeating, for you to feel depressed or suicidal if a person whom you care for doesn't happen to care for you). So feel as sad or sorry as you like—at least for a while! But since you are still *you,* no matter how many times you are spurned by others, and since you still can in all probability find *someone* you like who will accept you, rejection is hardly a catastrophe—unless you, definitionally, *make* it so. And if you refuse, as you pigheadedly can refuse, to make it so, you will eliminate one of the most serious emotional blocks to dating and mating.

Overcoming basic fears and hostilities

It is difficult to say which of the two basic neuroticizing emotions, acute anxiety or strong hostility, most interferes with loving and mating but it is pointless to speculate which is the worse of these traits, since they are commonly intertwined. This can be exemplified by the case of Marion D., who had more than her fair share of both destructive feelings.

Marion's greatest fear was that she was both stupid and incompetent, that the people with whom she associated were soon going to find this out, and then would never want to have anything to do with her. Actually, she was quite bright (though hardly brilliant) and she managed her business and personal affairs unusually well, in spite of the fact that she had been forced (by her father's poverty) to quit school in the tenth grade and had never (largely because of her dire needs to keep socializing) been able to gain any great amount of self-education.

Like most of us, however, Marion made numerous mistakes and blunders in her everyday life, considered each one as absolute proof of her own idiocy, and blamed herself enormously for being imperfect. Moreover, when any of her attempts to maintain deep friendships failed, she never even considered that the people whom she chose might possibly be amiss, but always took all the responsibility for the breakup on her own shoulders, and excoriated herself for what had happened. Then, tiring of self-flagellation, she reviewed the events of the breakup all over again, and usually came to the opposite conclusion: namely, that the people with whom she had been involved had been one hundred per cent wrong—and that she herself was no damned good for continually becoming attached to such obviously wrong people.

To make matters still worse, Marion became so sensitive, after a while, to the fact that her relations with others might end disastrously that she began to look for the nasty traits of everyone with whom she came in contact. She would find that this person was too untidy, that one stupid, the next one vicious, etc. And not only would she come to believe strongly in her criticisms of others — which, as was to be expected, were sometimes justified and sometimes exaggerated—but she would voice these criticisms to her new lovers, within a few minutes of meeting them.

She did this so often, moreover, that soon these friends began to say to themselves: "My God! there she goes again. Isn't there *anyone* she likes? When will I be *next* on her hate list?" And, of course, they ceased to think seriously of her as a permanent partner, and often stopped seeing her entirely.

Since Marion was basically more frightened than angry, and since she usually went out of her way to be exceptionally nice to each new mate, she couldn't understand why she lost so many of them so quickly. She had a picture of herself as a weak, exploited person; and didn't recognize her defensive hostility even when it was occasionally brought to her attention.

"Me hostile?" she would incredulously ask. "Why, that's ridiculous. I haven't a hostile bone in my body. In fact, I'm much *too* nice—as all my friends will tell you." And she *was* too nice, but was also too hostile as well—as all of her friends would also tell you, but would never dare to tell her.

I had quite a time convincing Marion that she was not altogether sweetness and light; but finally, by showing her how many nasty cracks she had made to me about others, and how many hostile remarks she had also parenthetically passed about me when I contradicted her in any way, I helped her see that perhaps she did have a hostile side, and that if she ever wanted to meet the right man and get him to care for her permanently, she'd better do something about changing her hostile attitudes.

"But how can I stop being angry if I usually don't even see that I am?" she asked me one day.

"By stopping your self-blaming, so that you can then permit yourself to see how hostile you are."

"You mean that I won't face my anger against others, because if I did I'd view myself as the sort of a person I wouldn't like to be, and that I would blame myself terribly for being this sort of a person?"

"That's exactly what I mean. And I also mean that your self-moralizing tendencies cause you to be defensive in the first place, and to become highly critical of others when you think that you are merely being nice."

"How so?"

"Well, as we've said many times before, you think that you've simply *got* to be approved by almost everyone you meet, especially the men you go out with. And you'll do anything whatever to get this approval—such as helping your first husband in those crooked deals he pulled, and going along with your last lover even though you knew that he was living off you and making no effort to get a job."

"Yes, you're right. And I hated myself for remaining in both those relationships."

"Yes, that's your second-level self-hatred. After you have nauseatingly kowtowed to some man in order to win or to keep his love, you beat yourself savagely for making such a fool of yourself. But there's a first-level self-hatred that even comes before that."

"You mean, that I hate myself right at the start, even before I start to give up my soul to these men to keep their love, or I should say their so-called love, for me?"

"Right. You define yourself, even before you meet a new mate, as a worthless creature who can only achieve some value by being adored by some man. And you look frantically for such a man to adore you. Then, when he seems to do so for a while, you forget entirely that he may well be the worst possible one for you—as both your husband and your last friend certainly were—and you feel temporarily worthy and are sure that this is it, that now you're fixed up for all time. What you really mean is that a dunce and an incompetent like you has finally been tied up and glued together by some great person, and that as long as he is around to keep adding a little more glue and mending tape from time to time, you won't fall apart at the seams. But it's never *you* who feel good in yourself—only his continued presence and acceptance that gives you a modicum of goodness."

"How right you are! Even when I think I am loved, and am relatively happy for a while, I still feel that I barely can make it, and that if my friend leaves me and fails, as you put it, to keep adding more glue and mending tape, I can't make it any longer, and must go back to my chronic state of falling apart."

"Yes. So you *start* with a feeling of self-deprecation; and, in fact, you are often goaded into beginning an affair in order to convince yourself, at least for a short while, that you are really not as horrible as you basically think you are—because someone else finds you at least partially acceptable. But because you are such a moralist, and look for and exaggerate every flaw you may have, you feel comfortable (especially when a loving man is not, at the moment, around) by moralizing about others, too, and looking for and overemphasizing their deficiencies. You thereby become angry as well as anxious.

"Finally, as we said before, you temporarily find approval, demean yourself to retain this approval at all costs, and then become more self-hating—and more angry at the man you are demeaning yourself for and at the world in general. A vicious circle of self-blame, blaming others, more self-blame, and then more blaming of others.

"And I'd better break this entire cycle if I am to get somewhere in ridding myself of my hostility. Is that what you were going to point out?"

"Yes, that's just what I was going to point out. If you are to try to get rid of the hostility, but still keep your self-blaming tendencies, you are practically doomed to failure from the start. For you *will* be hostile toward others if you are so extremely self-critical; you *will* use against them precisely the same overly moralistic perfectionistic attitudes that you take toward yourself. What is more, as long as you demean yourself so severely, you will lose one lover after another—for why should any man respect a woman who has so little respect for herself?—and then you will tend to be angry toward these men.

"I'd better attack my self-blaming tendencies first, then."

"Correct. First things first: You'd better forego self-deprecation if you are to start to get anywhere with either your anxiety or your hostility."

Marion, like so many of my other clients, had quite a time tackling her self-immolating tendencies. Before she even recognized what she was doing, she would find that she was damning herself for her appearance, her talk, her manner of approach to people, her work methods, and almost everything else she did. Then, when she discovered that she was doing this blaming, she would blame herself for that—for the blaming. Then, when she found that she was still beating herself, and was consequently still neurotic, she would severely castigate herself for that—for still being neurotic.

Whenever Marion narrated a simple event in her life, even one that had a fortunate outcome, I could usually pick up the self-criticism in her tone or her gestures; and I had to watch my step in bringing this to her attention, since she would almost immediately agree with my interpretation, but then excoriate herself for still being a blamer. After several more weeks of getting her to review her perfectionistic philosophies and getting her determinedly—rather than blamefully!—to challenge and contradict them, she finally began to become less self-hating. She came to me one day and said:

"Boy, what an experience I had last night. Everything possible went wrong. I knew it was wrong to go out with this particular man, Ed, in the first place, since I could see at the start that he wasn't for me. But I liked his looks, closed my eyes to his faults, and went out with him anyway. Then I made every mistake in the books. I stayed up with him too late, though I knew I had to get up early in the morning, and kept reminding myself that I must bid him goodnight. I went to bed with him, even though I didn't want to do so; but I let him talk me into it, and knew as I was giving in that I was selling myself short, because I was afraid he would be hurt, instead of thinking of myself first. And I even found myself having sex, at first, without using any contraceptive, since I let myself be sold on his line that he was sterile and that nothing could happen—though I've heard *that* line before, and I know damned well that it's usually the bull. Anyway, I soon stopped that nonsense, and got up to put in my diaphragm.

"Aside from that, I can't think of a thing I did right the whole evening. Some foolishness! Anyway, what I really want to say— and to thank you for, incidentally—is that after he left, I was able to review everything that had happened, to agree that I had been almost one hundred percent wrong, and then *not* give myself a hard time about having been wrong. I don't know *when* I was able to do that sort of thing before! But I just said to myself, "Look! No more of this kind of crap. None of that stuff again." And I turned on my side and went to sleep. And here, after working all day and thinking about it from time to time, I'm still not blaming myself for anything I did. I was wrong, all right: there's no escaping that. O.K.: so I was wrong! But for once I'm thinking of the *next time*—and how I'll manage to be less wrong then. And that sort of thinking is certainly revolutionary in *my* life!"

That was the real beginning of Marion's "conversion" from rampant self-blaming to fairly consistent self-acceptance. Since then, she has continued to make progress in this direction; and, without consciously ever knowing what her problems were or how she was tackling them, the men in her life have somehow noted a distinct change in her attitudes and behavior. She still hasn't met the one man she wants, but she is getting along much better with those she dates and for the first time has had several proposals from men whom she did not quite want. Better yet, where her relations with males used to be a continuous series of hassles, with consequent hurt and bitterness on her part and theirs, she is now fully enjoying these relations and gaining fine experiences through having them.

So may you, too, if you are plaguing yourself with basic anxiety or hostility.

Overattachment to your own family

Having close ties to your parents, siblings, or other family members can be a rewarding and beautiful thing; but it can also be an interference with mating urges. For one think, it can be a dependency rather than a mature love relationship. Your parents raised you from the time you were a pup, and they frequently would like you to remain a charming, dependent puppy. They consequently may easily forgive you all your nastinesses, encourage you to be financially dependent, take special care of you when you are sick or low in spirits, and otherwise baby you when you are long past the chronological time of childhood.

Males, naturally, are *not* very likely to do the same. They expect you to be reasonably able to take care of yourself—and often, in fact, to help care for them as well. They want you to be something of a responsible, self-initiating woman, and not to be eternally demanding of their time and attention. Consequently, they may be harsh and rejecting where your parents or siblings are mollycoddling and lenient; and you may well be tempted, after a man has asked you in no uncertain terms to become independent, to run back to Mama and Papa. This is dangerous for several reasons.

1. There is no real safety in being attached to your family members. Your mother and father are inevitably twenty or thirty years older than you are, and will not be around forever. Your brothers and sisters, although closer to you in age, may easily marry, move to distant places, or otherwise desert you. Although you may therefore feel temporarily secure in your family's support, in the long run you may well defeat yourself by relying on it.

2. Even when your family members stay around forever and keep helping you, you won't avoid being underlyingly anxious. For to be dependent means to be incapable of helping oneself, of relying on one's own abilities; and anxiety, lack of self-confidence, and often acute self-hatred tend to follow from your knowledge that you have not learned to help yourself.

3. No matter how satisfying the love that you receive from your family members may be, it is rarely an adequate substitute for forming a good heterosexual loving relationship. Love that you build between yourself and a man has many important aspects—including, of course, the sexual aspects—that are necessarily going to be missing from interfamily relations. Just because your lover is, at the start, essentially a stranger to you, and because you may have to *work* at adjusting to and remaining happy with him, the intimacy that exists between you will be considerably different from that between you and your parents. Achieving a mated love is the kind of experience that radically differs from

attaining most other kinds of love relations; and it is generally a decidedly worthwhile kind of experience—even when it is not entirely successful.

Conjugal love and family love, moreover, are not mutually exclusive. There is no reason why you cannot maintain a high degree of intimacy with your family and have a satisfactory relationship with your lover or husband *too*. If you are so closely involved with the former that there is just no room for the latter, that is usually a clear-cut loss, and you are depriving yourself of one of life's great potential satisfactions. Similarly, if you have a highly involved egotism-a-deux involvement with your mate that excludes all kinds of other love relations (including, perhaps, those with your own children) that, also, may become a loss, since there is room in life for *several* different kinds of attachments.

For several reasons such as these, remaining overattached to your parents or siblings is a dangerous, albeit sometimes advantageous, state. You can oppose this state by continually asking yourself:

Do I really need to be dependent on my family; or can I not enjoy myself better by learning to rely more on my own judgment, my own initiative? *Is* it truly awful that I must adjust to a member of the other sex, when my parents will give in to me so easily and make such adjustment unnecessary? *Can* I live fully and happily by withdrawing from heterosexual involvements and remaining only "safely" involved with members of my own family? *Will* I be satisfied with a perpetual nonsexual love affair with my father or mother, when I can maintain that kind of relationship and work at making a satisfying sexual partnership too?

If you keep questioning and challenging the basic premises that lie behind your overinvolvement with your family members and your "sour grapes" mechanism of staying away from erotic and conjugal intimacy, you probably will be able to take the risks of courting and marrying a suitable male, and that you will thereby add considerably to your enjoyment of living and loving.

Fear of responsibility

Many men notoriously refrain from mating because of the responsibilities that they would have to assume, or at least think they would have to assume. For the same reason, and to a much greater degree than is usually imagined, many women also shy away from living with a man.

Some women, for example, do not think that they would be able to run a household properly. Some feel that they would make exceptionally poor mothers. Some feel that being a steady companion, or bedmate, or having to help their man's career would place too much burden on them; and that therefore they would be much better off living the relatively carefree and irresponsible life of a single woman.

Some of these women who object to mating because of its responsibilities are of course correct: A steady union is kind of serious. Both partners do have to accept various restrictions on their freedom. But, by the same token, they presumably derive advantages that are not easily found in any other kind of prolonged relationship.

If you, then, really feel that it is going to be too hard for you to buckle down to domestic responsibilities, and that you can live just as happily in a state of singleness, by all means think seriously of *not* mating. But you cannot have your cake without baking it; and if you want the benefits of mating—which most women, for one reason or another, seem to want—then gracefully accept its discomforts in order to gain these benefits. If you find yourself unduly emphasizing domestic inconveniences, then it may well be that you are either fearful that you will fail in courtship and mating, and hence be "hurt"; or that you are childishly rebelling against some of the necessary frustrations of any state of togetherness.

Here again, don't rail against mating or against those lousy males who make it so terrible. Neither mating nor men is the real problem: *you* are. For it is you who keep telling yourself sentences like: "If I take a chance on living with Jim, and it turns out that he expects too much of me, and I just can't live up to his expectations what a nincompoop I'd show myself to be, and how loathsome I would find myself!" And: "I just can't *stand* the difficulties of adjusting to a man. Why should living together *have to be* so hard?"

If you would look, even for a moment, at these internalized sentences that you keep feeding yourself, you might quickly find how silly and self-defeating they are. For if by any chance you don't measure up to Jim's expectations—and the probability is at least ten to one that you could if you stopped believing that it would be so awful if you didn't—you could surely, at worst, leave Jim and benefit considerably by the honest try you had made. Or if you actually did find domestic relations too hard—which, again, you probably wouldn't if you stopped complaining about the difficulty and settled down to making it easier on yourself— you could arrange to have a nondomestic affair, or could live by yourself with a bunch of cats, or could find various other solutions to your problems.

The main point is that mating is a real responsibility; but that responsibility is hardly a horror or an impending catastrophe. At worst, it is a pain in the neck. At best, it is a vital absorbing interest that gives you something significant to which to commit yourself.

Responsibility, it is true, involves the possibility of failure: since, try as you may, you may not be able to meet your responsibilities perfectly, and may be blamed by others who think that you should be perfect. All right: so you may fail. So did Leonardo, when he tried to invent the airplane! So did Edison, when he invented cinematography a short while after a couple of others had beaten him to it. In point of fact, not only *may* you fail; you damned well, in the long run, *will*. We—at least we who try—all fail. So we fail! But at least, if we keep trying, if we keep making an effort to be responsible, we are almost bound to have some successes. And a fair *proportion* of successes is all we can hope for in this life.

So stop your crap! If you fail to be a responsible wife to Jim or a fine mother to Joe's children, that's too bad. But if you fail to *try* to be a responsible mate or mother, that's much worse: that's not living, not being *you*. In mating as in most things in life: 'tis better to have tried to be responsible and lost, than never to have tried at all.

Homosexual tendencies

If we are to believe the Freudians, almost all men and women who are blocked in mating are, whether they are aware of the fact or not, homosexually inclined; and it is their latent homosexuality which panics them when they are faced with marital situations and which induces them to find various rationalizations for not living with a member of the other sex.

True? To a slight degree, yes. A few persons who believe that they are heterosexually inclined are actually homoerotically oriented; and a few of these are even led to their homosexuality by a classic Oedipus or Electra complex: that is, the males are so horrified at their unconsciously lusting after their mothers, and the females by their unwittingly wanting to copulate with their fathers, that having sex relations with any member of the other sex reminds them of their unconscious incest desires, and makes them shy away from heterosexuality.

This kind of latent homosexuality, however, is quite a rarity today. Millions of men and women are more or less homosexual—but most of them tend to be consciously so. These overt homosexuals either have conscious blocks against mating with women; or in a surprisingly large number of instances, they mate for non-sexual reasons—e.g., to have children, or to lead a more stable and safer existence than they would be leading in the "gay" world.

But to believe that the average male who does not want to mate is always or even often a latent homosexual is to be unusually gullible: since it is much more likely that he is highly heterosexual and that he has figured out, and with good reason, that he will have a more uninhibited life if he is unmated than if he were tied to one particular woman.

The same thing, of course, may go for you. If you are somewhat free of conventional sex shackles, you will soon find that, as a single woman, you are in demand as a bedmate, and that you can practically write your own ticket when you want to sleep with Tom or Dick or Harry. Marrying one of these males, however, generally coerces you into giving up the others; and this you may not particularly care to do. Your real block against mating, if you have one, may not be your "latent homosexuality," but your heterosexuality; and in order to overcome this, you will have to convince yourself that a ring on your finger is worth half a dozen rings on your doorbell by different men each week.

Suppose, however, you *do* happen to be homosexually inclined, and you find yourself looking at and thinking about other women instead of men; and suppose that, nonetheless, you want to marry and raise a family. What then?

What you can do first of all, in that case, is to determine *why* you are so strongly attracted to women and not to men. The fact that you may like females, and even enjoy them sexually, is not unusual or important: since humans, as I point out in *The Art and Science of Love* and *Sex and the Liberated Man,* are plurisexual animals, who can easily get sexually excited by men, women, children, animals, inanimate objects, and whatnot. But it may be significant and may bear investigation if you don't enjoy sex with men.

It isn't homosexual behavior that makes a woman act in a disturbed or aberrant manner, but her being compulsively attached to that behavior, and therefore not able to engage in other types of behavior as well. Compulsive sex activity means doing that activity in a rigid, *must*urbatory manner rather than in a preferential, self-choosing way. Consequently, if you have some inclination toward having sex with females or even if you prefer homosexual to heterosexual acts, that is not in itself peculiar or "abnormal" as long as you act in terms of choice or preference, not compulsively.

If you are fixated on lesbian relations, this kind of compulsion would probably exist for one or more reasons. Thus, (1) You might have had an early puritanical upbringing which led you to fear heterosexual relations and to experience extreme guilt about having heterosexual affairs; therefore, you might now compulsively attach yourself only to lesbian relations. (2) You might have had early sexual traumas, such as seduction or attack by an older man during your childhood; and your overreactions to these traumas might make you falsely believe that sex with males could not possibly be exciting or pleasant, and you might therefore hang yourself up on only allowing yourself to have lesbian affairs. (3) You might have had poor or negative relations with your father or brothers; and from these you might make the foolish generalization that virtually *all* men are "bad" and that you have to remain hostile for the rest of your life to all of them, and cannot possibly, therefore, have sex-love relationships with any male. (4) You might be so taken in by your society's discriminations against you and other females that you might again generalize and insist that you must be a thoroughly butch-type woman who withdraws from the usual kind of "feminine" pursuits and only winds up doing "masculine" lesbian things. (5) You might, because of your overwhelming feelings of inadequacy, wrongly conclude that you could not possibly succeed heterosexually, as other women can do; and you might therefore withdraw to lesbian pursuits where you think that you *can* succeed. (6) You might down yourself for your specific sexual "frigidity" or "inadequacy" and consequently withdraw from heterosexual affairs and stick one-sidedly only to homosexual interests and sexuality. (7) You might have a neurotic fear of having children or of serving as a competent wife and mother; and you might therefore turn yourself into a lesbian who "cannot" make it as a competent, responsible partner to a male.

All these—and a good many more—reasons for your driving yourself exclusively into homosexual relations and withdrawing completely from heterosexual relationships would largely stem from a few main irrational Beliefs (iB's) that you would convince yourself of at point B, after you had had some early, adolescent, or later Activating Experiences (at point A). These irrational Beliefs (ib's) would tend to consist of the ideas that (1) "I cannot do well at my sex-love relations with males; and therefore I am a pretty rotten or worthless individual and had better stay away from the entire field of heterosexuality" and/or (2) "I cannot stand the horrible frustrations and difficulties that men place in my way; and therefore to hell with the bastards, I can only make it with females!"

Compulsive lesbianism, in other words, like compulsive heterosexuality, usually stems from deep-seated feelings of heterosexual anxiety and/or hostility and/or low frustration tolerance. It is by no means (as some "authorities" still erroneously believe) a specifically inherited trait. And it rarely arises from early childhood training. Like other forms of compulsion, and like other forms of *severe* self-downing, it originates in irrational Beliefs (iB's) that a woman *herself* creates and maintains—albeit often with the cooperation of encouragement of other people. And, like these other forms of compulsivity, it can be ameliorated and cured.

Can you fight your compulsive lesbian tendencies, if you happen to have them, on your own, or with a competent psychotherapist? You certainly can. If you will look for and discover the irrational Beliefs from which these tendencies are derived, and if you will act against the compulsive emotions and behaviors to which these irrational Beliefs lead, you can overcome them, and either opt for preferential or noncompulsive homosexual behavior or for noncompulsive heterosexuality.

All of which leads us to a consideration of other types of interferences with sexuality: such as dyspereunia or painful intercourse. Do you find coitus painful or revolting?

Try it enough times, with the kind of man you really like, and see if it remains so. Do males make love poorly, and usually leave you unsatisfied and frustrated? Get a willing partner, and instruct him carefully exactly what to do in order to satisfy you. Or seek an experienced lover who is only too willing to try those sex practices which especially send you. Continual practice at deindoctrinating yourself from the antimasculine or antisexual irrationalities that you have been consciously or unconsciously indoctrinating yourself with for years, and at forcing yourself to do and keep doing the sexual acts which you have previously avoided with males—this kind of practice will usually overcome your lesbian compulsions, if you really want to overcome them.

And if this kind of practice doesn't work? Then you are obviously not doing it correctly, and can get professional help. See an experienced psychotherapist—one who is *not* a classical Freudian, but who will actively-directively help you in a reasonable amount of time—and work with him to enjoy heterosexuality.

Attachments to ineligible males

In the course of my seeing hundreds of females during the last twenty years who say that they definitely want to mate but who have never got very close to doing so, I have found that one of the most common and serious blocks is the selection by these females of obviously ineligible males, followed by their compulsive attachment to them.

Gertrude R. is an excellent case in point. She was thirty-five when she first came to see me; was one of the few truly beautiful (as distinguished from pretty or attractive) women I have met; and was well-educated and highly cultured. Yet she had only been proposed to by a few males, who patently were not for her, and had never been asked to live with those men to whom she was considerably attracted.

Gertrude's problem was that she insisted on becoming attached to highly dedicated men who were more interested in their work than they were in her or in marriage. She found their dedication to some project or cause most appealing; and she also thought it a challenge to try to win a man who was so devoted to something outside himself.

At first, Gertrude usually succeeded: since the men she chose would become attracted to her, would willingly enter enter into a passionate affair, and would even neglect their work—for a while. But sooner or later they would be back at their central activity and their interest in her would wane. This she thought she could not stand, and would make herself miserable about. Instead, however, of leaving such a man, and going on to a more suitable lover, Gertrude would prolong the affair for months and months, trying to win back his attention and devotion; and the more she tried, the more her lovers would find her a real bother, and would want to break off the relationship. Eventually, they did; whereupon, she would look for a similar man again, and get herself into the same kind of bind.

Gertrude had two kinds of problems with men: (a) picking the wrong kind of man for her own mating requirements; and (b) staying with him much too long. The first of these characteristics might not have been so fatal if it had not been combined with the second but both together were poisonous. To make one of these errors is human; to make both of them is inhumanity to oneself.

There are many wrong kinds of choices that you can make in your love partnerships. Men, for example, who are many years older than you are will tend to be settled in their ways, already tied to previous wives and children, and often afraid to take on a much younger woman. Men who are several years younger than you will commonly be reluctant to mate even though they may find you a delightful companion and bed partner.

Men who are married will (as we noted in a previous chapter) frequently promise you the earth and the sky — and yet somehow will not break away from their wives. Men who are exceptionally handsome will sometimes be so spoiled and so adept at finding easy sex-love consorts, that they will be loath to mate. Men who are unusually wealthy will also have easy access to women and will sometimes be afraid that females want them primarily for their money. Men who are outstandingly talented may very well be (like Gertrude's lovers) so devoted to their talents that they have little time and energy for serious involvements.

This does not mean, now, that *none* of these males would make good partners. A man who is much older than you may be, just because he appreciates your youth and beauty, a more considerate and more loving mate than someone who is only a few years your senior. A man who is five or more years younger than you may find you more attractive than he finds women of his own age; and he may become a devoted and faithful husband.

In any given case, therefore, you should by all means consider the possibility of living with someone who, at first blush, looks like he would not make the best possible mate for you. Although mixed marriages, especially those between a devout member of one religion and an equally devout member of a different religion, are *generally* inadvisable, since they lead to additional difficulties which may not be present in unmixed marriages, they occasionally work out very well. By the same token, you may select a much older, a much younger, a much married, or a much work-preoccupied man and just happen to pick the right one for you.

Nonetheless: a man who has serious objections to mating, for any reasons whatever, usually is not usually going to change his mind within a reasonable short length of time; and even if he does, there is an excellent chance that he will not make a steady partner. When, therefore, you find that your current lover is not inclined to mate and that he probably will not change his inclinations your best bet may be to get the deuce away from him—and quickly! The longer you stay, the more you will tend to become attached, and the more deep-seated will become your habit patterns of being with him. No matter how great the *immediate* wrench of leaving him may be, you may be happier in the long run by breaking away and becoming involved with another man, one who offers the prospect of greater permanency.

Blocks to getting away from an ineligible male in a decently short period of time usually include: (a) convincing yourself that you simply *can't* live without him; (b) deluding yourself that he *will* be yours if you simply hang on to him long enough; (c) fearing that you just won't be able to get any other worthwhile man if you let this one go out of your life; (d) telling yourself that even though you could get another man, it would just be too much of a hassle getting back into the rat race and going to the trouble of meeting and winning him; and (e) believing that with all his faults, there just isn't nor ever will be anyone like the present man, and that therefore any possible substitute for him would be blah and unsatisfactory.

Virtually all these excuses—and many more like them which you may cook up to rationalize your staying with an ineligible male—are variations on the same major theme: namely, that you are really an awful hunk of garbage and that *therefore* you can't live without this man, can't get a better one, and might just as well not go to any trouble to try to get a man who would, as soon as he knew you, find out what garbage you were and refuse, just as this present one is doing, to unite with you.

If you believe this kind of rot, then your belief in it—and concomitant lack of belief in yourself—will actualize *what* you believe. If you tackle and challenge it you will see that it is not *you* who are incapable of winning a worthy companion, but that it is the false and self-deprecated "you" who will fail yourself.

Devotion to nonmarital interests

A great many women block themselves from mating by claiming that while they would be delighted to have a man and a family, their careers do not allow them the time or the opportunity to meet suitable prospects; and they let all their good chances pass by. Some are devoted to careers, such as medicine or teaching. Some spend large amounts of time pursuing a sport, such as tennis or swimming. Others are devoted bridge players, or church leaders, or amateur thespians.

Not only do some of these interest-absorbed females take time away from their social-sexual involvements to give to their careers or hobbies, but in many instances they virtually remove themselves from the society of eligible males in pursuing these interests. Thus, a woman who is a pediatrician will spend practically all her time with mothers and their young children. And a woman who is devoted to training horses or raising cats is not likely to find a suitable mate among the four-legged creatures with whom she fondly relates!

Feminine careers and vital absorptions, moreover, sometimes repulse men. Even among the relatively enlightened of today's males, nineteenth-century notions of male-female division of labor are sometimes prevalent. Some men, consequently, take a dim view of a woman's not being home to prepare meals when they come home from the office; and the fact that she may be saving patients' lives or winning a bridge championship is small comfort to them when they think in these old-fashioned ways.

What, then, is the vitally absorbed contemporary woman to do—give up all thought of having a career or an intense interest? Or stick to jobs and hobbies—such as joining the Woman's Army Corps or playing in chess tournaments—where she is likely to encounter a good many eligible males?

The first of these choices would be distinctly unhealthy, because (as we have previously noted) a woman's devotion to a career or an avocational interest is usually a sign of emotional health. Such devotion provides her with the very preoccupation that saves her from being overabsorbed with finding and winning a male, and from being frantically concerned with her love life.

Women who expend much of their time and energy pursuing some long-range project or goal may possibly have difficulty mating; but there is no evidence that they lead less happy lives than do millions of women who mate, but who never find a vital absorption outside of their relationships.

Indeed, a case could be made for the hypothesis that marriage-centered women are usually not as happy as career-centered women, and that if a female could have only one of these two central choices to make during her lifetime, she would be wiser to pick an intensely involving career.

Fortunately, however, this kind of either-or choice is not mandatory. It is quite possible, if a female plans her life intelligently, for her to have both.

You can manage this in either of two fairly common ways: first, by mapping out a major career or avocational interest and, while going about preparing for or working at this field, also managing to find and win a suitable mate who will not too seriously object to and interfere with your life's work. Second, by turning your efforts mainly toward mating and perhaps raising a family, and then, especially when your children are somewhat grown, devoting yourself to some significant field of endeavor and becoming an absorbed worker in this field.

Although the first of these choices is perhaps preferable—since it enables a woman to make an early start in her career and gives her a greater opportunity to get the proper training to follow it adequately—the second choice also has advantages, and is not to be minimized as a possible solution to this important problem.

The difficulty that often arises in connection with a woman's marrying and retaining outside interests is that of one-sidedness or of emotional blocking. Thus, she may become so absorbed, during her late teens and early twenties, with some arduous career or avocation that she may carelessly assume that her dating and mating will take care of themselves.

Driven to study hard, or to work long hours, such a woman

may forego dates, social affairs, dances, and other usual ways of getting to know and to become intimate with eligible males; and before she knows it, she finds that she is in her late twenties or early thirties, and that most of the males whom she would have found suitable are now husbands and fathers, while those who remain are hardly the best bets.

On the other side of the fence, a career-bound woman may at first try hard enough, even when she is in the midst of pursuing her vocational goals, to meet suitable males, and may do almost as well as her less career-minded sisters. But just as soon as a few affairs go sour—which, statistically speaking, is par for the course of love, she may feel so hurt and bitter that she *then* begins to use her vocational interests as an excuse for keeping herself from further courting.

If, especially, this career woman is not quite as bright or attractive as some other females, she may find herself handicapped in finding the kind of male she would like. Then, instead of doing everything possible to make up for her handicaps (such as making sure that she meets *more* men and makes *greater* efforts to charm them), she may take the "easier" way out, throw herself all the more into her career, and delude herself that this is the only thing that she really wants.

If you are unusually devoted to a career or to some other outside interest, and find that this devotion is interfering with your mating, what can you do? The first thing you can do is to review your basic interests, particularly in terms of timing. Is it, for example, absolutely necessary that you become the greatest physician or physicist who ever lived *right now*? Must you devote practically all of your *present* energies to getting ahead? Could you not, instead, work at a somewhat slower, though still steady, pace, and manage to get into some more social-sexual activity, too? And could you not plan, *after* you had managed to mate and perhaps even to have a child or two, to go full steam ahead in your chosen profession?

Various other aspects of your vital absorption may also be scheduled to fit in better with your love and marital goals. If, for example, you are determined to be a physician, one branch of medicine (such as, say, internal medicine) may be a better field in which you might make social-sexual contacts than another field (say, pediatrics). Or taking a job in a large hospital, where there are eligible male residents, might be better than taking one in a small hospital.

If this kind of practical timing and scheduling does not help, because you have more severe emtoional blocks concerned with your profession or vital interest, you can uncover and uproot the irrational philosophies of life that lie behind these blocks. Florence B. found that she was avoiding serious involvements with males because she was too occupied with studying to be a clinical psychologist and she felt sure that her work at school suffered whenever she carried on an active dating and courting pattern. Therefore, she preferred to put off almost all social activities until she had obtained her Ph.D. and was occupationally secure.

When Florence's motives for being a psychologist were psychotherapeutically investigated, however, she discovered that a good part of her interest stemmed from considering herself an inadequate person who had no good reason for living unless she devoted herself to others. Consequently, she had chosen clinical psychology as a profession, even though she personally preferred experimental work, so that she could have a picture of herself as a helping individual who made herself useful to others, and hence rated as worthwhile.

Florence also discovered, as we checked into her love-avoiding behavior, that she placed so little value on herself as a person in her own right that she was sure that no good man would accept her unless she did something outstanding—unless he could proudly introduce her to others as *Doctor* So-and-So. Both as an individual and as a potential mate, then, she believed that it was necessary for her to earn her right to existence and happiness by devoting her life to the service of others.

"I'm beginning to see it clearly now," she said to me during her ninth psychotherapy session. "I really think that in *myself* I have no purpose, and that I must make such a purpose by taking care of others and winning their undying appreciation. So why, with this set of beliefs, should I try to win a husband or to have children who would be good for *me* and make *me* happy? I only deserve to be happy when I am good to *others*. No wonder I have never tried to get what *I* want in life or to build the kind of relationship with a man that I would want for myself!"

"Yes, you are beginning to see this quite clearly," I agreed. "You've been doing this sort of thing all your life; but now you *see* what you have been doing; and now you can *stop* doing it. How, precisely, are you going to get around to stopping it?"

"Well, I'll tell you one thing I'm going to do, just as soon as the school term starts again. And that is to change my course immediately, get out of clinical psych—which may be all right for others but which is just not the thing for me—and get into experimental. Fortunately, I haven't gone so far yet that I will have lost very much by starting in clinical. But even If I had, I'd definitely change. After all, I'll probably be working in this field for another thirty or forty years. And I'm determined, now, to work at something that *I* definitely want to do during that long period of time.

"My parents, I'm sure, won't like it at all, my changing. They'd much rather see me as a practicing clinician than working with smelly rats. But that's *their* problem, and I don't intend to be unduly influenced by it. They'll just have to accept me as I am, rats and all!"

"And what will you do about men?"

"There, too, I'm determined to stop my nonsense and at least give myself a decent *chance* to get what I want. Maybe I never will get it, since my standards will probably remain pretty high, and I don't intend to live with *any* male who comes along and wants me. But I do intend to keep looking and looking—and for someone *I* want and who will accept me pretty much as I am.

"If any of my boyfriends, like my parents, want me to be a practicing psychologist, rather than an experimentalist, in order that *they* may boast to their friends what kind of a wife they have, so much the worse for them. There must be someone who will want me the way I am, even without my being of great and noble service to others, and that's the someone I'm going to look for. And, you know, this time, somehow, there's just something new in me that tells me that one of these days I'll find him."

Not all emotional blocks connected with vocational preoccupations are the same as Florence's. But many are. Behind the drive to get ahead in one's career, even at the cost of sacrificing love and mating, sometimes lurks a low estimation of oneself, with the concomitant conviction that one is not worthy of a good man unless and until one "proves" oneself vocationally and thereby wins his and also the world's esteem.

If you are mixed up in this regard, look into your own heart for your personal self-negating views. Do you think that you *must* succeed at work in order to be a worthwhile person? Do you feel that you simply *can't* get what you want in love until you have proven yourself in your career? If so, you'd better start forcefully asking yourself *why.* *Why* must you be a great career-woman to

be an estimable love partner or a worthy human? Who said so?
Why are you not deserving of the kind of sex-love relationship
you desire merely because you are you? Who said you aren't?
And who the hell is he or she who said it?

11

The Intelligent Person's Guide to Stubbornly Refusing to Make Yourself Miserable About Anything

Although this book is primarily addressed to women, and to helping yourself as a woman get what you want in the realm of dating and mating, it also is something of a primer on how you can use rational-emotive therapy (RET) as a self-help procedure when you are bothered by—or, rather, when you bother yourself with—virtually any emotional problem. As I note in one of the talks that I gave at the Institute for Rational Living in New York (it is available on the cassette recording, *How to Stubbornly Refuse to Make Yourself Miserable About Anything),* although life presents us with a fairly large amount of hassles and frustrations, we *choose* to take these difficulties overly seriously and we thereby *elect* or *decide* to make ourselves miserable (instead of merely sorry and annoyed) about these difficulties.

This is unethical! It is bad enough that we frequently have little or no control over the troubles and impediments that are placed in our way that often block us from fulfilling our healthiest and sanest desires. But it is far worse when we ourselves inanely and insanely place extra obstacles in our own paths and react with such agitation to the problems that others present that we gratuitously defeat ourselves and consequently obtain much less of what we want than is actually available.

Emotional self-sabotaging is highly immoral. For ideal morality consists of our first deciding that we want to live happily in the course of the one life that we most probably will ever have, and of our concomitantly deciding that we would also prefer to live enjoyably with other humans, and at least partly arrange for their happiness as well as our own. As Alfred Adler pointed out more than half a century ago, self-interest includes and abets social interest. If we are *entirely* obsessed with our own navels and therefore neglectful of other humans, we help create the kind of world in which we personally would not want to live, and we sabotage some of our most cherished goals.

RET, therefore, tries to help you get what you most want in life—including good relationships with others and including your abiding by the usual rules of social morality and thereby helping to fashion and maintain the kind of culture in which you would desire to live. And when I say "you," I automatically include, of course, your friends, your relatives, and your lover or lovers. For the more you help your close associates cope with themselves and their problems, the more mutually enjoyable are likely to be your contacts with them.

This book, then, is for intelligent women, but it is also for intelligent men. If you will use its principles correctly and persistently, you will probably help yourself considerably with your dating, mating, and other important problems. But consider your partners, too! The men you date can probably use the main teachings of RET just as you can. Don't hesitate to encourage them to read this book; and even consider reading portions of it aloud with them, and discussing some of the main points that have been presented in these pages.

As noted above, making yourself miserable is really unethical. As long as you live in a limited society with other fallible humans, you will be frustrated and hassled to a considerable degree; and not merely occasionally or rarely: all of your life. But you *don't* have to keep seriously upsetting yourself *about* the trials and tribulations of dating, mating, socializing, earning a living, building a career, improving your community, finding avocational enjoyments, or anything else. That kind of self-immolation, once again, is your *choice*, your *decision*. And you always have better emotional alternatives!

In this final chapter of a book largely designed to help you with the problems of dating and mating, let me go one step further and present some of the more general principles of RET that you can apply to just about any aspects of your life—and that can also be applied, if he wants to use them, by any man that you decide to mate with. You *can*, if you wish and if you work your butt off at implementing this determined wish, refuse to make yourself miserable about virtually anything that will ever occur—in the course of your entire lifetime. How? By admitting that you create your own misery. By seeking out the basic irrational Beliefs or underlying philosophies by which you make yourself anxious, depressed, hostile, and self-downing. By experimenting with oher Beliefs and with active pathways of implementing these Beliefs. By forcing yourself to change your emotions and your actions, no matter how uncomfortable you may at first feel in doing so, until you become comfortably adjusted to less self-defeating and more enjoyable ways of living. By working—yes, working, working, working!—at implementing your thinking about yourself and your planning to change your feelings and your behavior. And by following, as well as you can by yourself, and with a professional therapist if your own efforts are not sufficient, the rational-emotive teachings outlined in this book.

As a kind of summary of some of these main teachings, let me outline the main irrational Beliefs that you (and virtually all humans) frequently indoctrinate yourself with and that thereafter interfere with your healthy emotional and joy-producing functioning. Then I shall close with a set of cognitive, emotive, and activity-oriented rules by which you, and your lover, may recognize and cast aside these self-sabotaging irrationalities.

What are some of the fundamental irrational ideas that you may hold that will almost inevitably lead you to feel anxious, guilty, depressed, inadequate, or hostile? In my earlier writings, such as *Reason and Emotion in Psychotherapy* and the original edition of *A Guide to Rational Living*, written by Dr. Robert A. Harper and myself, ten or twelve basic irrationalities are listed that tend to lead to human disturbance. In my later writings, including *How to Live With—and Without—Anger* and the *Handbook of Rational-Emotive Therapy*, I emphasize three major irrational Beliefs, but each of them has several subheadings. These Beliefs may be outlined as follows:

> *Irrational Idea No. 1:* "I MUST do well and HAVE TO win the approval of others, especially of males in whom I am seriously interested, or else I will rate as a ROTTEN PERSON!"

1a. "I MUST have sincere love and approval almost all the time from virtually all the people who I find significant or important."

1b. "I MUST prove myself a thoroughly competent and adequate achiever or at least have a real skill or talent in something important to me."

1c. "I MUST succeed in avoiding noxious or unpleasant situations. My emotional misery comes almost completely from external pressures that I have little ability to change or control. Unless these pressures change, I cannot help making myself feel anything but anxious, depressed, self-downing, or hostile."

1d. "I MUST never encounter events that put me in real danger or that threaten my life, as I would have to make myself totally preoccupied with and upset about them."

1e. "I MUST continue to think, feel, and behave as I have in the past. My past life influenced me immensely and remains crucial today because if something once strongly affected me, it must continue to determine and affect my present feelings and behavior. My early childhood gullibility and conditioning still remain, and I cannot surmount these tendencies and truly think for myself without being strongly swayed by early influences."

1f. "I MUST find a high degree of order, certainly, or predictability in the universe in order to feel comfortable and to perform adequately."

1g. "I MUST continue to rely and depend on other people. Because I remain weak in this respect, I shall also continue to need and to rely on certain forms of superstitions and religious ideas in order to survive times of great stress."

1h. "I MUST understand the nature and secrets of the universe to live happily in it."

1i. "I can and SHOULD give myself a global rating as a human, and I can rate myself as good and worthy ONLY if I perform well, do worthwhile things, and have people generally approve of me."

1j. "I MUST never make myself depressed, anxious, ashamed, or angry, for if I do give in to these feelings of disturbance, I become a thoroughly weak and rotten person since I then perform incompetently and shamefully."

1k. "I MUST never question the beliefs, attitudes, or opinions held by respected authorities or by my society, family, or peer group because they certainly are valid. If I do question them, people should rightly condemn and punish me."

If you hold the above irrational Beliefs (iB's) or similar ones, you will often to make yourself feel anxious, depressed, guilty, ashamed, and self-hating. If you hold the following iB's you will tend to make yourself feel angry, over-rebellious, hostile, and homicidal:

Irrational Idea No. 2: "Others MUST treat me considerately and kindly and in precisely the way I want them to treat me. If they don't, society and the universe should severely blame, damn, and punish them for their horrible behavior!"

2a. "Other people MUST treat everyone, but especially me, in a fair and considerate manner. If they act unfairly and inconsiderately, they are rotten people who deserve punishment and damnation, which society should see that they get."

2b. "Other people MUST not behave incompetently or stupidly. If they do, they are thorough idiots who ought to feel ashamed of themselves and who deserve none of the good things in life."

2c. "People who have the ability to perform well MUST not choose to shirk or avoid their responsibilities. They absolutely OUGHT to accept and carry out their duties. They are thoroughly rotten and should feel utterly ashamed of themselves if they don't. People MUST achieve their potential for a happy and worthwhile life, or else they have no real human worth or value."

2d. "Other people MUST not unjustly criticize me! If they do, they are rotten people who deserve practically nothing good in life!"

Finally, in its newer formulations, rational-emotive therapy (RET) posits a third major irrational Belief (iB) that leads to a low frustration tolerance, discomfort anxiety, and self-pity:

Irrational Idea No. 3: "The world (and the people in it) MUST arrange the conditions under which I live so that I get everything that I want when I want it! And, further, conditions MUST exist so that I practically never get what I don't want. Moreover, I usually MUST get what I want quickly and easily, without having to work too hard to get it."

3a. "Things MUST go the way I would like them to go because I NEED what I want and life is AWFUL, HORRIBLE, and TERRIBLE when I do not get what I NEED!"

3b. "I MUST continually preoccupy myself thinking about dangers or about fearsome people or things and upset myself about them. In that way, I increase my power to control or change them. And I MUST control or change them!"

3c. "I MUST avoid, rather than face and deal with, many of life's difficulties and responsibilities since I NEED immediate comfort and cannot discipline myself or go through present pain to achieve future gain."

3d. "People SHOULD act better than they do; and if they act badly or create needless hassles for me, they are AWFUL and HORRIBLE; and I CAN'T STAND the difficulties which they thereby create!"

3e. "I MUST continue to suffer endlessly if I have handicaps. I can do practically nothing to overcome any serious handicaps, and life is so HORRIBLE when I have them that it is hardly worth living!"

3f. "I MUST not have any difficulty in changing obnoxious or unpleasant things in my life! Such difficulties OUGHT not exist! I find it TOO HARD to do anything about them, and I might as well not try to change them since the situation is more or less hopeless!"

3g. Justice, fairness, equality, and democracy MUST prevail; and when any condition is unfair to me, I CAN'T STAND it and life seems too unbearable to continue!"

3h. "I MUST find correct and perfect solutions to my problems and to those of other people for whom I care! If I don't, castastrophe and horror will surely ensue!"

3i. "I MUST remain a helpless victim of anxiety, depression, feelings of anxiety, and hostility unless the conditions that cause my misery change and allow me to stop feelings disturbed."

3j. "Since I was born into this world and still manage to stay alive, my life MUST continue forever or for just as long as I want it to continue! I find it completely unfair and HORRIBLE to think about the possibility of dying and of no longer having any existence. I also find it horrible to think about the death of those whom I love. Death, except for my enemies, MUST not exist!"

3k. "As long as I remain alive, my life MUST have some unusual or special meaning or purpose; and if I cannot create such a meaning or purpose for myself, the universe or some supernatural or magical force in it MUST create it for me!"

3l. "I CANT' STAND uncomfortable feelings like anxiety, depression, guilt, and shame; and if I really went crazy and found myself in an institution, I could never stand that horror or make the adjustment back to normal life."

3m. "When things have really gone badly for me for a period of time and when there are no guarantees that they will change or that anyone will make life better for me, I simply CAN'T BEAR the thought of living any longer and may seriously contemplate killing myself!"

Most of the irrational ideas just listed are an integral part of our culture and are continually propounded to us by our parents, teachers, clergymen, fairy tales, books, TV shows, films, stage dramas, etc. But that is NOT the main reason, probably, why we believe them. We mainly subscribe to them because we have strong innate tendencies, as humans, to invent them: to think in absolutistic, MUSTurbatory ways. Our parents and our culture, in fact, mainly teach us standards—tell us what is DESIRABLE and PREFERABLE to do and not to do. Such as: try to mate with an attractive, strong, productive man. Such as: get good marks in school and have something of a career of your own. Such as: learn to enjoy sex and have intense orgasms with your partners.

Some of these standards are sensible and realistic; and some of them are not. But as long as we keep them as DESIRES and

PREFERENCES, we are not likely to get into serious trouble. For if we then mate with the wrong man, fail in school, and never have a single orgasm, those things may be UNdesirable and UNpreferential—but they obviously won't kill or maim us.

Just like our parents did before us, however—because, again, we are HUMAN and are NATURAL crooked-thinkers—we inflate innumerable desires and preferences into MUSTS, SHOULDS, and OUGHTS, into NEEDS AND NECESSITIES. And that is where our irrational Beliefs (iB's) mainly come from: our own crooked thinking, our own MUSTurbation, though aided, to be sure, by social rules and customs, by superstitions and unrealistic expectations modeled for us on our mass media screens and printed pages.

If you insist, then, on accepting the nutty ideas of your parents and your culture, and you insist on creating more crazy ideas of your own, you will almost certainly make yourself guilty, ashamed, anxious, self-downing, and hostile.

Instead of creating or sticking with, the kinds of irrational Beliefs just outlined, can you acquire a reasonably sane philosophy that will help you live with a minimum of anxiety and hostility, and keep you from seriously blocking yourself emotionally. Yes, there is such a philosophy, and many of our wisest thinkers—such as Epictetus and Marcus Aurelius in ancient times, Spinoza in the seventeenth century, and Bertrand Russell, Robert S. Hartman and Paul Tillich in modern times—have outlined some of its main tenets. After many years of studying the views of these sages and of doing intensive psychotherapy with hundreds of individuals, I would summarize a good working philosophy in these terms:

> I. Do not try to eradicate all or even most of your wish for approval and love by others, since humans are animals who naturally and normally thrive on warmth. But do try to eradicate your inordinate, all-consuming love *needs*. Realize that true self-respect does not come from the plaudits of others but from accepting yourself and following your own fundamental interests *whether or not* others approve of your doings.

> 2. When you are not appreciated or approved by those you care for admit that this is annoying and frustrating but refrain from convincing yourself that it is horrible and catas-

trophic. To the extent that it is desirable and practical for you to win the love of others, try to do so in an intelligent, planful way rather than in a frantic, hit-and-miss manner. To this end, realize that one of the best methods of winning love is unstintingly to give it.

3. Try to *do* things that you enjoy rather than kill yourself insisting that you must do well. Focus on savoring the *process* rather than only the result of what you do. When you do try to perform well—which is permissible, since there are real advantages from succeeding at certain events—do not insist on always doing *perfectly* well. Try, on most occasions, for *your* best rather than *the* best; and try to do well for your *own* sake rather than to please or to best *others*.

4. Learn to welcome your mistakes and errors—rather than to become horrified at them—and thereby to put them to good account. Make yourself practice, practice and practice the things you want to succeed at; often force yourself to do what you are afraid to fail at doing; and fully accept the fact that humans are limited ainimals and that you, in particular, have distinct fallibilities.

5. Do not criticize or blame others for their misdeeds (although you may point out to them their mistakes), but realize that they usually err out of stupidity, ignorance, or emotional disturbance. Try to accept people when they act stupidly and to help them when they behave ignorantly or in a disturbed manner.

6. When people blame you, first ask whether you have really done anything wrong; and if you have, try to improve your behavior. Don't condemn yourself. If you made the mistakes of which you are accused try to realize that other people's criticism is often *their* problem and stems from defensiveness or disturbance on their part.

7. Try to understand *why* people act the way they do. Try to see things from *their* frame of reference when you think they are behaving badly. If there is no way of changing them (as is all to frequently true!) convince yourself that it is too bad that people are the way they are, but that's all it is— too bad. It is *not* terrible, horrible, or catastrophic.

8. When frustrating or painful circumstances raise, determine whether they are truly annoying or whether you are imagining or highly exaggerating their irritating qualities. If certain circumstances are distinctly unpleasant, do your best to face and to work at improving them. If you cannot for the present, improve conditions, philosophically accept them or resign yourself to their existence. Instead of convincing yourself that you *can't stand* these conditions, show yourself that it's too bad that they exist, but that you *can* gracefully lump them.

9. Whenever you believe that people are bothering or upsetting you, ask yourself whether it is they who are disturbing you or whether it is *your* atttitude toward them that is causing you to be upset. Track down your anxieties and hostilities to the exclamatory sentences that *you* keep telling yourself *about* various irritating persons and things; think about these sentences; and logically parse and forcefully question and challenge them until you become convinced that they are definitional, contradictory, and untenable.

10. Realize that practically all your worries are caused not by external dangers that may occur but by your telling yourself "Wouldn't it be awful *if* this danger occurred?" Instead of continuing to worry endlessly about something, force yourself to examine your catastrophizing sentences and to change them for the saner and more realistic philosophy: "It would be a distinct nuisance or a bad thing if this danger occurred; but it would *not* be awful, and I *could* cope with it if I had to do so."

11. Recognize that most of your anxieties arise from the fear of what others think of you; and question and challenge this fear and make yourself see how silly it is. Realize that it certainly may be inconvenient if So-and-So does not like you or thinks you are wrong; but that that's *all* it normally is: inconvenient.

12. As often as possible, actually *do* the things you are most afraid to do—such as speaking in public, telling your lover what you really think about something, or standing up for your own rights—in order to prove to yourself that there *is* nothing frightful about doing these things. Force yourself,

as much as you can, to be *yourself,* rather than some pale reflection of what you think *others* would like you to be.

13. Uncomplainingly do desirable but onerous tasks no matter how much you dislike doing them, while at the same time figuring out intelligent methods of avoiding the unnecessarily painful aspects of living. If, at present, you have to work at an unpleasant job in order to earn a living, that's tough: you'd better do it. But there's no reason why you can't plot and scheme so that in the future you *won't* have to do this kind of work.

14. If you find that you are goofing on various life problems and responsibilities, don't carelessly assume that you are just naturally "lazy," but realize that behind such goofing there usually exists a chain of your own anxious or rebellious sentences.

15. Accept the fact that your past experiences didn't make you disturbed but possibly helped to influence you in some ways. But also acknowledge that *your present is your past of tomorrow* and that, by working at and changing this present, you can make your future significantly different from, and in many ways more satisfactory than, today.

This, in simple outline, is a rational way of living—and one that will, if you follow it, not only prevent you from being emotionally blocked in regard to dating and mating, but will help you to rid yourself of other anxieties and hostilities. For a more detailed description of the techniques for disputing irrational beliefs you may refer to the appendix.

Being neurotic is exceptionally difficult, and requires immense amounts of time and effort. It *seems* easy to be continually anxious and hostile; but it's really quite a job—and one that pays worse than any other known form of occupation. If, therefore, you must work so hard at destroying yourself, and blocking your own fondest sex-love desires, don't you think that it might well be worth at least a little effort to *stop* the nonsense you keep telling yourself to create and maintain your neurotic blocks?

Why not try it and see?

Bibliography

Items in this bibliography that are preceded by an asterisk (*) are particularly directed toward the principles and practice of rational-emotive therapy and rational living. Most of these starred items can be ordered from the Institute for Rational Living, Inc., 45 East 65th Street, New York, N.Y. 10021, which continues to make available these and other materials, as well as to present talks, seminars, workshops, and other presentations in the area of human growth, sexuality, and rational living. Interested readers may send for its current list of publications and events.

Adler, Alfred. *What life should mean to you.* New York: Putnam, 1931, 1959.

*Alberti, R. E., & Emmons, M. L. *Your perfect right..* San Luis Obispo, California: Impact, 1971.

Anderson, Camilla M. *Saints, sinners and psychiatry.* Portland, Ore.: Durham Press, 1962.

Ansbacher, Heinz, & Ansbacher, Rowena. *The individual psychology of Alfred Adler.* New York: Basic Books, 1956.

Anthony, Rey (pseud). *The housewife's handbook on selective promiscuity.* Tucson, Ariz.: Seymour Press, 1960.

*Ard, Ben N., Jr. *Counseling and psychotherapy.* Palo Alto, Calif.; Science and Behavior Books, 1976.

*Beck, A. T. *Cognitive therapy and the emotional disorders.* New York: International Universities Press, 1976.

*Bedford, Stewart. *Instant replay.* New York: Institute for Rational Living, 1974.

Brown, Helen Gurley. *Sex and the single girl.* New York: Geis, 1962.

Clark, LeMon. *Sex and you.* Indianapolis: Bobbs-Merrill, 1949.

Comfort, Alex. *The joy of sex.* New York: Crown, 1972.

Comfort, Alex. *More joy.* New York: Crown, 1975.

Dreikurs, Rudolf. *Psychodynamics, psychotherapy and counseling.* Chicago: Alfred Adler Institute, 1974.

DuBrin, Andrew J. *The singles game.* Chatsworth, Calif.: Books for Better Living, 1974.

*Dyer, Wayne. *Your erroneous zones.* New York: Avon, 1977.

Ehrmann, Winston W. *Premarital dating behavior.* New York: Holt, 1960.

Ellis, Albert. Is the vaginal orgasm a myth? In Pillay, A. P., & Ellis, Albert (Eds.), *Sex, society and the individual.* Bombay: International Journal of Sexology Press, 1953.

Ellis, Albert. *The American sexual tragedy.* New York: Twayne Publishers, 1954. Rev. ed.: New York: Lyle Stuart and Grove Press, 1962.

*Ellis, Albert. *How to live with a "neurotic."* New York: Crown, 1957. Rev. ed.: New York: Crown, 1975.

*Ellis, Albert. *Sex without guilt.* New York: Lyle Stuart, 1958. Rev. ed.: New York: Lyle Stuart and Hollywood: Wilshire Books, 1965.

Ellis, Albert. *The intelligent woman's guide to man-hunting.* New York: Lyle Stuart and Dell Books, 1963.

*Ellis, Albert. *Reason and emotion in psychotherapy.* New York: Lyle Stuart, 1962. Paperback ed.: New York: Citadel Press, 1977.

*Ellis, Albert. *The art and science of love.* Rev. ed.: New York: Lyle Stuart and Bantam Books, 1969.

Ellis, Albert. *Sex and the single man.* New York: Lyle Stuart and Dell Books, 1963.

*Ellis, Albert. *Growth through reason.* Palo Alto: Science and Behavior Books, 1971. Hollywood: Wilshire Books, 1974.

*Ellis, Albert. *Executive leadership: a rational approach.* New York: Citadel Press, 1972.

*Ellis, Albert. *The sensuous person.* New York: Lyle Stuart and New American Library, 1972.

*Ellis, Albert. *Humanistic psychotherapy: the rational-emotive approach.* New York: Julian Press and McGraw-Hill Paperbacks, 1973.

*Ellis, Albert. *How to stubbornly refuse to be ashamed of anything.* Cassette recording. New York: Institute for Rational Living, 1973.

*Ellis, Albert. *Conquering the dire need for love.* Cassette recording. New York: Institute for Rational Living, 1975.

*Ellis, Albert. *Sex and the liberated man.* New York: Lyle Stuart, 1976.

*Ellis, Albert. *Conquering low frustration tolerance.* Cassette recording. New York: Institute for Rational Living, 1976.

*Ellis, Albert. *A garland of rational songs.* Cassette recording and song book. New York: Institute for Rational Living, 1977.

*Ellis, Albert. *How to live with—and without—anger.* New York: Reader's Digest Press, 1977.

Ellis, Albert. *How to stubbornly refuse to make yourself miserable about anything.* Cassette recording. New York: Institute for Rational Living, 1979.

Ellis, Albert, & Abarbanel, Albert (Eds.). *The encyclopedia of sexual behavior.* New York: Jason Aronson, 1971.

*Ellis, Albert, & Grieger, Russell. *Handbook of rational-emotive therapy.* New York: Springer, 1977.

*Ellis, Albert, & Harper, Robert A. *Creative marriage.* New York: Lyle Stuart, 1961. Paperback: *A guide to successful marriage.* Hollywood: Wilshire Books, 1971.

*Ellis, Albert, & Harper, Robert A. *A new guide to rational living.* Englewood Cliffs, N.J.: Prentice-Hall and Hollywood: Wilshire Books, 1975.

*Ellis, Albert, & Knaus, William. *Overcoming procrastination.* New York: Institute for Rational Living, 1977.

*Ellis, Albert, Wolfe, Janet L., and Moseley, Sandra. *How to raise an emotionally healthy, happy child.* Hollywood: Wilshire Books, 1972.

*Farrell, Warren. *Sex and the liberated man.* New York: Bantam Books, 1974.

*Epictetus. *The works of Epictetus.* Boston: Little, Brown, 1899.

Fensterheim, Herbert, and Baer, Jean. *Don't say yes when you want to say no.* New York: Dell, 1975.

Fisher, Seymour. *The female orgasm.* New York: Basic Books, 1973.

*Friedan, Betty. *The feminine mystique.* New York: Norton and Dell Books, 1962.

Freud, Sigmund. *Standard edition of the complete pyschological works of Sigmund Freud.* London: Hogarth, 1965.

Friday, Nancy. *My secret garden.* New York: Trident, 1973.

Fromm, Erich. *The sane society.* New York: Rinehart, 1950.

Fromm, Erich. *The art of loving.* New York: Harper, 1956.

*Garcia, Edward, & Pellegrini, Nina. *Homer the homeley hound dog.* New York: Institute for Rational Living, 1974.

Gillette, Paul. *Sexual cybernetics.* New York: Pinnacle, 1973.

*Goldfried, Marvin R., & Davison, G. C. *Clinical behavior therapy.* New York: Holt, Rinehart and Winston, 1976.

*Goodman, David, & Maultsby, Maxie C., Jr. *Emotional well-being through rational behavior training.* Springfield, Ill.: Thomas, 1974.

Gornick, V., & Moran, B. (Eds.) *Woman in sexist society.* New York: New American Library, 1971.

*Greenburg, Dan. *How to make yourself miserable.* New York: Random House, 1966.

*Greenwald, Harold. *Decision therapy..* San Diego: Edits, 1977.

*Grossack, Martin. *You are not alone.* Boston: Marlborough, 1974.

*Grossack, Martin. *Love and reason.* Boston: Institute for Rational Living, 1976.

Guyon, Rene. *The ethics of sexual acts.* New York: Knopf, 1934, 1950.

Guyon, Rene. *Sexual freedom.* New York: Knopf, 1950.

Hamilton, Eleanor. *Sex before marriage.* New York: Meredith, 1969.

Harper, Robert A. *The new psychotherapies.* Englewood Cliffs, N.J.: Englewood Cliffs, N.J.: Prentice-Hall, 1959.

Harper Robert A. *The new psychotherapies.* Englewood Cliffs, N.J.: Prentice-Hall, 1975.

Hartman, Robert S. *The measurement of value.* Carbondale: Southern Illinois University Press, 1967.

Hartman, William, & Fithian, Marilyn. *Treatment of sexual dysfunction.* Long Beach, Cal.: Center for Marital and Sexual Studies, 1972.

*Hauck, Paul. *Overcoming depression.* Philadelphia: Wekstminster Press, 1973.

*Hauck, Paul. *Overcoming frustration and anger.* Philadelphia: Westminster Press, 1974.

*Hauck, Paul. *Overcoming worry and fear.* Philadelphia: Westminster Press, 1975.

Heiman, Julia, LoPiccolo, Leslie, and LoPiccolo, Joseph. *Becoming orgasmic: a sexual growth program for women*. Englewood Cliffs, N.J.: Prentice-Hall, 1976.

Herschberger, Ruth. *Adam's rib*. New York: Pellegrini and Cudahy, 1948.

Hite, Shere. *The Hite report*. New York: Macmillan, 1976.

Horney, Karen. *Collected writings*. New York: Norton, 1972.

J. (pseud. for Terry Joan Garrity). *The sensuous woman*. New York: Lyle Stuart and Dell Books, 1969.

Johnson, Stephen. *First personal singular*.

Johnson, Wendell. *People in quandaries*. New York: Harper, 1946.

*Kelly, George. *The pyschology of personal constructs*. New York: Norton, 1955.

Kinsey, Alfred C., Pomeroy, Wardell B., Martin, Clyde E., & Gebhard, Paul H. *Sexual behavior in the human female*. Philadelphia: Saunders and New York: Pocket Books, 1953.

Klemer, Richard H. *A man for every woman*. New York: Macmillan, 1959.

*Knaus, William. *Rational emotive education*. New York: Institute for Rational Living, 1974.

Korzybski, Alfred. *Science and sanity*. Lancaster, Pa.: Lancaster Press, 1933.

*Kranzler, Gerald. *You can change how you feel*. Eugene, Oregon: Author, 1974.

*Lange, Arthur, & Jakubowski, Patricia. *Responsible assertive behavior*. Urbana, Illinois: Research Press, 1976.

*Lazarus, Arnold A. *Behavior therapy and beyond*. New York: McGraw-Hill, 1971.

*Lazarus, Arnold A. *Multimodal therapy*. New York: Springer, 1976.

*Little, Bill L. *This will drive you sane*. Minneapolis: CompCare, 1977.

*Mahoney, Michael. *Cognition and behavior modification*. Cambridge: Ballinger, 1974.

*Marcus Aurelius. *Meditations*. Boston: Little, Brown, 1890.

Masters, William H., & Johnson, Virginia E. *Human sexual inadequacy*. Boston: Little, Brown, 1970.

*Maultsby, Maxie C., Jr. *Help yourself to happiness*. New York: Institute for Rational Living, 1975.

*Maultsby, Maxie C., Jr., & Ellis, Albert. *Technique for using rational-emotive imagery*. New York: Institute for Rational Living, 1974.

*Maultsby, Maxie C., Jr., & Hendricks, Allie, *Cartoon booklets*. Lexington, Kentucky: Rational Behavior Training Center, 1974.

McCary, James Leslie. *Human sexuality*. Second ed. New York: Van Nostrand, 1973.

*Meichenbaum, Donald. *Cognitive behavior modification*. New York: Plenum, 1977.

*Morris, Kenneth T., & Kanitz, H. Mike. *Rational-emotive therapy*. Boston: Houghton Mifflin, 1975.

Phillips, E. L. *Psychotherapy*. Englewood Cliffs, N.J.: Prentice-Hall, 1956.

*Powell, John. *Fully human, fully alive*. Niles, Ill.: Argus, 1976.

*Raimy, Victor. *Misunderstandings of the self*. San Francisco: Jossey-Bass, 1975.

Reich, Wilhelm. *The sexual revolution*. New York: Orgone Institute Press, 1945.

Reiss, Ira L. *Premarital sexual standards* in America. Glencoe, Ill.: Free Press, 1960.

Rimm, David C., & Masters, John C. *Behavior therapy*. New York: Academic Press, 1974.

Rogers, Carl R. *On becoming a person*. Boston: Houghton Mifflin, 1961.

*Russell, Bertrand. *The conquest of happiness*. New York: Pocket Books, 1950.

Shibles, Warren. *Emotion*. Whitewater, Wisc.: Language Press, 1974.

*Silverstein, Lee. *Consider the the alternative*. Minneapolis: Comp Care, 1978.

Smith, Manual J. *When I say no, I feel guilty*. New York: Bantam, 1975.

Thorne, Frederic C. *Personalty: a clinical eclectic view*. Brandon, Vt.: Journal of Clinical Psychology Press, 1961.

Tillich, Paul. *The courage to be*. New York: Oxford University Press, 1953.

*Tosi, Donald J. *Youth: toward personal growth, a rational-emotive approach*. Columbus, Ohio: Merrill, 1974.

Watts, Alan W. *Nature, man and sex*. New York: New American Library, 1959.

Weekes, Claire. *Peace from nervous suffering* New York: Hawthorn, 1972.

*Wolfe, Janet L. *Rational-emotive therapy and women's problems*. Cassette recording. New York: Institute for Rational Living, 1974.

Wolfe, Janet L. *Aggression vs. assertiveness. Practical Psychology for Physicians*, 1975, 2(1), 44.

*Wolfe, Janet L. Rational-emotive therapy as an effective feminist therapy. *Rational Living, 1976*, 11(1), 2-7. Reprinted: New York: Institute for Rational Living, 1976.

*Wolfe, Janet L. *How to be sexually assertive*. New York: Institute for Rational Living, 1976. Pamphlet

Wolfe, Janet L., & Fodor, Iris G. A cognitive-behavioral approach to modifying assertive behavior in women. *Counseling Psychologist*, 1975, 5(4), 45-52.

Wolfe, Janet L., & Fodor, Iris G. Modifying assertive behavior in women: a comparison of three approaches. *Behavior Therapy*, 1977, 8, 567-574.

Wolpe, Joseph, & Lazarus, Arnold. *Behavior therapy techniques*. New York: Pergamon, 1966.

*Young, Howard. *A rational counseling primer*. New York: Institute for Rational Living, 1974.

Youngson, Jeanne. Places to meet people in and around New York. New York: Author, 1970. Mimeographed.

APPENDIX

Techniques for Disputing
Irrational Beliefs
(DIBS)

If you want to increase your rationality and reduce your irrational beliefs, you can spend at least ten minutes every day asking yourself the following questions and carefully thinking through (not merely parroting!) the appropriate answers. Write down each question and your answers to it on a piece of paper; or else record the questions and your answers on a tape recorder.

1. What irrational belief do I want to dispute and surrender?

Illustrative Answer: I must receive love from someone for whom I really care.

2. Can I rationally support this belief?

Illustrative Answer: No.

3. What evidence exists of the falseness of this belief?

Illustrative Answer: Many indications exist that the belief that I must receive love from someone for whom I really care remains false:

　　a) No law of the universe exists that says that someone I care for *must* love me (although I would find it nice if that person did!).

b) If I do not receive love from one person, I can still get it from others and find happiness that way.

c) If no one I care for ever cares for me, I can still find enjoyment in friendships, in work, in books, and in other things.

d) If someone I deeply care for rejects me, that will seem most unfortunate; but I will hardly die!

e) Even though I have not had much luck in winning great love in the past, that hardly proves that I *must* gain it now.

f) No evidence exists for *any* absolutistic *must*. Consequently, no proof exists that I must have *anything,* including love.

g) Many people seem to exist in the world who never get the kind of love they crave and who still lead happy lives.

h) At times during my life I know that I have remained unloved and happy; so I most probably can feel happy again under nonloving conditions.

i) If I get rejected by someone for whom I truly care, that may mean that I possess some poor, unloving traits. But that hardly means that I rate as a rotten, worthless, totally unlovable individual.

j) Even if I had such poor traits that no one could ever love me, I would still not have to down myself as a lowly bad individual.

4. Does any evidence exist of the truth of this belief?

Illustrative Answer: No, not really. Considerable evidence exists that if I love someone dearly and never get loved in return that I will then find myself disadvantaged, inconvenienced, frustrated, and deprived. I certainly would prefer, therefore, not to get rejected. But no amount of inconvenience amounts to a *horror.* I can still *stand* frustration and loneliness. They hardly make the world *awful.* Nor does rejection make me a turd! Clearly, then, no evidence exists that I *must* receive love from someone for whom I really care.

5. What worst things could actually happen to me if I don't get what I think I must (or do get what I think I mustn't)?

Illustrative Answer: If I don't get the love I think I must receive:

a) I would get deprived of various pleasures and conveniences that I might receive through gaining love.

b) I would feel inconvenienced by having to keep looking for love elsewhere.

c) I might *never* gain the love I want, and thereby continue indefinitely to feel deprived and disadvantaged.

d) Other people might down me and consider me pretty worthless for getting rejected—and that would prove annoying and unpleasant.

c) I might settle for pleasures other than and worse than those I could receive in a good love relationship; and I would find that distinctly undesirable.

f) I might remain alone much of the time: which again would prove unpleasant.

g) Various other kinds of misfortunes and deprivations might occur in my life—none of which I need define as *awful, terrible,* or *unbearable.*

6. What good things could I make happen if I don't get what I think I must (or do get what I think I mustn't)?

a) If the person I truly care for does not return my love, I could devote more time and energy to winning someone else's love—and probably find someone better for me.

b) I could devote myself to other enjoyable pursuits that have little to do with loving or relating, such as work or artistic endeavors.

c) I could find it challenging and enjoyable to teach myself to live happily without love.

d) I could work at achieving a philosophy of fully accepting myself even when I do not get the love I crave.

You can take any one of your major irrational beliefs—your *shoulds, oughts,* or *musts*—and spend at least ten minutes every day, often for a period of several weeks, actively and vigorously disputing this belief. To help keep yourself devoting this amount of time to the DIBS method of rational disputing, you may use operant conditioning or self-management methods (originated by B. F. Skinner, David Premack, Marvin Goldfried, and other psychologists). Select some activity that you highly enjoy that you tend to do every day—such as reading, eating, television viewing, masturbation, or social contact with friends. Use this activity as a reinforcer or reward by ONLY allowing yourself to engage in it AFTER you have practiced Disputing Irrational Beliefs (DIBS) for at least ten minutes that day. Otherwise, no reward!

In addition, you may penalize yourself every single day you do NOT use DIBS for at least ten minutes. How? By making yourself perform some activity you find distinctly unpleasant—such as eating something obnoxious, contributing to a cause you hate, getting up a half-hour earlier in the morning, or spending an hour conversing with someone you find boring. You can also arrange with some person or group to monitor you and help you actually carry out the penalties and lack of rewards you set for yourself. You may of course steadily use DIBS without any self-reinforcement, since it becomes reinforcing in its own right after a while. But you may find it more effective at times if you use it along with rewards and penalties that you execute immediately after you practice or avoid practicing this rational-emotive method.

Summary of Questions
to Ask Yourself in DIBS

1. What irrational belief do I want to dispute and surrender?

2. Can I rationally support this belief?

3. What evidence exists of the falseness of this belief?

4. Does any evidence exist of the truth of this belief?

5. What worst things could actually happen to me if I don't get what I think I must (or do get what I think I mustn't)?

6. What good things could I make happen if I don't get what I think I must (or do get what I think I mustn't)?

About the Author

ALBERT ELLIS, born in Pittsburgh and reared in New York City, holds a bachelor's degree from the City College of New York and M. A. and Ph.D. degrees in clinical pyschology from Columbia University. He has an appointment as Visiting Professor of Psychology at Rutgers University and at the United States International University. He served as Chief Psychologist of the New Jersey State Diagnostic Center and later as Chief Psychologist of the New Jersey Department of Institutions and Agencies. He has practiced psychotherapy, marriage and family counseling, and sex therapy for over thirty years and continues this practice at the Institute for Rational-Emotive Therapy in New York City, where he also serves as Executive Director (as well as Executive Director of the Institute for Rational Living).

A fellow of many professional societies, Dr. Ellis served as President of the Division of Consulting Psychology of the American Psychological Association, as President of the Society for the Scientific Study of Sex, as Vice-President of the American Academy of Pscyhotherapists, and as a member of the Executive

Boards of the American Association of Marriage and Family Counselors and of the New York Society of Clinical Psychologists. Several societies have given him special awards, including the American Humanist Association, the Division of Psychotherapy of the American Psychological Association, and the American Association of Sex Educators, Counselors and Therapists.

Dr. Ellis has served as Associate Editor of many professional journals, including the *Journal of Contemporary Psychotherapy*, the *Journal of Indvidual Psychology*, the *Journal of Marriage and Family Counseling*, the *Journal of Sex Research, Rational Living*, and *Cognitive Therapy and Research*. He has published over five hundred papers in psychological, psychiatric, and sociological journals and anthologies; and has authored or edited forty books and monographs, including *Sex Without Guilt, How to Live with a "Neurotic," The Art and Science of Love, Reason and Emotion in Psychotherapy, Growth Through Reason, Executive Leadership: A Rational Approach, Humanistic Psychotherapy: The Rational-Emotive Approach, A New Guide to Rational Living, Sex and the Liberated Man, How to Live With—and Without—Anger, Overcoming Procrastination,* and *A Handbook of Rational-Emotive Therapy.*